WKC LEARNING CENTRES

KU-534-447

FRANK WOOD'S

BUSINESS ACCOUNTING BASICS

PEARSON

We work with leading authors to develop the
strongest educational materials in business and finance,
bringing cutting-edge thinking and best
learning practice to a global market.

Under a range of well-known imprints, including
Financial Times Prentice Hall, we craft high quality print and
electronic publications which help readers to understand
and apply their content, whether studying or at work.

To find out more about the complete range of our
publishing, please visit us on the World Wide Web at:
www.pearsoned.co.uk

FRANK WOOD'S

BUSINESS ACCOUNTING BASICS

Frank Wood

and

David Horner

**Financial Times
Prentice Hall
is an imprint of**

WKC
KX Learning Centre
Acc no. SY170994
Class no. 657 WOO
Type BS
Date 07/9/10

Harlow, England • London • New York • Boston • San Francisco • Toronto • Sydney • Singapore • Hong Kong
Tokyo • Seoul • Taipei • New Delhi • Cape Town • Madrid • Mexico City • Amsterdam • Munich • Paris • Milan

Pearson Education Limited
Edinburgh Gate
Harlow
Essex CM20 2JE
England

and Associated Companies throughout the world

Visit us on the World Wide Web at:
www.pearsoned.co.uk

First published 2010

© Pearson Education Limited 2010

The rights of Frank Wood and David Horner to be identified as authors of this work have
been asserted by them in accordance with the Copyright, Designs and Patents Act 1988.

All rights reserved. No part of this publication may be reproduced, stored in a
retrieval system, or transmitted in any form or by any means, electronic, mechanical,
photocopying, recording or otherwise, without either the prior written permission of the
publisher or a licence permitting restricted copying in the United Kingdom issued by the
Copyright Licensing Agency Ltd, Saffron House, 6–10 Kirby Street, London EC1N 8TS.

All trademarks used herein are the property of their respective owners. The use of any
trademark in this text does not vest in the author or publisher any trademark ownership rights
in such trademarks, nor does the use of such trademarks imply any affiliation with or
endorsement of this book by such owners.

Pearson Education is not responsible for third party internet sites.

ISBN: 978-0-273-72500-8

British Library Cataloguing-in-Publication Data
A catalogue record for this book is available from the British Library

Library of Congress Cataloging-in-Publication Data
Wood, Frank, 1926–2000.
  Business accounting basic / Frank Wood and David Horner.
      p. cm.
  ISBN 978-0-273-72500-8 (pbk.)
1. Accounting.   I. Horner, David, 1970–   II. Title.
  HF5636.W858 2010
  657—dc22

                                    2010013482

10 9 8 7 6 5 4 3 2 1
14 13 12 11 10

Typeset in 10.5/12.5pt ITC Garamond Book by 35
Printed and bound by Rotolito Lombarde. Italy

Contents

Supporting resources
Visit **www.pearsoned.co.uk/wood** to find valuable online resources

For instructors
- Complete Instructor's Manual

For more information please contact your local Pearson Education sales representative or visit **www.pearsoned.co.uk/wood**

Preface

Notes for teacher and lecturers

This textbook has been written to provide a concise but comprehensive introduction to financial accounting.

It is suitable for beginners to this subject area and provides an introduction to the major topics covered within an introductory bookkeeping or financial accounting course. The textbook would be ideal for those studying for A and AS level, IGCSE, Scottish Higher Qualifications, Association of Accounting Technicians, university undergraduate degree courses and professional accountancy qualifications.

The textbook is based on the International Financial Reporting Standard (IFRS) and the International Accounting Standard (IAS) framework, meaning it can be used by students across the world rather than any one country in particular.

Each chapter begins with learning objectives which outline what skills and techniques will be acquired by completion of the chapter. The chapter will explore each topic in sufficient detail with explanation of each topic accompanied by fully worked-out examples accompanied by explanations and reference to the relevant international accounting standards throughout.

Frequent learning checks appear throughout each chapter in the form of review questions. These are included in each chapter and follow a scale of increasing challenge. This provides accessibility for all students whilst providing the relevant challenge for the student who is keen to practice further as the chapter progresses. Answers for each of the review questions appear at the end of the textbook.

The textbook is written on the assumption that the user of the book has limited or no knowledge of accounting. Although each chapter is largely self-contained, the chapters are arranged in a sequential order. This means that review questions in later chapters will require the completion of the subject metier in the earlier chapters. Where review questions require prior knowledge, this is highlighted.

Although the textbook is written to comply with international standards so as to maximise its usefulness for students of accounting across the globe, the chapter on Value Added Tax is based on the UK rate as at May 2010 of 17.5%.

An Instructor's Manual, which contains further guidance on the how to use the textbook, how to approach particular topics, as well as additional review questions for each chapter, is available from www.pearsoned.co.uk/wood.

Notes for students

This textbook is designed to provide a full and comprehensive guide as you begin your study of bookkeeping and financial accounting. It is meant to serve as an introduction to financial accounting, which means that you are not expected to have read any other textbooks in advance of using this particular one.

When using this textbook, we would recommend that you always stick to the following guidelines:

- Always read the learning objectives as you begin to study a new chapter. These objectives give you clear targets for each chapter, which you can check on completion.
- Ensure that you attempt all the review questions when you have completed the relevant section of each chapter. The questions are designed to be completed as you finish a relevant section so you don't have to wait until the end of the chapter.
- Answers to the review questions appear at the end of the textbook. However, we strongly recommend that you only use these answers to review your own progress after you have completed all the questions. Your progression in terms of learning will be severely restricted if you constantly check the answers before you have firmly grasped a topic. As a minimum, you should complete the entire relevant section before you check your own answers.
- If you are unsure on how to complete a review question, then revisit the relevant section in the chapter. The fully worked-out examples and explanation should provide guidance on how to reach the correct solution.

Although financial accounting can seem very complex when undertaking study of the subject for the first time you should see clear improvement as you progress through each chapter. Regular practice through the review questions will help to consolidate your knowledge and understanding of the subject area.

Finally, we wish you luck with your studies. Financial accounting is not the easiest subject to get to grips with, but with this textbook, a calculator and some dedication on your part, we are sure that you will be successful.

Acknowledgements

I would like to dedicate this book to my parents, Mollie and Harold Horner. However, there are also a number of people I would like to thank for support in various ways:

Matthew Smith deserves great thanks – for his positive support and encouragement, particularly in the early stages of this book. I owe him.

I would also like to thank Sally Nower, John Bellwood and Ian Yates for their suggestions they made in the writing of this book – more often than not, they were spot on.

However, great credit must go to the students of Colchester Sixth Form College who, without fail, have made the teaching of Accounting never a bore, and surprisingly fun.

CHAPTER 1

Introduction

Learning objectives

By the end of this chapter you should be able to:

- Understand the different sectors in the economy
- Understand the main forms of business organisation within the private sector
- Understand how the accounting equation can be used and what it represents.

Introduction

The purpose of this book is to introduce you to the basics of business accounting. This book will cover the basics of the system of financial accounting – from the basics of double-entry bookkeeping to the construction of the financial statements for a simple small business. Although much of this book is aimed at the financial accounts of the sole trader, we will also have a look at the financial accounting practices employed by the limited company.

This opening chapter aims to prepare you for what lies ahead. We will consider the various types of business organisation that you come across in your studies and what their major aims are as businesses. Accounting is often seen as a jargon-heavy subject and in this chapter we will also introduce you to some of the terms and concepts that you will be coming across throughout this textbook. This is potentially a confusing area – not helped by changes in some of the terminology over recent years. This textbook uses the most up-to-date terminology possible but at the same time will keep you informed of older terminology.

Sectors in the economy

It is common to classify economic activity into two sectors: the public sector and the private sector.

The public sector

The public sector is owned and controlled by the government. This covers all levels of government – from local to central government – and includes all the organisations which are funded by the taxpayer. The public sector is not as large as, say, thirty years ago, due to successive governments pursuing a policy of privatisation (transferring organisations from the public to the private sector), but it still accounts for a significant proportion of the business activity in the UK. Examples of public sector activity in the UK include the National Health Service and the provision of libraries.

The private sector

The private sector consists of businesses owned and controlled by private individuals acting either on their own or in groups. Although private sector organisations have to comply with laws and regulations set out by the government, these businesses are free to pursue their own ends. It is business organisations within the private sector that this textbook will be exploring.

Types of business organisation

There are three main types of business organisation within the private sector.

Sole traders

A sole trader is a one-person business (the business is owned by one person but others can be employed to work within the business). The sole trader is an **unincorporated business organisation**. This means that the legal status of the business is no different to that of the owner. If the business cannot pay its debts then it would be up to the owner to clear the debts even if this meant selling personal (non-business) assets to clear the business debt. Sole traders are generally small organisations but are very common – mainly due to the ease of setting up as a sole trader.

Partnerships

Partnerships are also unincorporated businesses. Historically, a partnership was owned by between two and twenty partners, although the limit on the maximum number of partners was relaxed in 2002. A greater number of owners potentially allows a greater contribution of capital into the business thus increasing the chances of success and minimising risk of failure. However, partners may still have to sell their own possessions to clear the debts of the partnership in certain circumstances.

A limited partnership was a variant on the partnership. This form of organisation allowed some (but not all) partners to enjoy **limited liability**, which meant that they avoided the risk of selling personal possessions.

The Limited Liability Partnerships Act of 2000 created a new type of partnership. The *Limited Liability Partnership (LLP)* is closer in many respects to a limited company in that all members of the LLP (partners) enjoy limited liability. However, the profits are treated as income for the partners rather than that of the organisation which is similar to how other unincorporated organisations (sole traders and ordinary partnerships) are treated.

Limited companies

A company has undergone the process of incorporation. This means a company exists separately from those who own the company. This means that the company will carry on independently from the owners. The owners of limited companies are known as shareholders.

There are two types of limited company: public limited companies and private limited companies. They are run by directors elected by the shareholders. It is appropriate to talk of a 'separation of ownership from control' – it is the shareholders who own the company, but it is the directors and managers who actually run the company. This can potentially cause a conflict of interest as the two groups may have differing objectives. This conflict highlights the importance of having clearly presented and understandable financial statements for user groups to examine and assess.

As stated above, this textbook is primarily concerned with the accounts of sole traders, but limited companies will be briefly explored in Chapter 15.

You should now attempt review questions 1.1 to 1.4.

Business objectives

The objectives of the business refer to the long-term aims of the business. It is commonly assumed that all businesses in the private sector have profit maximisation as their prime objective. This means that business activity will be focused on increasing the profits of the business. The objective of profit maximisation has a certain logic to it – after all, businesses are often set up to generate a return for the owner of the business. In the case of limited companies, the objective of profit maximisation is more formally built into the activities of the business. A limited company is owned by shareholders who often buy shares in a company purely to generate as high a return as possible. Therefore the directors of the company will ensure that the activities of the business are focused on maximising profits.

It is argued that businesses in reality do not always focus on profit maximisation as their prime objective. Sole traders and partnerships may have other objectives such as any of the following:

● Survival
● Personal objectives
● Market share growth.

Objectives can change over time. A business trading in a period of reduced economic activity (especially a recession) may focus on survival rather than profit maximisation. This switch in objectives may mean that decisions are taken which would not normally be considered (e.g. selling assets at a loss simply to raise cash).

Fundamentals of financial accounting

As mentioned earlier, accounting is often seen as a jargon-heavy subject. First-time students of accounting are often discouraged by the number of new terms that have to be committed to memory. At the end of each chapter there is a list of key terms with brief definitions or explanations. In this chapter we will be introducing you to some of the terms which are seen as crucial and underpinning much of what follows. There are three terms which underpin much of the system of financial accounting: assets, liabilities and capital (or equity).

Term	Description
Assets	Assets are the resources which are used by the business as part of the activities of the business (e.g. property, equipment and cash).
Liabilities	Liabilities represent the debts of the business – i.e. what is owed by the business to others. These may be short-term debts which are to be repaid soon or long-term debts which may be outstanding and owing for many years (e.g. a mortgage).
Capital (or equity)	Capital refers to the resources supplied to the business by the owner(s) of the business. This capital could be in the form of money or as other assets.

You should now attempt review questions 1.5 to 1.8.

The accounting equation

In Chapter 2 you will be introduced to the system of double-entry bookkeeping. One of the principles that underlie much of the financial accounting within this book is the principle of **duality**. This relates to the idea that accounting transactions can be considered from two different perspectives.

The accounting equation encapsulates this duality and is as follows:

$$\textbf{Assets = Capital + Liabilities}$$

What this equation represents is the two sides of the business – the physical side of the business (i.e. the assets) and the financial side of the business (i.e. the capital and the liabilities).

If you think about it the equation must always be true; if there is an increase in the assets of the business then these assets must have been financed through either more resources from the owner (i.e. more capital) or more resources that have been borrowed (i.e. more liabilities). (In Chapter 3 we consider how capital can be increased by the generation of profits earned by the business.)

If the equation always holds then we can ascertain the value of the assets of the business (or any other component of the equation) if we know the value of the capital and liabilities (or any other two components).

The accounting equation underpins the statement of financial position of the business (see Chapter 3). It also indirectly influences the rules of double-entry bookkeeping (see Chapter 2).

You should now attempt review questions 1.9 to 1.12.

International standards

Accounting systems must follow rules. You may be surprised to find that there are different ways of recording and presenting accounts and financial statements. Rules and regulations are not as important for the purpose of internal accounts as they are for those for external publication and external use. However, it is good practice and useful to see how the rules and regulations which apply to larger business organisations would also apply to those of a small organisation.

Accounting standards are a set of continually evolving documents which provide guidance on various aspects of financial accounting. This textbook will be based on the international standards (IASs and IFRSs) rather than those set out in UK GAAP. This is covered in Chapter 7.

Terminology

Terminology has evolved over time and unfortunately there are multiple terms used for the same concept. The following table outlines some of the old terms that are used and their equivalent new term. It will be well worth checking with the syllabus requirements of your particular course as there may be some flexibility in which terminology is used.

Old term	New term
1 Profit and loss account (or income statement)	Statement of comprehensive income
2 Balance sheet	Statement of financial position
3 Fixed assets	Non-current assets
4 Long-term liabilities	Non-current liabilities
5 Stock	Inventory/inventories
6 Debtors (or accounts receivable)	Trade receivables
7 Creditors (or accounts payable)	Trade payables
8 Sales revenue	Turnover
9 Shareholders' funds	Equity
10 Profit and loss account (appearing as a revenue reserve)	Retained earnings

Summary

Studying accounting can seem daunting at times. It is a challenging subject to study. However, you will quickly realise that there is a certain logic to the accounting techniques and procedures, which can be picked up relatively quickly.

A lot of the content of an accounting course can be reduced to simple rules. Commit these rules to memory – use them through practical application and a lot of the difficulties you may face studying accounting will be overcome.

It is vital that you don't study accounting passively. This textbook has many questions designed to test your understanding. Work with the text and complete the review questions as you progress. We wish you good luck with your studies.

Chapter review

By now you should understand the following:

- The different types of business organisation
- What is meant by the accounting equation and how it can be used
- Differences in terminology used within accounting.

Key terms

Public sector Sector in the economy owned and controlled by the government

Private sector Sector in the economy owned and controlled by private groups and individuals

Sole trader A business organisation owned and controlled by one person

Partnership A business organisation owned and controlled by a small group of people

Unincorporated business A business organisation in which the owners and the business are, in legal terms, the same as each other

Limited liability Where one is limited to losing no more than their original investment in a company

Limited company A business organisation which has undergone incorporation and therefore exists as a legal entity separate from its owner(s)

Business objectives The aim or purpose of a business – i.e. what it is trying to achieve

Profit maximisation Where a business aims to generate as much profit as is possible

Assets Resources used within a business (e.g. equipment)

Liabilities Debts and other borrowings of a business

Capital (or equity) Resources provided to a business by the owner(s) of the business

REVIEW QUESTIONS

1.1 Outline three advantages of operating as a sole trader as compared to operating as a partnership.

1.2 Give three reasons why a sole trader may wish to convert into a partnership with others.

1.3 Suggest three reasons why one may prefer to operate as a company rather than as a sole trader.

1.4 Explain what is meant by a 'separation of ownership from control' in the context of limited companies.

1.5 Explain why profit maximisation is likely to be the prime objective of a company.

1.6 Classify the following into assets or liabilities:

(a) Business premises
(b) Bank overdraft
(c) Money owed by others to the business
(d) Equipment owned by the business
(e) Mortgage on premises
(f) Cash held in till
(g) Unpaid bill.

1.7 Classify the following into assets or liabilities:

(a) Money owed to suppliers
(b) Vehicles used by the business
(c) Goods bought with the intention of their being sold for a profit
(d) Computer used in the business
(e) Bank loan to be repaid within the next year
(f) Amount owing for office fixtures bought on credit.

1.8 Classify the following into assets or liabilities:

(a) Amount that business will need to pay another business for purchases of equipment
(b) Cash in bank account
(c) Balance on savings account
(d) Bill paid in advance
(e) Amount due to be paid in next month for business rates
(f) Delivery van.

1.9 Complete the gaps in the table below:

	Assets £	Liabilities £	Capital £
(a)	?	4,100	1,300
(b)	3,870	?	2,680
(c)	9,875	?	8,680
(d)	?	543	637
(e)	6,767	1,107	?

1.10 Complete the gaps in the table below:

	Assets £	Liabilities £	Capital £
(a)	12,231	?	7,887
(b)	23,434	18,312	?
(c)	?	23,111	51,312
(d)	54,524	9,090	?
(e)	31,231	?	20,022

1.11   Complete the gaps in the table below:

	Assets £	Liabilities £	Capital £
(a)	?	31,221	33,343
(b)	?	23,123	76,990
(c)	64,564	?	54,693
(d)	76,575	11,200	?
(e)	86,788	31,231	?

1.12   A business provides the following figures.

	£
Property	54,000
Equipment	8,200
Bank	1,150
Loan	15,900

Based on the above data ascertain the size of the capital of the business.

CHAPTER 2

Double-entry bookkeeping

Learning objectives

By the end of this chapter you should be able to:

- Understand the nature and content of double-entry accounts
- Enter transactions correctly into accounts for a variety of transactions
- Balance off accounts at the end of the accounting period.

Introduction

Business transactions are recorded in **accounts**. The maintenance and recording of transactions within these accounts is known as **double-entry bookkeeping**. The 'double-entry' term is used because each transaction can be seen to have two separate effects on the business. For example, buying a new machine for cash would affect both the asset of machinery, and the asset of cash. Similarly, selling inventory on credit would affect the asset of inventory, and the liability of trade payables.

A double-entry account would normally appear as follows:

A double-entry account

Account name

Debit side (Dr)		Credit side (Cr)	
Date Account details	Amount (£)	Date Account details	Amount (£)

What does the account show?

Given the 'T' shaped appearance of the accounts they are often referred to as 'T' accounts. Each of these accounts will show the following:

- *Account name*
  The name of the account refers to the type of transaction. For example, if the account is dealing with buying or selling machinery, then the account could simply be known as '*machinery*'. This means that each different type of transaction would be recorded in a separate account.

- *Debits and credits*

  The debit side (Dr) and credit side (Cr) refer to the left-hand and right-hand sides of each account. These terms can be used to refer to how entries are made. For example, if we talk of '*debiting*' an account, all we mean is that we would be placing an entry on the debit side – the left-hand side – of the account.

- *Account details*

  The details element of each side of the account will contain the name of the other account which the transaction also affects. As a form of symmetry, each transaction will affect two accounts – hence the term 'double-entry' – and the details included in each account will refer to the other account to be affected.

There are some basic principles that must be applied when recording double-entry transactions:

1 Every transaction requires two entries to be made in separate accounts.
2 Every transaction requires one debit entry and one credit entry to be made in each of the two accounts.

Rules for double-entry transactions

It is vital that transactions are recorded correctly. For this we need to establish on which 'side' of the account each transaction needs to be recorded – i.e. should we 'debit' or 'credit' an account? This will depend on the type of account that we are dealing with.

In Chapter 1 we were introduced to the terms asset, liability and capital. To start with we will consider three separate types of account: for assets, liabilities and capital. The rules for recording the double-entry transactions are as follows:

all Asset accounts

Debit	*Credit*
INCREASES entered HERE	DECREASES entered HERE

all Liability accounts

Debit	*Credit*
DECREASES entered HERE	INCREASES entered HERE

all Capital accounts

Debit	*Credit*
DECREASES entered HERE	INCREASES entered HERE

These rules will make more sense if we see some examples of them in action.

Example 2.1

On 1 November, the owner places £5,000 of her own money into the bank account of the new business.

Explanation
The asset of bank has increased – so we debit that account.
The capital of the business has increased – so we credit that account.

Bank

	£			£
1 Nov Capital	5,000			

Capital

	£			£
		1 Nov Bank		5,000

Notice how the detail of each transaction cross-references the other account to be affected – providing a useful way of locating the other account that is to be affected by the transaction.

Example 2.2

On 3 November, machinery is purchased for £2,000, payment made by cheque.

Explanation
The asset of machinery has increased – so we debit that account.
The asset of bank has decreased due to the payment made – so we credit that account.

Machinery

	£			£
3 Nov Bank	2,000			

Bank

				£
		3 Nov Machinery		2,000

Example 2.3

On 9 November, equipment is purchased on credit from Perkins Ltd for £320.

Explanation
The asset of equipment has increased – so we debit that account.
The liability of creditor* Perkins Ltd has increased – so we credit that account.

Equipment

	£			£
9 Nov Perkins Ltd	320			

Perkins Ltd

				£
		9 Nov Equipment		320

* **Note**: A creditor is someone the business owes money to who is likely to be repaid in the near future.

Example 2.4

On 14 November, the £320 owing to Perkins Ltd is paid by cheque.

Explanation
The asset of bank has decreased – so we credit this account.
The liability of creditor has decreased – so we debit this account.

Bank

			£
	14 Nov	Perkins Ltd	320

Perkins Ltd

		£	
14 Nov	Bank	320	

Further information for double-entry bookkeeping

The books which contain the accounts that record these transactions are known as **ledgers**.

In reality, most accounts will contain more than one transaction and one single account could easily take up many pages in the ledger. In Chapter 4 we show how these ledgers are sub-divided.

When completing questions that involve maintaining double-entry accounts, it is a good idea to read through the complete list of transactions first so as to get a rough idea of how many entries will be needed in each account. This will mean that you can leave sufficient space to make all the entries in that account – it will start to look untidy if you have to restart an account later on in your workings due to leaving insufficient space for transactions.

Typically, the bank and cash accounts are used frequently, whereas the capital account is only affected by one or two entries.

You should now attempt review questions 2.1 to 2.7.

Accounting for inventory

Goods that are bought with the intention of being sold are referred to as **inventory**. Inventory is an asset and will therefore follow the rules of an asset account. However, bookkeeping for inventory is not as straightforward as you might think.

Consider the following account:

Inventory

2010		£	2010		£
8 Apr	Purchases	300	6 May	Sales	300

It would be tempting to think that the balance on this account is zero – with the inventory purchased in April all being sold in May. However, it is likely that the selling price of the inventory differed from the purchase price of the inventory (i.e. it was sold for a profit) and, as a result, we cannot actually determine how much inventory is left within the business.

The solution is to have separate accounts for different movements of inventory. There are four separate accounts to record different movements in inventory:

The four accounts for inventory	
1 **Purchases**	– for purchases of inventory
2 **Sales**	– for sales of inventory
3 **Returns inwards**	– when a customer returns inventory to the firm.
4 **Returns outwards**	– when the business returns inventory to the supplier.

What do we mean by inventory?

Initially we will use examples where firms are not manufacturers of goods. Profits are earned by these businesses trading in goods: buying goods and selling these goods on to customers. This may be unrepresentative of many businesses today, but it simplifies matters to start with.

Inventory refers to goods that the firm buys with the intention of selling at a profit. What is counted as inventory will depend on the type of business we are dealing with. For example, a business buying and selling computers would count purchases of computers as inventory – and would enter these into the purchases account. However, another firm may see the purchase of a computer as the purchase of an asset and the entry for this purchase would be in a 'computer' account.

Many accounting students are initially unsure whether something counts as the purchase of an asset or the purchase of inventory. This distinction between purchases of assets and purchases of inventory is important as it has implications later on for calculating the profit of the business.

Double-entry transactions for inventory

Inventory is an asset and will therefore follow the rules of an asset account. It is possible that both **purchases** and **sales** will be either for immediate payment or receipt – these would be referred to as 'cash transactions'. However, they may be on 'credit terms' where the payment or receipt is made at a later date.

It is worth pointing out that the term 'cash' – as in 'cash sales' – can include payment or receipt by cheque; it is only referred to as 'cash' to distinguish it from credit terms.

Nature of inventory transaction	
Cash transaction	= Immediate payment
Credit transaction	= Payment made at a later date

Credit terms are normally offered when one business trades with another business. The credit period offered can vary, but 30 days is a typical period offered. The double-entry transactions for credit transactions will be completed in two stages: firstly, the initial credit transaction, and secondly, the payment made or received in final settlement of the account owing or owed.

Example 2.5: purchases of inventory

On 10 November, the business purchases £450 of inventory.

Whether the firm pays for this immediately by cheque, or purchases it on credit terms, can be shown easily in the following accounts.

The purchase of inventory will require a debit entry into the purchases account as an asset has increased, but there are two options for the corresponding credit entry:

A = Cash purchase
B = Credit purchase

A Cash purchases

Purchases

	£		£
10 Nov Bank	450		

Bank

	£		£
		10 Nov Purchases	450

Explanation
If the inventory is paid for immediately, then a credit entry will be made in the bank account – an asset has decreased.

B Credit purchases

Purchases

	£		£
10 Nov Creditor	450		

Creditor

	£		£
		10 Nov Purchases	450

Explanation
If the inventory is bought on credit, then a credit entry will be made in the creditor's account – a liability has increased.

Example 2.6: sales of inventory

On 19 April, the business sells £870 of inventory. Again, we can illustrate the accounts for both cash sales and for credit sales.

The sale of inventory will require a credit entry in the sales account as the asset of inventory is being reduced. Again, there are two options for the corresponding debit entry:

A = Cash sale
B = Credit sale

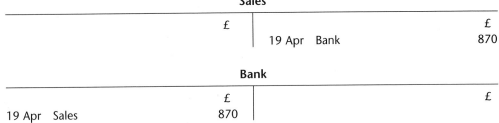

A Cash sales

Sales

	£			£
		19 Apr	Bank	870

Bank

	£		£
19 Apr Sales	870		

Explanation

If the sale is for immediate receipt, we would debit the bank account – as an asset is being increased.

B Credit sales

Sales

	£			£
		19 Apr	Debtor	870

Debtor

	£		£
19 Apr Sales	870		

Explanation

If the sale is on credit then we would debit the account of the debtor,* as an asset is being increased.

* **Note**: Debtors are people or other businesses that owe the business money – usually for sales made to them on credit. The repayment of the amount owing is expected in the near future.

Returns of inventory

It is possible that goods will be returned to the original supplier. This is not something that the supplier will allow automatically, but if there is some issue with the order, such as the order itself being incorrect, or the items faulty, then it is normal practice for the goods to be returned.

Both returns inwards and returns outwards are asset of inventory accounts and will therefore follow the rules of an asset account.

Returns inwards refer to the goods which are sent back to the firm from the customer. For this reason they are also known as **sales returns**.

Example 2.7

Goods previously sold on credit to C Smith for £189 were returned to the firm on 12 March due to the goods being faulty.

Returns inwards

	£		£
12 Mar C Smith	189		

C Smith

	£		£
		12 Mar Returns inwards	189

The returns inwards represent an increase in the asset of inventory which means we will debit that account. By returning goods C Smith will owe the firm less money which reduces the asset of debtor which means we credit Smith's account.

Returns outwards refer to the goods which the business returns to the original suppliers. They are purchases that are unsuitable and for this reason are also known as **purchases returns**.

Example 2.8

Goods previously purchased from L McCormack for £212 were found to be faulty and were subsequently returned to him on 5 April.

Returns outwards

	£		£
		5 Apr L McCormack	212

L McCormack

	£		£
5 Apr Returns outwards	212		

Returns outwards represent a decrease in the asset of inventory which will mean we credit this account. By returning goods we will owe McCormack less money which reduces the liability of trade payables which means we debit McCormack's account.

Returns	
Returns inwards (sales returns)	*Inventory returned **to** the business from the customer*
Returns outwards (purchases returns)	*Inventory returned **by** the business to the supplier*

You should now attempt review questions 2.8 to 2.14.

Drawings

In Example 2.1 we looked at the owner of the business adding resources to the business in the form of extra capital. However, it is perfectly possible that the owner will take resources out of the business for personal use. Resources taken out of the business by the owner are known as **drawings**.

As the owner will be withdrawing assets from the business, the relevant asset account will be credited; the debit entry is in the drawings account. Hence, the double-entry for drawings is completed as follows:

Account to be debited	Account to be credited
Drawings	Asset withdrawn by owner

Example 2.9

On 1 October, the owner of the firm takes out £500 from the business bank account for her own use.

Drawings

	£		
1 Oct Bank	500		

Bank

			£
		1 Oct Drawings	500

The total drawings for the year would be transferred to the capital account at the end of the trading period. This will adjust the existing capital of the business to give us the new capital account balance for the following trading period – this adjustment will also appear on the statement of financial position.

Income and expenses

Businesses will incur expenses as part of their normal trading operations. Common expenses incurred by businesses would include rent, insurance and wages. In addition, the business may have other income in addition to the sales revenue earned from selling goods. Additional forms of income for the business may include rental income (known as rent received).

The double-entry account transactions to record income and expenses are straightforward. It is often easier to think of these transactions in terms of their effect on the bank or cash account – as a payment will involve the bank or cash account being credited, the debit entry for this transaction must be in the relevant expense account.

Similarly, if money is received as business income then we would debit either the cash account or the bank account. This means that the credit entry for this transaction would be in the relevant income account.

For expenses:

Account to be debited	Account to be credited
Expense	Bank or cash

For income and other revenues:

Account to be debited	Account to be credited
Bank or cash	Income

Example 2.10

On 9 March, the firm paid wages of £140 in cash.

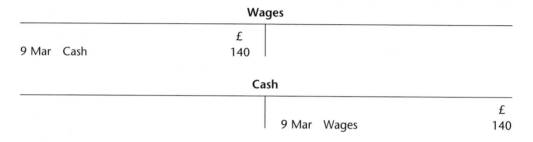

Wages

	£
9 Mar Cash	140

Cash

	£
	9 Mar Wages 140

Example 2.11

On 9 March, the firm received a cheque for £250 in respect of rent received.

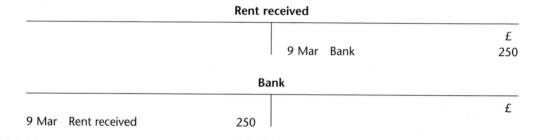

Rent received

	£
	9 Mar Bank 250

Bank

	£
9 Mar Rent received 250	

How many different expense accounts should be opened?

An account should be opened for each separate expense generated by the business. However, it is possible that some of the smaller expenses that are incurred, for example tea or coffee costs for a staff office, could be kept in a 'general' or a 'sundry' expenses account.

It is better to keep each expense separate so as to provide information for the managers of the business as to what expenses are being incurred, and thus give them information that can be used to control these costs and prevent them rising too quickly.

Another way of separating out the accounts is to ensure that expense and income accounts remain separate. For example, some firms will have an account for both rent as an expense, and rent as an income. Here, two separate accounts are maintained with the account dealing with rental income referred to as rent received, and the account dealing with the expense of rent simply referred to as rent.

If there is any doubt in knowing whether you are dealing with an income or an expense account then just look at the entries made within the account – the expense account will have the debit entry referring to the means of payment – as in the above example. Incomes will be credited to the income account as the money received for the income would be debited to either bank or cash.

You should now attempt review questions 2.15 to 2.19.

Balancing accounts

At the end of a given accounting period (which could be weekly, monthly or yearly), the double-entry accounts will be balanced. The main purpose of balancing the accounts is so that the financial statements of the business can be produced.

Balancing off accounts involves comparing the totals of the debit entries in the individual accounts with the total of the credit entries. The balance on an account arises where there is a difference between the total of the debits and the total of the credits. The different ways in which accounts can be balanced are as follows:

Example 2.12: where no balance exists

Some accounts will exist where the totals of the debits and credits are equal. In these cases, there is *no balance* on the *account*.

Bank

2010		£	2010		£
Jan 8	Sales	86	Jan 11	Purchases	345
Jan 15	Cash	112	Jan 14	Wages	290
Jan 18	Equipment	750	Jan 19	Vehicle	2,313
Jan 26	Loan	2,000			
		2,948			2,948

S Moorcroft

2010		£	2010		£
Jan 17	Sales	112	Jan 24	Cash	112

In these two cases, the total of the debits is equal to the total of the credits. The technique to finish the accounts is as follows:

Where there are multiple entries in the account (e.g. see the bank account above):

- Total up each column and write the totals alongside each other – on the same line down.
- Double underline these totals.

Where there is only one entry on each side of the account (e.g. the account of S Moorcroft above):

● Double underline the account.

Example 2.13: entries only on one side of the account

Some accounts will exist where there are only entries on one side of the account.

Where the totals on each side are not the same then there is a *balance* on each account.

Purchases

2010		£	2010		£
Feb 2	R Johns	13	Feb 28	Balance c/d	411
Feb 8	F Spencer	76			
Feb 12	O Tye	230			
Feb 20	I Shipsom	92			
		411			411
Mar 1	Balance b/d	411			

I Shipsom

2010		£	2010		£
Feb 28	Balance c/d	92	Feb 20	Purchases	92
			Mar 1	Balance b/d	92

In the purchases account we enter the *balancing figure* (the amount needed to ensure the two sides are equal) on the credit side. In the account of I Shipsom, there is only one entry in the account (on the credit side) and so we only need the equivalent entry on the debit side of the account. The insertion of these balancing items means the totals of each side now equal and the totals and ruling off can take place as in the earlier example.

The term 'balance c/d' refers to the balance on the account to be carried down to the next period of time. Confusingly, this term is the '*balancing amount*' but not the balance. Notice that on the two accounts above, the balancing figure is then brought down ('balance b/d') to the opposite side of the account for the next period of time. This is the *actual* balance – in the case of Purchases, it is a *debit balance of £411*. In the case of I Shipsom, there is a *credit balance of £92* on the account.

Be careful here: it is the balance b/d which represents the actual balance on the account, not the balance c/d which is simply the balancing figure.

It is good practice to always bring the balance down to the start of the next accounting period – even if not asked for.

Example 2.14: entries on both sides of the account

In some accounts there will be multiple entries in the accounts and the totals of each side will not be equal, as in the following account:

C Flint

2010		£	2010		£
Apr 5	Sales	24	Apr 7	Returns inwards	11
Apr 19	Sales	36	Apr 12	Bank	56
Apr 24	Sales	28			

To balance off this account we would complete the account as follows:

C Flint

2010		£	2010		£
Apr 5	Sales	24	Apr 7	Returns inwards	11
Apr 19	Sales	36	Apr 12	Bank	56
Apr 24	Sales	28	Apr 30	Balance c/d	21
		88			88
May 1	Balance b/d	21			

In the above account, there is a debit balance of £21. This means that C Flint owes the business £21 – a debit balance reflects the fact that the above account receivable is an asset of the business.

General rules for balancing accounts

Although balancing accounts is fairly straightforward, it can initially cause problems. Most problems can be avoided if the following points are remembered:

- Balances *only* exist if there is a difference between the totals on each side of the account.
- The totals of each side of the account are not the balances.
- The balancing figure on the account will be the amount needed to ensure the totals of each side are equal.
- Ensure that the totals of the accounts are written on the same line down.
- Bring the balance down on to the opposite side of the account from the balancing figure.

You should now attempt review questions 2.20 to 2.22.

Chapter review

By now you should understand the following:

- How to record basic transactions for asset, liability and capital accounts
- How to account for inventory transactions in the accounts
- How to account for drawings, income and expenses
- How to balance off accounts.

Handy hints

The following hints will help you avoid errors.

- Always ensure that you make **two** entries for each double-entry transaction.
- Always complete one debit entry and one credit entry for each transaction.
- Memorise the basic rules for asset, liability and capital accounts – use a prompt card until you can memorise these rules.
- Leave plenty of room when drawing up accounts – for extra entries and also room for balancing off the account.
- Inventory is accounted for just as any other asset.
- Each separate expense should be kept in a separate account.
- Incomes and expenses should be kept in separate accounts and not combined.

Key terms

Bookkeeping   The system of recording and maintaining financial transactions in accounts

Double-entry   The system by which accounting entries are recorded in two accounts

Debit   Accounting entry on the left-hand side of an account

Credit   Accounting entry on the right-hand side of an account

Account   A place where a particular type of transaction is recorded

Ledger   A book containing double-entry accounts

Inventory   Goods purchased with the intention of being sold by the business for a profit

Debtor   A person or business that owes a business money and will repay in the near future

Creditor   A person or business that a business owes money to and that is expected to be repaid within the near future

Purchases   Inventory purchased by a business for the purpose of resale

Sales   Inventory sold by a business

Returns inwards   Inventory previously sold by a business which is returned to the firm by the customer (usually because of unsuitability of the inventory)

Returns outwards   Inventory previously purchased by a business which is returned to the original supplier (usually because of unsuitability of the inventory)

Drawings   Resources (e.g. cash) taken out of a business by the owner for private use

Expenses   Costs incurred by a business in the day-to-day running of the business

Income   Revenue earned by a business as part of the business's operations

Balance   The outstanding amount remaining when an account is balanced – measured by the difference between the totals of the debit column and the credit column in an individual account

REVIEW QUESTIONS

2.1 For the following transactions state which accounts should be debited, and which should be credited.

(a) Equipment bought on credit from M Sparks.
(b) Motor car bought and payment made by cheque.
(c) Owner pays own money into bank account.
(d) Fixtures sold on credit to J Harker.
(e) Cheque sent to A Johnson, a creditor.
(f) Cash received from P Shortland, a debtor.

2.2 Write up the following transactions in double-entry accounts of J White.

1 March White places £900 of his own money into the cash till for business use.
4 March He places £500 of the cash into a business bank account.
8 March White buys £400 of machinery, paying by cheque.
12 March White buys shop fittings for £200 on credit from M Yeates.
13 March Machinery worth £200 is sold for the same value for cash.
19 March White decided to bring his own computer into the business at a valuation of £380.

2.3 Record the following transactions for S Vernon's first month of business operations.

2009
2 January £25,000 of owner's money placed into business bank account.
7 January Premises are bought for £15,000, payment made by cheque.
14 January £900 from bank paid into cash till.
17 January Fixtures are purchased for £4,000 on credit from C Platt.
19 January Office supplies bought for cash £500.
23 January Fixtures worth £750 sold for the same amount on credit to D Hammond.

2.4 Write up the following transactions in the double-entry accounts for S Nower for April 2011.

8 April Bank loan taken out for £18,000 which is paid directly into the bank account.
11 April Plant purchased for £4,000 payment made by cheque.
15 April Nower brings her own car into the business at a valuation of £8,000.
18 April Machinery bought on credit from J Bellwood for £2,500.
23 April Plant sold on credit to C Roberts for £800.
26 April Bellwood paid in full by cheque.

2.5 Write up the following transactions in the double-entry accounts for K Johnson for August 2012.

2 August Johnson places £950 of her own money into the cash till.
3 August Johnson borrows £1,200 from J Tahoulan – which is placed into the bank account.
7 August A delivery van is bought on credit for £1,000 from S Wells.
12 August Machinery is purchased for £340 cash.
19 August Johnson sends Tahoulan a cheque for £600 as part repayment of the loan.
27 August A cheque for the full amount is posted to Wells – with £400 cash paid into the bank account to cover the cheque.

2.6 Record the following transactions in ledger accounts for R Wheatcroft for July 2013.

1 July Wheatcroft places £300 of his own money into the business cash till.
3 July Wheatcroft places £1,000 of his own money into the business bank account.

5 July Machinery is bought for £400 with payment made by cheque.

12 July Equipment is bought on credit for £250 from B Street.

14 July A motor car is bought on credit for £1,300 from C Alexander.

18 July A cheque is sent to B Street for £250.

21 July Wheatcroft places £200 of the cash into the bank.

2.7 Record the following transactions in ledger accounts for I Sharp for March 2009.

1 March Owner borrows £10,000 from the Essex Bank which is immediately paid into bank.

3 March Machinery is purchased for £950, payment to be made by cheque.

5 March Sharp transfers £1,000 from the bank into the cash till.

12 March Equipment is purchased from T Wilson on credit for £450.

14 March Motor vehicle for £2,000 is purchased by cheque.

19 March Sharp sends £200 of equipment back to Wilson – it was faulty.

24 March Sharp settles his account with Wilson by making payment by cash.

2.8 For the following transactions, state the accounts to be debited and credited.

(a) Firm buys inventory and pays immediately by cheque.

(b) Goods returned to the original supplier, A Rahman, due to them being faulty.

(c) Garage purchases cars for resale on credit from Autocars Ltd.

(d) Greengrocer purchases fruit for cash.

(e) Garage sells a recovery vehicle that had been used within the business on credit to Rescuecars Ltd.

2.9 For the following transactions state the accounts to be debited and credited.

(a) Goods sold to K Jones on credit are returned due to unsuitability.

(b) Butcher purchases new bacon slicer, paying by cheque.

(c) Baker sends buns back to A Francis, the original supplier, due to them being stale.

(d) Fast food outlet sells pizzas for cash.

(e) Local shop sells counter on credit to E Polley.

2.10 Draw up the double-entry accounts to record the following transactions.

1 Mar Goods bought on credit for £32 from T Burke.

3 Mar Goods bought on credit for £81 from W Randlesome.

9 Mar We return goods to Burke worth £12.

12 Mar We pay Randlesome by cheque for the full £81.

15 Mar We settle our account with Burke by a cash payment of £20.

2.11 Write up the following transactions in the double-entry accounts in the books of M Cousins for the month of December 2014.

1 Dec Cousins opens a business bank account with £8,000 of his own money.

4 Dec Fixtures and fittings purchased for £2,200 on credit from P Lambert.

11 Dec Goods purchased on credit from K Symons for £85.

13 Dec Goods purchased for £41 – payment made by cheque.

15 Dec Goods sold on credit to G Williams for £95.

17 Dec Goods sold on credit to P Parkinson for £124.

22 Dec Williams returns £23 of goods due to them being faulty.

2.12 Write up the following transactions in the double-entry accounts of J Lam for the month of February 2009.

    2 February Lam places £400 of his own money into the cash till.

    3 February Purchases made on credit for £47 from P Jackson.

    5 February Purchases made on credit for £43 from K Sage.

    8 February Goods returned to Jackson worth £11.

14 February Sales of good for cash – £102.

17 February Sales of goods on credit for £95 to L Burrell.

21 February Cash paid to Jackson – £36.

24 February Burrell returns goods worth £28.

2.13 Construct the ledger accounts for S Gillespie from the following transactions.

2015

    1 June Gillespie places £6,000 of his own money into the business bank account.

    4 June Gillespie borrows £4,000 from M Lockwood – money paid into the bank account.

    8 June Purchases on credit: £76 from P Reid, £65 from C Coyne.

16 June Premises purchased for £50,000 – financed entirely by a mortgage from Woodseats Building Society.

21 June Sales made on credit: £240 to P Baldwin, £340 to J Dunne.

25 June Sales for cash – £250.

26 June Purchase of equipment for £950 – payment made by cheque.

29 June Baldwin returns goods worth £50.

2.14 Write up in the following transactions in the double-entry accounts of J Jackson.

2008

    1 September Jackson transfers £4,500 of his own money into the business bank account.

    3 September Jackson purchases goods for resale from S Painter for £123 and from C Throup for £89.

    5 September Goods are sold for £121 cash.

12 September Jackson buys a motor vehicle for £2,900, payment by cheque.

13 September Jackson returns goods worth £87 to Painter.

18 September Jackson sells goods on credit to J Brown for £187.

21 September Brown returns goods worth £31.

27 September Jackson pays Throup in full by cheque.

29 September Brown settles her account in full by cash.

2.15 For the following transactions state which accounts should be debited, and which should be credited.

(a) Rent paid by cheque.

(b) Goods for resale purchased for cash from S Barnes.

(c) Goods sold on credit to A Stacey.

(d) Commission received paid into the business bank account.

(e) Owner takes a computer used by the business to use as her own personal computer.

(f) Cash held in till paid into bank.

2.16 For the following transactions state which accounts should be debited, and which should be credited.

(a) Insurance paid in cash.

(b) Goods previously purchased returned to J Nesbit.

(c) Cash banked.

(d) Purchases on credit from G Thompson.

(e) Marketing costs paid by cheque.

(f) Car used in business sold for cash.

2.17   For the following transactions state which accounts should be debited, and which should be credited.

    (a) Private car to be used in future within business.
    (b) Wages paid by cash.
    (c) Goods purchased for resale taken by owner for private use.
    (d) Rental income received by cheque.
    (e) Goods returned by J Spillane, a customer.
    (f) R Hinds lends the business £400 cash.

2.18   Will Pierce runs a small business. Construct the ledger accounts from the following transactions.

2014
    1 August Pierce borrows £5,000 from K Johnson and places this into the bank.
    1 August Pierce transfers £1,000 from the bank into cash.
    3 August Wages paid by cheque – £320.
    4 August Pierce purchases goods on credit from D Rooney for £52.
    11 August Cash sales – £340.
    15 August Pierce pays insurance of £85 in cash.
    20 August Pierce pays his private car insurance using business cash of £28.

2.19   The following transactions relate to the business of J Clover for the month of May 2009. From the details, construct the ledger accounts.

2009
    1 May Goods purchased on credit from C Donner for £32.
    3 May Goods purchased on credit from J Holmes for £74.
    5 May Cash sales of £318 paid directly into the bank.
    6 May Rent of £54 received in cash.
    8 May Clover returns goods to Donner worth £12.
    11 May Advertising of £19 paid by cheque.
    14 May Fixtures and fittings bought on credit for £820 from J Read.
    19 May Sales on credit to N Bell for £93.
    23 May Holmes paid in full in cash.
    24 May Clover withdraws £100 from the bank for personal use.

2.20   Construct the double-entry accounts of Helen Clews from the following transactions and balance off each account at the end of the month.

2010
    1 November Clews opens a business bank account with £8,500 of her own money.
    3 November Machinery is bought for £1,500, payment made by cheque.
    4 November Machinery insurance of £95 is paid by cheque.
    7 November Purchases on credit are made as follows: £65 from M Hodge, and £21 from B Bolder.
    10 November A vehicle is bought for £4,300 on credit from Mark Sterland.
    14 November Sales on credit are made of £272 to M Smith.
    16 November Goods worth £34 are returned to Hodge.
    18 November Smith sends Clews a cheque for the full amount.
    21 November Clews pays Bolder £21 by cheque.
    24 November Sales are made for £180 on credit to T Curran.

2.21   Post the following transactions to the double-entry accounts of D Weir and balance off the accounts at 30 April 2017.

2017

1 April   Owner places £500 of her own money into the business bank account.

4 April   Goods purchased on credit from J Sheridan for £67.

5 April   Goods purchased on credit from P King for £98.

8 April   Sales made on credit to C Turner for £99.

12 April   Owner returns goods worth £22 to King.

16 April   Commission received £45 cash.

18 April   Sales made on credit to R Nilsson for £178.

20 April   Nilsson returns £58 of the goods that he purchased.

24 April   Owner withdraws £100 from the bank for own private use.

25 April   Cash received totalling £50 from Turner.

28 April   Wages paid by cheque £134.

2.22   Construct the double-entry accounts for the following transactions of N James, a sole trader, and balance off each account at the end of the month.

2016

1 January   Business is started with opening up of a bank account with private money totalling £3,000.

3 January   Fixtures bought on credit from K Wesson for £870.

5 January   Goods purchased on credit from S Johnson for £96.

9 January   Goods purchased on credit from P Jones for £45.

13 January   Money transferred to the cash till from the bank totalling £600.

14 January   Jones paid in full in cash.

16 January   Insurance paid by cheque £33.

19 January   Advertising paid by cash £45.

20 January   Sales on credit of £205 to S Welsh.

22 January   Rent received of £70 cash.

26 January   Welsh returned £60 of goods.

28 January   Cheque received from Welsh for £100.

CHAPTER 3

Financial statements

Learning objectives

By the end of this chapter you should be able to:
- Construct a trial balance from a set of ledger accounts
- Understand the uses and limitations of a trial balance
- Understand the meaning and different measures of profit
- Construct the statement of comprehensive income
- Construct the statement of financial position.

Introduction

One of the most important uses of the double-entry system of bookkeeping is to produce the **financial statements** of the business (also known as the **final accounts** of the business). These statements provide crucial information on business performance. According to IAS 1, the following are classified as the financial statements:

- Statement of comprehensive income
- Statement of financial position
- Statement of changes in equity
- Statement of cash flows
- Notes providing a summary of accounting policies and other explanations.

According to IAS 1, the objective of the financial statements is to provide information about the financial position and financial performance of the business for a period of time. In this chapter we will only be looking at the following:

- Statement of comprehensive income
- Statement of financial position.

Once the double-entry accounts have been balanced off (see Chapter 2) then it is possible to construct a **trial balance** for the business which will facilitate our construction of the financial statements.

In this chapter we will be looking at the financial statements of a **sole trader** – that is an organisation owned by one person. Although accounting standards do not apply to sole traders as they would to limited companies we will still introduce some of the terminology used in the presentation of limited company accounts.

Trial balance

Double-entry accounts are used to calculate the level of profit earned by a business. They can also be used to take a measure of the business's size and financial structure. Before any of this is completed it is customary to extract a trial balance.

The trial balance is simply a list of the closing balances on each individual ledger account. The debit balances and credit balances are listed in separate columns. If the double-entry bookkeeping has been conducted correctly then the totals of these columns should 'agree', that is, should total the same amount. This is no coincidence.

It is logical that the totals of each column should be the same. For every debit entry, a credit entry of equal amount was made in an account. In other words, every time we added an amount to the debits we always added an equal amount to the credits – meaning it has to be the case that the debits and credits agree in total. It doesn't matter which accounts have been affected because the trial balance looks at the system as a whole.

A trial balance that fails to agree would indicate that mistakes have been made in the double-entry bookkeeping. Common errors shown up by the trial balance would include:

● Only entering half of a transaction (i.e. missing out a debit or a credit entry)
● Entering two debits or two credits for a transaction rather than one of each
● Entering different amounts for the two entries.

However, even if a trial balance agrees this does not mean that the bookkeeping has been error-free. For example, any of the following errors would *not* prevent the trial balance agreeing:

● Missing out a whole transaction (i.e. both the debit and the credit entry)
● Entering the same incorrect figure on both halves of the transaction
● Reversing the debit and credit entries.

These types of errors and how errors are corrected in general are explored in Chapter 11. A trial balance will normally appear as follows:

I Fraser
Trial balance as at 31 December 2008

	Dr £	Cr £
Sales		12,000
Purchases	8,000	
Insurance	1,300	
Lighting and heating	900	
General expenses	240	
Machinery	4,200	
Trade receivables*	1,780	
Trade payables*		1,960
Bank	3,940	
Rent received		220
Administration expenses	260	
Drawings	1,560	
Capital		6,000
Loan (repayable in 2015)		2,000
	22,180	22,180

* Covered later.

Inventory at 31 December 2008 was valued at £600.

In the trial balance there will be a mixture of balances from different types of accounts. Some accounts will have no outstanding balance and therefore will not appear in the trial balance.

Any inventory left unsold at the end of the period would be treated as an asset and would be stated outside the trial balance (as there is no individual account for inventory).

For financial statements, it is important to get the correct format of the title. Think of this as a three-part process:

- Who? – the name of the person or business
- What? – what type of statement
- When? – for what time period

This may be referred to as the three Ws.

Whether the financial statement is for a particular point in time (i.e. a day) or for a period of time (e.g. a year) is an important distinction to make and be aware of.

The focus of some examination questions will be on constructing or correcting a trial balance, which means that is important that you can remember the balances of particular types of account – whether debit or credit. The common balances are as follows:

Common balances in the trial balance	
Debit balances	**Credit balances**
Assets	Liabilities
Drawings	Capital
Expenses	Revenues
	Provisions*

* Covered later in the book.

Some balances can be debit or credit. For example, the bank balance can be either be a debit balance if there is money in the bank or a credit balance if there is an overdrawn balance.

You should now attempt review questions 3.1 to 3.4.

Statement of comprehensive income

The **statement of comprehensive income** is the statement which shows the profit or loss earned by a business for a particular period of time. For many years, this was known as the **profit and loss account**. More recently, it was also known as the **income statement** of the business. In this chapter we will use the IAS 1 terminology for the full statement of comprehensive income.

As we construct this statement we will refer to the two sections of the statement as the trading account and the profit and loss account respectively. In fact, some older texts still refer to the statement of comprehensive income as a 'trading and profit and loss account'. Although the introduction of alternative names for this one statement may seem confusing, this is designed to make understanding the full statement and how it is constructed easier.

*A **statement of comprehensive income** is also known as*
*a **profit and loss account***
or
*an **income statement**.*

Calculation of profit

Profit maximisation – where managers and owners aim to make as much profit as possible – is the main objective of many businesses. Even if a business has other objectives, such as growth or survival, the calculation of profit will be of great importance for the following reasons:

- *Calculation of tax* – tax paid to the government will be based on the profits earned
- *Obtaining credit* – lenders (such as banks) will want to see that they will be repaid and profit is a good indicator of this ability
- *Expansion* – profits enable a firm to grow.

Profit is measured over a period of time. The calculation of the profit will involve calculation of both total income and total expenses generated for a particular time period with profit being the difference between these two. The profit of a business is calculated in the **statement of comprehensive income**. However, there is more than one measurement of profit which can be calculated.

Difference between gross and net profits

Although the final profit figure is important, managers and owners will also want to know the size of the profit made on the actual sales that have been made before any other expenses are deducted. As a result, statements of comprehensive income are normally split into two sections, the trading account and the profit and loss account.

Sections found in the statement of comprehensive income	
Trading account	Calculates the **gross profit** – calculated as the profit made on the buying and selling of goods.
Profit and loss account	Calculates the **net profit** – calculated as the profit remaining after all other expenses are deducted.

Given that the gross profit is only calculated as the profit made on the buying and selling of goods, it is possible that a firm earns a gross profit, but still ends up with a net loss. It is also possible (though unlikely) that the business makes a gross loss, which would make it highly unlikely that they would make anything other than a net loss.

The information needed to calculate gross and net profits will come from the trial balance. For the purpose of the next few examples, we will continue to use the trial balance of I Fraser.

I Fraser
Trial balance as at 31 December 2008

	Dr £	Cr £
Sales		12,000
Purchases	8,000	
Insurance	1,300	
Lighting and heating	900	
General expenses	240	
Machinery	4,200	
Trade receivables	1,780	
Trade payables		1,960
Bank	3,940	
Rent received		220
Administration expenses	260	
Drawings	1,560	
Capital		6,000
Loan (repayable in 2015)		2,000
	22,180	22,180

Inventory at 31 Dec 2008 was valued at £600.

The statement of comprehensive income will be constructed from many of the balances found on the trial balance.

To calculate profit we need the balances from the accounts that refer to flows of income and expenditure – look for the balances that are not dealing with assets, liability or capital – these will be the balances that we need. (The asset of inventory will be the only asset balance which is used within the statement of comprehensive income – it is needed in the calculation of the cost of goods sold.)

The unused balances will be used when we construct the statement of financial position and appear in blue to indicate that they are not used in this stage.

Trade receivables and **trade payables** are the names given to the totals of debtors and creditors respectively. In the double-entry accounts these balances would appear as the name of the relevant debtor or creditor.

In each of the ledger accounts that appear in the statement of comprehensive income the balance on the account would be transferred to the income statement. In effect, each ledger account is 'emptied' into the statement of comprehensive income (though this doesn't apply to all accounts).

Trading account

In the trading account we calculate the **_gross profit_**. This is calculated as the difference between sales and the **cost of goods sold**.

Gross profit = Sales less Cost of goods sold

The cost of goods sold refers to the cost of any purchases made by the firm. However, we would not include any purchases that remain unsold at the end of the period so we would always subtract the value of any closing inventory from this purchases figure. In our example, the cost of goods sold would be £8,000 – £600 = £7,400 (i.e. purchases – closing inventory).

In this case, the trading account section of the statement of comprehensive income would look as follows:

I Fraser
Trading Account for year ended 31 December 2008

	£	£
Sales		12,000
Less Cost of goods sold:		
Purchases	8,000	
Less Closing inventory	600	7,400
Gross profit		4,600

Statements of comprehensive income and the trading account can be shown either in what is known as 'horizontal' or 'vertical' presentation. The example above shows the trading account in its vertical format. In this book we will stick to using the vertical format as it is more in line with how financial statements are presented in annual reports.

Note that the title of the trading account contains the three Ws – who, what and for when.

The trading account should not really be thought of as an account. Think of it as part of the business's financial statements – a section of the statement of comprehensive income.

Profit and loss account

The second section of the statement of comprehensive income is sometimes referred to as the profit and loss account. Once we have calculated the gross profit (or gross loss) of the business, it is now time to include all the other expenses that the business has incurred so as to arrive at the net profit.

Net profit = Gross profit – Expenses

It is important that we only include the income and expenses belonging to the particular time period we are concerned with. This means that we must be careful not to include the purchase of any non-current assets as expenses. How we account particularly for non-current assets will be dealt with in Chapter 10.

As with the sales account, the expenses and other income accounts have their balances transferred to the profit and loss section of the statement of comprehensive income. The profit and loss section will appear as follows:

I Fraser
Profit and loss account for the year ending 31 December 2008

	£	£
Gross profit		4,600
Add: Rent received		220
		4,820
Less: Expenses		
Insurance	1,300	
Lighting and heating	900	
General expenses	240	
Administration expenses	260	2,700
Net profit		2,120

Any additional income – in this case 'rent received' – would be added on to the gross profit before we deduct the total of the expenses.

The total of gross profit (with any additional income added on) is greater than the total of the expenses. This means that the business has made a net profit for the year.

The full statement of comprehensive income would appear as follows:

I Fraser
Statement of comprehensive income for the year ending 31 December 2008

	£	£
Sales*		12,000
Less Cost of goods sold:		
Purchases	8,000	
Less Closing inventory	600	7,400
Gross profit		4,600
Add: Rent received		220
		4,820
Less: Expenses		
Insurance	1,300	
Lighting and heating	900	
General expenses	240	
Administration expenses	260	2,700
Net profit		2,120

* **Note**: In the published version of these accounts, sales are referred to as '**revenue**'. Here we will continue to use the term '**sales**' as this enables you to see more closely the link between the statement of comprehensive income and the double-entry bookkeeping.

Although the trading account and profit and loss account can be shown separately (and can appear separately in assessment questions) It is normal to combine the two accounts into one overall accounting statement – the statement of comprehensive income.

The net profit of £2,120 does not mean that the firm has this amount of money in the bank – a common confusion by students new to the subject. The profit earned could have already been 'spent' on new assets, inventory, or taken as personal drawings.

All the profit represents is that the business generated more in income than it managed to spend on business expenses for that period of time.

You should now attempt review questions 3.5 to 3.6.

Statement of financial position

The other main part of a set of financial statements is the **statement of financial position** (previously known as the **balance sheet**). This is also constructed from the balances found on the trial balance. Again, we will use the trial balance of I Fraser.

Balances remaining unused after the construction of the statement of comprehensive income will be used to construct the balance sheet.

The balances appearing on the statement of financial position will be those of assets, liabilities and capital accounts.

The balances that are not being used in the construction of the statement of financial position appear in blue on the version of the trial balance below.

Trade receivables and **Trade payables** are the names given to the totals of debtors and creditors respectively. In the double-entry accounts these balances would appear as the name of the relevant debtor or creditor.

I Fraser
Trial balance as at 31 December 2008

	Dr £	Cr £
Sales		12,000
Purchases	8,000	
Insurance	1,300	
Lighting and heating	900	
General expenses	240	
Machinery	4,200	
Trade receivables	1,780	
Trade payables		1,960
Bank	3,940	
Rent received		220
Administration expenses	260	
Drawings	1,560	
Capital		6,000
Loan (repayable in 2015)		2,000
	22,180	22,180

Inventory at 31 Dec 2008 was valued at £600.

Sections within the statement of financial position

A statement of financial position can be thought of as a list of the assets of the business. It shows the assets of the business and how those assets were financed. Assets can be financed by either the owner's own resources – capital – or by borrowing – liabilities. As we know from Chapter 1, the total value of assets should always be equal to the combined total of capital and liabilities. Given that the statement of financial position reflects this it will always balance.

Rather than simply list assets, liabilities and capital, further subdivisions are shown on a statement of financial position.

Non-current assets

Non-current assets (also known as **fixed assets**) are those assets which are not bought with the intention of resale. They are often bought to be used within the business, either to facilitate production or, in the case of investments, to generate further income. Common examples of non-current assets would include property, plant and equipment. More detail about the accounting treatment of non-current assets is given in the accounting standard IAS 16.

Non-current assets
are also known as
fixed assets.

Current assets

Current assets are assets which are likely to be converted into cash before the end of the current year (i.e. before the date of the next statement of financial position). Liquidity is used to refer to how easily an asset can be converted into cash (without any significant loss in value). Current assets are deemed to be liquid assets. Common examples of current assets would include inventory, trade receivables, bank and cash.

Current liabilities

In line with IAS 1, current liabilities would be those expected to be settled before the date of the next statement of financial position – in other words, in the next year. Common examples of current liabilities would include trade payables, overdrafts and any other short-term borrowings.

Non-current liabilities

Non-current liabilities include any debts that the business incurs which are not due for repayment until at least after the date of the next statement of financial position (i.e. at least one full year away). Common examples of non-current liabilities would include non-current loans, mortgages and debentures (though debentures are only available for limited companies).

Non-current liabilities
are also known as
long-term liabilities.

Capital

In our example the double-entry account for capital would be updated as shown opposite. It will be affected by the net profit earned for the year and will also be reduced by any drawings taken during the period. (NB: Any net loss would be debited to the capital account.)

Capital

2008		£	2008		£
Dec 31	Drawings	1,560	Jan 1	Balance b/d	6,000
Dec 31	Balance c/d	6,560	Dec 31	Net profit	2,120
		8,120			8,120

The statement of financial position will now appear as follows:

I Fraser
Statement of Financial Position as at 31 December 2008

	£	£
Non-current assets		
Machinery		4,200
Current assets		
Inventory	600	
Trade receivables	1,780	
Bank	3,940	
	6,320	
Current liabilities		
Trade payables	1,960	
Working capital		4,360
		8,560
Less **Non-current liabilities**		
Bank loan		2,000
Net assets		6,560
Capital		6,000
Add Net profit		2,120
		8,120
Less Drawings		1,560
		6,560

Note that the title of the statement of financial position contains the three Ws – who, what and for when. However, the 'when' aspect of the title is a specific date as the statement of financial position can only represent a point in time (i.e. a day) and not a period of time.

Working capital is presented as the difference between current assets and current liabilities.

The top section of the statement of financial position represents the **net assets** of the business which are calculated as follows:

> **Non-current assets**
> **+ Current assets**
> **− Current liabilities**
> **− Non-current liabilities**

The bottom section of the statement of financial position represents the capital of the business, which is adjusted by adding any net profit and deducting any drawings.

Use of the statement of financial position

The statement of financial position provides the following uses:

- It gives an estimate for the overall value of the business (this would not include any value of the business which cannot be measured – such as the value of a brand name).
- The financial structure of the business can be examined. For example, a business that relies on loans and other borrowings for its non-current finance will often be seen as a greater risk for investment purposes.
- Working capital is a useful calculation in providing information about the overall liquidity position of the business. A business with low levels of working capital may face problems in the future.

You should now attempt review questions 3.7 to 3.11.

Bringing the statements together

The statement of comprehensive income and the statement of financial position are normally constructed together – with the statement of comprehensive income being constructed first.

The net profit from the statement of comprehensive income will be added to the capital balance on the statement of financial position. As a result, if a mistake is made in calculating the net profit of the business it is unlikely that the statement of financial position will balance.

If the statement of financial position does not balance then don't forget to check the statement of comprehensive income – the mistake might be there!

You should now attempt review questions 3.12 to 3.15.

Further adjustments to the statement of comprehensive income

Opening inventory

So far we have looked at a business in its first year of trading. Once a business trades for more than one accounting period of time then it will be likely we will have inventory in hand at the start of the period (opening inventory) as well as inventory at the end of the period (closing inventory).

Opening inventory is available for use and resale so it will be added into the cost of goods sold calculation. The opening inventory will be a debit entry in the trial balance (closing inventory will always be found in the additional information to the trial balance).

Carriage

Carriage is an expense relating to the transport of goods. There are two types of carriage, and their treatment is as follows:

Treatment of carriage		
Type of carriage	Definition	Appears as expense in
Carriage inwards	The cost of transporting goods from suppliers into the business	Trading account
Carriage outwards	The cost of transporting goods from the business to customers	Profit and loss account

The reason why the two types of carriage expense are treated in different ways is that carriage inwards is connected with the cost of getting goods ready for sale and therefore belongs in the cost of goods sold calculation.

Returns

We have already dealt with the accounting entries for both returns inwards and returns outwards in Chapter 2. However, we will also need to make adjustments in the trading account for the returns. These adjustments are as follows:

Adjustments needed for returns	
Returns inwards	Deduct from sales
Returns outwards	Deduct from purchases

This means that the full cost of goods sold calculation would appear as follows:

Adjustments needed for the cost of goods sold	
Opening inventory Add Purchases Add Carriage inwards Less Returns outwards Less Closing inventory Equals Cost of goods sold	The order in which the cost of goods sold is adjusted for returns outwards and carriage is not important. However, it is good practice to show your full workings when the adjustments are made.

Example

Consider the following trial balance extract:

S Preston
Trial balance (extract) as at 31 December 2009

	Dr £	Cr £
Inventory at 1 January 2009	5,750	
Sales		28,000
Purchases	15,000	
Returns inwards	550	
Returns outwards		320
Carriage inwards	240	
Carriage outwards	410	

Inventory at 31 December 2009 was valued at £4,300.

The trading account – with all these further adjustments – would appear as follows:

S Preston
Trading account for the year ending 31 December 2009

	£	£
Sales		28,000
Less Returns inwards		550
Net turnover		27,450
Less Cost of goods sold:		
Opening inventory	5,750	
Add Purchases	15,000	
	20,750	
Add Carriage inwards	240	
	20,990	
Less Returns outwards	320	
	20,670	
Less Closing inventory	4,300	16,370
Gross profit		11,080

Some points to note:

- In the above example the term **net turnover** is introduced for the difference between sales and returns inwards.
- The carriage outwards would appear with the other business expenses in the profit and loss section of the statement of comprehensive income.

You should now attempt review questions 3.16 to 3.27.

Chapter review

By now you should understand the following:

- How to produce a trial balance and assess its uses and limitations
- How to construct a statement of comprehensive income and consequently calculate profit for the business
- How to construct a statement of financial position.

Relevant accounting standards

IAS 1   Presentation of Financial Statements
IAS 16   Property, Plant and Equipment

Handy hints

The following hints will help you avoid errors.

- The trial balance will always agree – there is no reason for each column to total different amounts.
- Use full workings when constructing a statement of comprehensive income – try not to list items without showing the necessary additions or subtractions.
- Keep columns of data aligned – use margins to stop columns drifting.
- For the statement of financial position, ensure that items belong in the appropriate section.
- Remember – the statement of financial position must balance.
- Again, show full workings in calculations – especially for the capital section.

Key terms

Financial statements   The statements produced by a business to provide a summary of the overall performance and the financial position of the business

Statement of comprehensive income   A statement which shows the profits (or losses) of a business calculated by comparing revenues and expenses

Statement of financial position   A statement which shows the assets, liabilities and capital of a business, enabling an assessment to be made of the strength of the business

Trial balance   A list of all the balances from the double-entry accounts providing an arithmetical check on the accuracy of the bookkeeping

Gross profit   The difference between sales revenue and the cost of the goods sold, before taking other expenses into account

Net profit   The profit earned by deducting *all* expenses from the revenue for the period

Trade receivables   The collective term used to represent the total of the debtors of a business

Trade payables   The collective term used to represent the total of the creditors of a business

Non-current assets   Assets held within a business in order to generate future economic benefits

Current assets   Liquid assets which are held as part of the operations of a business, and which are unlikely to be held continuously for more than the next year

Current liabilities   Short-term borrowings and other debts incurred by a business which are to be repaid in the next year

Non-current liabilities   Borrowings by a business which are not expected to be repaid in the next year

Carriage inwards   The cost of delivering goods (purchases) into a business

Carriage outwards   The cost of delivering goods (sales) to the customers of a business

Working capital   The circulating capital of a business which is used to finance its day-to-day operations, calculated as current assets less current liabilities

Net assets   The total value of all assets of a business less the total value of any liabilities

3.1 Produce a trial balance from the data in question 2.20.

3.2 Produce a trial balance from the data in question 2.21.

3.3 Produce a trial balance from the data in question 2.22.

3.4 The following trial balance has been completed but errors have been made. You are to redraft the trial balance in correct form. You can assume that the balance on the suspense account will be zero in the correct version.

	Dr £	Cr £
Sales		118,944
Purchases		76,574
Returns inwards	432	
Returns outwards		342
Equipment	21,000	
Rent received		1,220
Office expenses		314
Motor vehicles	12,300	
Inventory at 1 January 2011		9,950
Inventory at 31 December 2011	8,722	
Trade payables	6,900	
Trade receivables	8,786	
Bank overdraft	2,246	
Wages and salaries		12,330
Insurance	841	
Capital	26,000	
Drawings	13,125	
Suspense	119,322	
	219,674	219,674

3.5 Construct a statement of comprehensive income for C Palmer for the year ended 31 March 2009 from the following data.

	£
Sales	81,400
Purchases	74,750
Closing inventory	5,890
Business rates	1,800
Electricity	975
Salaries	3,800
Rent	4,200

3.6   Construct a Statement of Comprehensive Income for C Woods for the year ended 30 June 2001 from the following data.

	£
Sales	87,450
Purchases	65,264
Closing inventory	9,810
Heating and lighting	4,310
Marketing	7,866
Wages and salaries	11,721
Commission received	1,045
Rent	3,290

3.7   From the following, produce a statement of financial position for J Harkes as at 30 June 2005.

	£
Property	56,000
Equipment	9,870
Inventory	9,020
Trade receivables	3,422
Bank	1,878
Trade payables	4,321
Capital	67,000
Net profit for year	17,656
Drawings	8,787

3.8   From the following data construct a statement of financial position for D Wilson as at 30 April 2019.

	£
Fixtures and fittings	18,500
Equipment	3,400
Inventory	5,322
Trade receivables	2,324
Bank	1,122
Trade payables	3,413
Cash	98
Capital	16,000
Net profit for year	4,786
Drawings	3,433
Long-term loan	10,000

3.9 From the following, produce a statement of financial position for L Madden as at 31 December 2008.

	£
Premises	75,000
Fixtures and fittings	12,500
Inventory	4,995
Trade receivables	7,212
Bank	3,323
Trade payables	5,788
Capital	62,132
Net profit for year	14,343
Drawings	4,233
Long-term loan	25,000

3.10 From the following data construct the statement of financial position for T Quinn as at 30 June 2012.

	£
Buildings	133,000
Machinery	19,342
Inventory	7,565
Trade receivables	6,285
Bank	4,324
Trade payables	9,797
Cash	314
Loan repayable in 2017	54,000
Capital	95,000
Drawings	11,390
Net profit for year	23,423

3.11 From the following data construct the statement of financial position for N Pearson as at 28 February 2011.

	£
Premises	105,000
Machinery	13,700
Motor vehicles	9,100
Inventory	9,800
Trade receivables	4,543
Trade payables	7,565
Bank overdraft	3,423
Cash	323
Capital	88,434
Net profit for year	23,434
Drawings	7,390
Loan repayable in 2014	27,000

3.12 Below is the trial balance extracted from the books of R Grime as at 30 September 2015.
Construct a statement of comprehensive income for the year to 30 September 2015 and a statement of financial position as at that date.

	Dr £	Cr £
Sales		323,423
Purchases	234,354	
Property	194,000	
Delivery van	18,700	
Trade receivables	18,793	
Trade payables		20,912
Bank	12,346	
Heating expenses	4,233	
Salaries	16,565	
Office expenses	2,131	
Rent and rates	19,213	
Long-term loan		50,000
Capital		144,798
Drawings	18,798	
	539,133	539,133

Inventory was valued at 30 September 2015 at £23,223.

3.13 From the following data construct a statement of comprehensive income for D Ferdinand for the year ending 31 December 2016 and a statement of financial position as at that date.

	Dr £	Cr £
Sales		42,321
Purchases	35,188	
Insurance	345	
Machinery	8,000	
Fixtures and fittings	3,422	
Trade receivables	6,453	
Trade payables		7,585
Bank		1,415
Heating	2,425	
Staff wages	9,891	
Sundry expenses	881	
Marketing	2,866	
Capital		29,808
Drawings	8,745	
Maintenance	2,667	
Cash	246	
	81,129	81,129

Inventory was valued as at 31 December 2016 at £1,890.

3.14 From the following trial balance construct the statement of comprehensive income for P Miller for the year ended 31 December 2007 and a statement of financial position as at that date.

	Dr £	Cr £
Sales		265,000
Purchases	210,450	
Carriage outwards	1,100	
Premises	100,000	
Equipment	15,900	
Trade receivables	7,520	
Trade payables		6,980
Bank	6,500	
Administration	4,300	
Wages and salaries	15,328	
Rates and insurance	3,432	
Repair costs	2,450	
Capital		120,000
Drawings	16,500	
Motor van	8,500	
	391,980	391,980

Inventory as at 31 December 2007 was valued at £9,450.

3.15 Below is a trial balance for A Bantick. Construct a statement of comprehensive income for the period ending 30 November 2011, and a statement of financial position as at that date.

	Dr £	Cr £
Sales		342,312
Purchases	311,769	
Vehicle expenses	3,212	
Premises	87,000	
Motor vehicle	13,000	
Trade receivables	27,878	
Trade payables		29,090
Bank	4,354	
Heating and lighting	7,891	
Wages and salaries	23,141	
Rent and rates	6,543	
Advertising	2,313	
Capital		155,121
Drawings	12,188	
Repairs	4,234	
Plant	23,000	
	526,523	526,523

Inventory as at 30 November 2011 was valued at £27,655.

3.16 From the following data, construct a trading account for the year ended 31 December 2010.

	£
Carriage inwards	332
Sales	15,432
Purchases	9,807
Opening inventory	2,341
Closing inventory	3,298

3.17 Copy out the following trading account filling in the necessary missing figures:

	£	£
Sales		54,353
Less Returns inwards		??????
Net turnover		54,231
Less Cost of goods sold		
Opening inventory	8,798	
Add Purchases	??????	
	54,232	
Add Carriage inwards	767	
	??????	
Less Returns outwards	453	
	54,546	
Less Closing inventory	??????	41,773
Gross profit		??????

3.18 From the following data, construct the trading account for the year ended 30 June 2007.

	£
Sales	43,555
Purchases	27,800
Opening inventory	3,780
Returns outwards	763
Closing inventory	2,943
Returns inwards	544

3.19 From the following data, construct a trading account for the year ended 31 March 2006.

	£
Sales	86,500
Purchases	49,800
Returns inwards	390
Returns outwards	1,010
Carriage inwards	540
Opening inventory	5,670
Closing inventory	6,500

3.20 From the following data, construct a trading account for the year ended 31 October 2012.

	£
Sales	17,424
Purchases	12,342
Returns inwards	123
Returns outwards	432
Carriage inwards	787
Opening inventory	3,189
Closing inventory	4,123

3.21 From the following data, construct a statement of comprehensive income for D Hirst for the year ended 31 December 2014.

	£
Sales	143,244
Purchases	105,400
Returns inwards	780
Returns outwards	1,010
Carriage inwards	650
Opening inventory	14,300
Closing inventory	17,630
Advertising	3,230
Insurance	2,767
Wages	22,321
Rent received	1,899
Carriage outwards	812

3.22 From the following balances, construct the statement of comprehensive income for P Warhurst for the year ended 31 December 2003.

	£
Sales	243,233
Purchases	165,764
Returns inwards	2,122
Returns outwards	3,413
Carriage inwards	1,898
Opening inventory	43,545
Closing inventory	39,898
Heating costs	2,865
Office salaries	16,754
Wages	26,323
Rent and rates	8,778
Carriage outwards	976

3.23 From the following data construct a statement of comprehensive income for C Hopkins for the year ended 31 March 2011.

	£
Sales	43,244
Purchases	28,879
Returns inwards	342
Returns outwards	453
Inventory at 1 April 2010	4,346
Heating	3,423
Insurance	2,767
Wages	8,787
Carriage	1,568

Additional information:

(a) Inventory as at 31 March 2011 was exactly 50% higher than the inventory one year earlier.
(b) Carriage inwards accounted for £756 out of the total cost for carriage.

3.24 From the following data construct a statement of comprehensive income for R Millward for the period ended 31 December 2014, and a statement of financial position as at that date.

	Dr £	Cr £
Sales		78,678
Purchases	56,545	
Carriage	666	
Inventory as at 1 January 2014	8,984	
Machinery	15,000	
Fixtures and fittings	8,450	
Trade receivables	9,876	
Trade payables		5,676
Bank overdraft		5,344
Gas and electricity	4,212	
Wages	14,234	
General expenses	1,254	
Advertising	3,221	
Capital		48,740
Drawings	9,899	
Maintenance	2,667	
Commission received		870
Equipment	4,300	
	139,308	139,308

Additional information:

(a) Inventory at 31 December 2014 was valued at £5,467.
(b) Carriage inwards accounts for £321 of the total carriage expense.

3.25 From the following trial balance construct the statement of comprehensive income for D Wilcox for the year ended 31 July 2015 and a statement of financial position as at that date.

	Dr £	Cr £
Sales		141,000
Purchases	96,500	
Returns inwards	321	
Returns outwards		423
Carriage inwards	433	
Carriage outwards	534	
Inventory as at 1 August 2014	6,788	
Machinery	13,200	
Vehicles	7,800	
Trade receivables	8,232	
Trade payables		7,564
Bank	3,453	
Lighting and heating	4,233	
Wages and salaries	14,312	
Insurance	2,131	
Rent	7,705	
Long-term loan		7,000
Capital		15,000
Drawings	5,345	
	170,987	170,987

Inventory at 31 July 2015 was valued at £5,454.

3.26 From the following trial balance for E Soormally, produce a statement of comprehensive income for the period ending 30 September 2017 and a statement of financial position as at that date.

	Dr £	Cr £
Sales		534,534
Purchases	412,312	
Returns inwards	5,435	
Returns outwards		4,233
Carriage inwards	989	
Carriage outwards	2,123	
Inventory as at 1 October 2016	67,809	
Plant	55,000	
Motor van	19,800	
Trade receivables	43,242	
Trade payables		32,132
Bank	19,809	
Power costs	23,432	
Wages	42,423	
Business rates	8,723	
Marketing expenses	5,132	
Debentures		75,000
Capital		121,211
Drawings	27,656	
Maintenance	6,805	
Sundry income		18,980
Equipment	45,400	
	786,090	786,090

Inventory at 30 September 2017 was valued at £53,673.

3.27 From the following data construct a statement of comprehensive income for S Rogers for the year ending 31 July 2018 and a statement of financial position as at that date.

	Dr £	Cr £
Sales		765,755
Purchases	545,343	
Returns inwards	5,424	
Returns outwards		6,562
Carriage inwards	1,213	
Carriage outwards	5,343	
Inventory as at 1 August 2017	63,443	
Machinery	88,500	
Fixtures and fittings	49,600	
Trade receivables	42,540	
Trade payables		53,453
Bank	23,123	
Heating and lighting	24,211	
Wages and salaries	43,243	
General expenses	8,787	
Distribution costs	5,989	
Loan (repayable in 2023)		25,000
Capital		99,700
Drawings	24,343	
Maintenance	2,667	
Commission received		8,676
Equipment	24,500	
Cash	877	
	959,146	959,146

Inventory at 31 July 2018 was valued at £75,343.

CHAPTER 4

Day books and ledgers

Learning objectives

By the end of this chapter you should be able to:

- Explain the use of day books and ledgers
- Construct and maintain a cash book of two or three columns
- Construct and understand the uses of a petty cash book
- Make appropriate entries and maintain the main day books
- Enter transactions into the journal when necessary.

Introduction

For very small businesses all the double-entry accounts can be kept in one book – one ledger – which will be sufficient for the business's financial records. However, for most businesses, keeping all the accounts in one ledger would not be the most efficient in terms of organisation as it would become time-consuming to track down individual entries when required. Therefore some amendments are made to the accounting system once a business moves beyond a certain size.

Ledgers

Once a business goes beyond a certain size it makes sense to divide the ledgers up according to the type of account in which the transactions are to be entered. It is common practice to have three distinct ledgers: a **sales ledger**, a **purchases ledger** and a **general (or nominal) ledger**.

Name of ledger	Accounts contained within the ledger
1. Sales ledger	*Contains all the personal accounts of credit customers (debtors)*
2. Purchases ledger	*Contains all the personal accounts of credit suppliers (creditors)*
3. General ledger (or nominal ledger)	*Contains all other accounts not contained in the sales or purchases ledger*

Ledger accounts only provide a small amount of information about transactions. It is useful to have a separate source of information about each transaction which provides back-up to the ledgers. This extra information is contained with the business's day books.

Day books

Day books (also known as **journals** or **books of original entry**) are where transactions are first recorded. These day books are not accounts. (The cash book is the only day book which serves jointly as both a day book and an account.) They are simply books that record details of transactions as and when they happen – almost like diaries of transactions.

There are several day books, each of which will be used for a particular type of transaction. The day books which are used are as follows:

Name of day book	Type of transaction recorded
Sales day book	All credit sales of goods
Purchases day book	All credit purchases of goods with the intention of resale
Return inwards day book	Returns inwards of goods previously sold
Returns outwards day book	Returns outwards of goods previously purchased
Cash book (and petty cash book)	All cash (and bank) transactions
The journal	Any transaction not covered by the other day books

Posting transactions from the day book

Part of the purpose of the day-book system is to provide back-up to the ledgers. It also provides order to the ledgers by linking up transactions. When a transaction is entered into the day book, one half of the double-entry transaction can be entered into the day book, with the second posted to the ledger account. This prevents the individual accounts within the ledgers becoming cluttered with many frequent entries.

You should now attempt review questions 4.1 to 4.3.

Cash books

The cash book acts as a combination of the cash and bank accounts of the business. It therefore records all bank and cash transactions made by the business. Consider the following example of a cash and bank account for a business for the month of January 2011.

Example 4.1

Cash Account

2011		£	2011		£
Jan 1	Balance b/d	165	Jan 4	Stationery	18
Jan 3	Sales	33	Jan 7	Purchases	54
Jan 8	Sales	52	Jan 15	Wages	120
			Jan 22	Electricity	42
			Jan 31	Balance c/d	16
		250			250

Bank Account

2011		£	2011		£
Jan 7	F Bentos	95	Jan 1	Balance b/d	260
Jan 12	L Martins	56	Jan 9	Machinery	250
Jan 16	Loan	300	Jan 21	W Skelton	88
Jan 31	Balance c/d	189	Jan 27	R Verge	42
		640			640

To construct a cash book, we simply combine the above two accounts. The cash book for these accounts would appear as follows:

Cash book

2011		Cash £	Bank £	2011		Cash £	Bank £
Jan 1	Balance b/d	165		Jan 1	Balance b/d		260
Jan 3	Sales	33		Jan 4	Stationery	18	
Jan 7	F Bentos		95	Jan 7	Purchases	54	
Jan 8	Sales	52		Jan 9	Machinery		250
Jan 12	L Martins		56	Jan 15	Wages	120	
Jan 16	Loan		300	Jan 21	W Skelton		88
Jan 31	Balance c/d		189	Jan 22	Electricity	42	
				Jan 27	R Verge		42
				Jan 31	Balance c/d	16	
		250	640			250	640
Feb 1	Balance b/d	16		Feb 1	Balance b/d		189

All we have done here is to superimpose the two accounts so they appear as one account, albeit an account with two columns of data for both the debit side and the credit side. As a result the above would be known as a **two-column cash book**.

There are two opening balances and two closing balances on the cash book – one for the cash account and one for the bank column. These can be either debit or credit balances for the bank account but can only be debit balances for the cash column.

Contra entries

One entry that can cause some initial confusion in the cash book is that known as a **contra entry**. A contra entry occurs when both parts of the double-entry transaction are contained within the same account. In the cash book, the contra entry would include cash withdrawn from the bank, or cash deposited into the bank. There is nothing special about either of these transactions. Both will require a debit and a credit entry to be made.

For example, depositing cash into the bank account would require a debit entry in the bank column (because the asset of bank is being increased) and a credit entry in the cash column (because the asset of cash is being reduced).

You should now attempt review questions 4.4 to 4.7.

Cash and trade discounts

Businesses will trade with other businesses. It is common practice for intra-business trade to include two types of discounts.

Trade discounts are discounts which are offered to other businesses with no particular conditions attached. The trade discount may show up on the invoice but would not appear in any of the ledger accounts.

Cash discounts are given by businesses to another business with the intent of encouraging prompt settlement of any outstanding invoice. They are usually given as a percentage of the outstanding invoice (once any trade discount has been deducted). These discounts will show up in the ledger accounts as follows:

Discounts allowed Discounts that the business gives to customers settling amounts owing to the business

Discounts received Discounts given by other business when the business settles the amounts it owes to its suppliers

When recording these discounts there are two different approaches: firstly, entries can be made in the ledger accounts for each individual transaction; alternatively, monthly totals for each type of cash discount can be posted to the ledger accounts. This second approach requires the use of a three-column cash book.

Example 4.2

On 2 May we sell £180 of goods on credit to D Lindley. We offer a 5% discount for full settlement within 14 days. On 8 May Lindley settles her account in full by sending a cheque totalling £171 (i.e. £180 less 5%).

D Lindley

	£			£
2 May Sales	180	8 May	Bank	171
		8 May	Discounts allowed	9

Discounts allowed

	£		£
8 May D Lindley	9		

As you can see, after the payment has been made, the account of D Lindley has no outstanding balance, i.e. Lindley no longer owes the business.

Example 4.3

On 18 May, we buy £240 of goods on credit from C Zaori. A 2.5% discount is offered if we settle within seven days. On 24 May we send cash of £234 to Zaori in full settlement.

C Zaori

		£			£
24 May	Bank	234	18 May	Purchases	240
24 May	Discounts received	6			

Discounts received

	£			£
		24 May	C Zaori	6

Once again, the discount received allows us to have no outstanding amount with regards to Zaori's account.

Three-column cash books

Although it is perfectly acceptable to record discounts in the manner outlined above, a speedier way of recording discounts is to introduce a third column to the cash book – the extra column recording discounts, both allowed and received.

Example 4.4

If we use the above data from Examples 4.2 and 4.3 then we can show how these would appear in a three-column cash book.

Cash book

		Discount £	Cash £	Bank £			Discount £	Cash £	Bank £
8 May	D Lindley	9		171	24 May	C Zaori	6		234

Note that the column for discounts on the debit side of the cash book represents the **discounts allowed** by the business, and the discounts column on the credit side of the cash book represents the **discounts received** by the business.

Whereas both the cash and bank columns will be balanced off in the normal manner, the discounts columns are not balanced off. The discounts columns are simply totalled and these totals are transferred to the ledger accounts for discounts allowed and discounts receivable.

You should now attempt review questions 4.8 to 4.12.

Petty cash book

Some businesses actually keep a separate cash book *and* a petty cash book. The petty cash book is used for dealing with small items of money. It may be the case that the firm has lots of transactions which involve relatively small amounts of money (e.g. petrol costs, postage costs and so on). If these were all entered in the main cash book then it would quickly become cluttered up with entries for small amounts of money. To prevent this, a petty cash book deals with these items. At the end of each month the monthly totals can then be transferred to the main cash book. This has the other advantage of allowing other members of staff (usually junior workers) the responsibility of dealing with the petty cash book alone and this frees up time for the main cashier of the firm to deal with the main cash book.

Some very large firms may actually use the petty cash book for dealing with all cash items of expenditure. The main cash book would then only be used for bank transactions.

Imprest system

The most common system used to maintain the petty cash book is known as the imprest system. This involves co-ordination between the cashier responsible for the cash book and the cashier responsible for the petty cash book.

The cashier will give the petty book cashier just enough money to cover the petty cash transactions of a period of time – usually one month. At the end of the month, the amount actually spent will be totalled up and the amount will be refunded from the main cashbook as follows:

Entries needed to refund amount spent on petty cash	
Debit	*Credit*
Petty cash book	Cash book

In this way, the balance on the petty cash book will always be the same at the start of each period. This opening balance is known as the **float** or **imprest**. The float can be changed if it is observed that the petty cash is being spent too quickly, or is not being spent at all. The idea is that the float should cover the period's expenses.

Most firms that maintain petty cash books will do so in a format which categorises different types of petty cash expenditure. This is known as an analytical petty cash book because it analyses the different types of expenditure (different types of expenditure appear under different column headings).

The petty cash book still follows the rules of any double-entry account. However, the credit side of this account will be split into the various categories of expenditure.

Example 4.5

The following are details of petty cash transactions for the month of February 2004. The business transactions that occur are as follows:

Feb 1   The chief cashier debits the petty cash book with £70 to restore the float.

			£
Feb 4	Petrol costs	10
Feb 5	Stationery	4
Feb 8	Coffee for office	3
Feb 9	Bus fares	6
Feb 15	Milk and tea	2
Feb 16	Rail fares	17
Feb 21	New paper for printer	9
Feb 24	Folders for office	4

Feb 28   The chief cashier debits the petty cash book with £55 to restore the float.

The £55 received on February 28 is exactly the amount that was spent during February on petty cash transactions.

The analysis columns that are to be used in this example are:

● Travel expenses
● Stationery
● Miscellaneous.

There are no strict rules on what columns should be used or how many of them there should be. It makes sense not to have too many because it may become confusing when filling in the petty cash book.

The petty cash book will appear as in Exhibit 4.1.

Exhibit 4.1

Receipts	Date	Details	Voucher	Total	Travel costs	Stationery	Misc.
£				£	£	£	£
70	Feb 1	Cash					
	Feb 4	Petrol costs	12	10	10		
	Feb 5	Stationery	13	4		4	
	Feb 8	Coffee for office	14	3			3
	Feb 9	Bus fares	15	6	6		
	Feb 15	Milk and tea	16	2			2
	Feb 16	Rail fares	17	17	17		
	Feb 21	Paper for printer	18	9		9	
	Feb 24	Folders for office	19	4		4	
				55	33	17	5
55	Feb 28	Cash					
	Feb 28	Balance c/d		70			
125				125			
70	Mar 1	Balance b/d					

Notice the following:

1 The receipts and the total columns in effect represent the debit and credit columns of the petty cash book.

2 On Feb 1 and Feb 28, the petty cash book is debited with the amount needed to restore the float.

3 Each analysis column is totalled up separately. This would then be transferred to the actual account for each category of expenditure in the general ledger. Thus these individual ledger accounts, such as travel costs, are only entered with monthly totals and not the individual entries.

4 The vouchers are used by staff to reclaim the amount spent out of petty cash. For example, it may be the case that a member of staff purchases an item for the business out of their own money. To reclaim this amount, a voucher must be filled out before it can be taken out of the petty cash. Of course, it is important that these transactions are verified by the petty cashier, otherwise the business may find that money is being taken without reason.

Advantages of maintaining a petty cash book

1 It stops the main cash book being cluttered up with small items of expenditure.
2 It allows the firm to delegate these small items to a junior member of staff, which frees up the time of the main cashier to concentrate on other areas.

You should now attempt review questions 4.13 to 4.14.

Sales day book

The **sales day book** records all transactions resulting from credit sales. This must only include sales relating to goods bought with the specific intention of resale. For example, a firm that sells computers would not include the credit sale of office furniture in the sales day book and would only include the credit sales of computers (and other equipment that related to the business's main trading area, e.g. printers or scanners).

For each sale made, the business will issue an **invoice**. This is a written document which contains details of the sale, such as the goods to be ordered, the value of the sale and any relevant trade or cash discounts. The sales invoice would be issued to a customer when the sale is made. From the invoice, the details of each sale would be collated and written up into the sales day book. A sample page of a sales journal would appear as follows:

Sales day book

Date	Invoice No.	Details	Total
2013			£
03 March	1011	C Scanlon	89
06 March	1012	S Hanley	113
18 March	1013	M Brammah	150
29 March	1015	C Scanlon	54
Total			406

For the sales day book, only the information relevant for the accounts is recorded.

The invoice number relates to the number on each invoice – usually rising in sequential order.

The details relate to the name of the account in which the sale will be recorded.

The total will be after any trade discount has been deducted but before any cash discount has been taken.

In Chapter 2, the double-entry for each credit sale was recorded by crediting the sales account, and by debiting the account of the customer. However, to save time we now introduce a more efficient way of recording the credit sales. This is completed as follows: for each credit sale, we record the details in the sales day book. We then post the details to the sales ledger by debiting the accounts of the customers. However, we only debit the sales account in the sales ledger with the monthly total for sales. The resulting entries would be as follows:

Sales Ledger

C Scanlon

2013		£	2013	£
3 Mar	Sales	89		
29 Mar	Sales	54		

S Hanley

2013		£	2013	£
6 Mar	Sales	113		

M Brammah

2013		£	2013	£
18 Mar	Sales	150		

Total of debit entries = £406.

General Ledger

Sales

2013	£	2013		£
		31 Mar	Total for month	406

Total of credit entries = £406.

You should now attempt review questions 4.15 and 4.16.

Purchases day book

The **purchases day book** consists of all credit purchases of goods for resale. For example, a business selling office furniture would not include the purchase of a delivery van as purchases as this is an asset to be used within the business.

The sales invoice sent by the business to the customer can also be thought of as the purchase invoice by the business which is buying the goods. When the business which is purchasing goods receives the invoice this would be used to construct the purchases invoice.

For the purchases day book, only the information relevant for the accounts is recorded.

Purchases day book

Date 2013	Invoice No.	Details	Total £
02 March	564	J Nunn	34
05 March	565	C Smith	12
11 March	566	C Smith	26
22 March	567	A Butcher	55
Total			127

The invoice number simply relates to the numerical order of each purchase.

The details relate to the name of the account in which the sale will be recorded.

The total will be after any trade discount has been deducted but before any cash discount has been taken.

As with the sales day book, it is only the entries in the personal accounts which are entered individually. The entry in the general ledger (i.e. the entry in the purchases account) is only entered as a monthly total. The entries in this example would appear as follows:

General Ledger

Purchases

2013	£	
31 Mar Purchases for month	127	

Total of debit entries = £127.

Purchases Ledger

J Nunn

2013	£	2013	£
		2 Mar Purchases	34

C Smith

2013	£	2013	£
		5 Mar Purchases	12
		11 Mar Purchases	26

A Butcher

2013	£	2013	£
		22 Mar Purchases	55

Total of credit entries = £127.

You should now attempt review questions 4.17 to 4.20.

Returns day books

Both purchases and sales may, if allowed, be returned to the original supplier. In this case, the return would be recorded in the relevant day book. There is a return book for the each of the two types of return:

Returns inwards day book   for recording returns inwards (or sales returns)
Returns outwards day book   for recording returns outwards (or purchases returns)

For each of these, the method used is the same as used in the sales and purchases day books:

General ledger account – only enter the monthly total
Personal ledger account – enter details of each transaction individual.

The following two examples will be based on and will follow on from the transactions above.

Example 4.6

Returns inwards day book

Date 2013	Note No.	Details	Total £
18 March	1/3	C Scanlon	34
26 March	2/3	M Brammah	12
Total			46

The note number simply relates to the **credit note** which is a document issued by the business to the customer when it is agreed to accept the returns made by the customer.

The term credit note is useful as it indicates that we are to credit the personal account of the customer (i.e. reduce the amount owing to us).

Each entry in the returns inwards day book will require an entry to be made in the personal account of the customer in the sales ledger.

Sales Ledger

C Scanlon

2013		£	2013		£
3 Mar	Sales	89	18 Mar	Returns inwards	34
29 Mar	Sales	54			

M Brammah

2013		£	2013		£
18 Mar	Sales	150	26 Mar	Returns inwards	12

General Ledger

Returns Inwards

2013		£	2013	£
31 Mar	Total for month	46	2013	£

Notice how the returns inwards entry will reduce the balance on each account.

Example 4.7

Returns outwards day book

Date 2013	Note No.	Details	Total £
13 March	3/100	C Smith	23
17 March	3/101	J Nunn	10
Total			<u>33</u>

Goods returned to the original supplier may often be accompanied by a **debit note**. This note will give details of the goods and the reason for returning them.

The entries in the returns outwards day book will be posted in the purchases ledger to the accounts of the business's suppliers.

As with the purchases day book, it is only the entries in the personal accounts which are entered individually. The entry in the general ledger (i.e. the entry in the purchases account) is only entered as a monthly total. The entries in this example would appear as follows:

General Ledger

Returns outwards

		2013 31 Mar Total for month	£ 33

Purchases Ledger

J Nunn

2013	£	2013	£
17 Mar Returns outwards	10	2 Mar Purchases	34

C Smith

2013	£	2013	£
13 Mar Returns outwards	23	5 Mar Purchases	12
		11 Mar Purchases	26

You should now attempt review questions 4.21 to 4.24.

The journal

Nearly all business transactions will be dealt with in the cash book and the four main day books outlined so far in this chapter. Trying to imagine a transaction which does not involve those is not easy. However, there are transactions which require the use of another day book, and this day book would be known as the journal.

The journal is used mainly for unusual transactions which would not occur on a frequent basis. As a result the layout of a journal is not the same as that of the four main day books.

Common uses of the journal are as follows:

1 Buying and selling fixed assets on credit
2 Writing off bad debts (see Chapter 9)
3 Correcting errors (see Chapter 11).

The layout of the journal is as follows:

Journal Entry

	Dr £	Cr £
Date Name of account to be debited	Amount	
Name of account to be credited		Amount
Narrative – a brief explanation of the transaction entered above		

The name of the account to be debited must always come first – followed by the name of the account to be credited slightly indented underneath. There is no point getting these mixed up as any deviation in the layout would be incorrect.

The narrative should provide detail needed to understand the transactions. It does not need to contain detail such as the accounts used, or amounts, as these are entered in the actual journal entry. However, it should provide sufficient detail so the transaction can be understood, as it is possible that the transactions could have more than one explanation.

Example 4.8

On 12 November, we purchase a delivery van from Sharp Ltd on credit for £3,700.

The Journal (extract)

	Dr £	Cr £
Nov 12 Delivery van	3,700	
Sharp Ltd		3,700
Asset bought on credit for business use		

Example 4.9

On 8 December, we write off a debt of £120 owing to us from J Dolman as bad. We received a payment of 20p in the £ in full settlement.

In this situation, we will receive one-fifth (i.e. 20p out of every £1 owed) of the amount owing and the remainder is written off (i.e. lost) as a bad debt.

The Journal (extract)

	Dr £	Cr £
Dec 8 Bad debt	96	
Bank	24	
J Dolman		120
Debt partly written off as bad with residual amount received as a cheque		

In the above example you can see that the debit entry is split into two entries. This is perfectly appropriate as long as the totals of the debit entries equal the totals of the credit entries.

You should now attempt review questions 4.25 to 4.31.

The use of folio columns

Each double-entry account will contain the name of the other account in which the other half of the transaction is contained. Except in very small firms, this does not necessarily make it any easier to locate the other account – there may be hundreds of separate accounts.

A method of speeding up the finding of an account is the use of folio columns. These are found both in accounts and in day books. An extra column, usually quite small, is placed beside the details of each transaction. In this folio column is placed an abbreviated reference to which ledger or day book the transaction can be located in, and on what page of the relevant book.

For example, if a credit sale was recorded in the sales day book with the folio reference SL54, then this would tell us that the customer's account could be found on page fifty-four of the sales ledger. If we actually looked at this relevant account then we would see that it also had a folio reference sending us back to the sales day book itself.

Common abbreviations are as follows:

SL   Sales ledger
PL   Purchases ledger
GL   General ledger
CB   Cashbook

If the entry 'C' appears in the folio column then this refers to a **contra entry**. This means that both halves of the transaction are contained in the same account. An example of this is dealt with in the section on cash books.

Chapter review

By now you should understand the following:

- How transactions are classified according to type in both ledgers and day books
- How to produce a cash book of either two or three columns
- How to maintain a petty cash book
- How to enter transactions into the main day books and post to the correct ledger
- The use and layout of the journal, and how to enter transactions in it.

Handy hints

The following hints will help you avoid errors.

- For the cash book – remember that the opening and closing balances can be both debit and credit and are not necessarily on the same side as each other.
- The discount columns are not to be balanced and are simply totalled up.
- Only monthly totals are transferred to the accounts in the general ledger.
- Ensure that the debit entry always comes before the credit entry in the journal.
- Check carefully if narratives are required for the journal entries.

Key terms

Sales ledger   A book containing all the accounts of the credit customers of the business

Purchases ledger   A book containing all the accounts of the credit suppliers of the business

General ledger   A book containing all accounts of the business that are not found in the sales or purchases ledgers

Day book   Place where transactions are first classified and recorded according to type before they are posted to the ledger accounts

Cash book   A day book and combined account recording all bank and cash transactions

Trade discount   Reduction in invoice total given to a customer – usually between businesses – which does not show up in the bookkeeping

Cash discount   Discount given to a customer in order to encourage prompt payment

Discounts allowed   A reduction in the invoice total given to those owing the business money – treated as a revenue expense in the financial statements

Discounts received   A reduction in the invoice total received by the business when paying trade payables – treated as revenue income in the financial statements

Imprest   System for running a petty cash book where the amount spent is reimbursed each month so as to restore the float

Float   The amount to be maintained at the start of each period in the petty cash book

Sales day book   Day book where all credit sale transactions are first recorded

Sales invoice   Document issued by the business making a sale containing detailed information about the sale

Purchases day book   Day book where all credit purchase transactions are first recorded

Purchases invoice   Sales invoice viewed from the perspective of the business making the purchase

Returns inwards day book   Day book used to record all goods sold that are returned to the business

Credit note   Document issued by the business when accepting returns inwards

Returns outwards day book   Day book used to record all goods that are returned by the business to the original supplier

Debit note   Document issued when goods are returned to their original supplier

Journal Day book used to record transactions (likely to be more unusual transactions) not contained within the other main day books

Folio reference An abbreviated reference accompanying an entry in a ledger or day book, which helps to locate where the transaction has been entered

Contra A transaction in which both halves of the double-entry are contained within the same account

REVIEW QUESTIONS

4.1 For each of the following, state in which day book the transaction would be recorded.

(a) Sales made on credit.
(b) Goods previously purchased by the business sent back to the original supplier.
(c) Stock taken out of business for private use.
(d) Cheque paid out to settle account relating to the purchase of goods for resale.
(e) Fixed asset sold with payment received by cheque.
(f) Furniture bought on credit specifically for resale.

4.2 For each of the following, state in which day book the transaction would be recorded.

(a) Purchases made for immediate payment.
(b) Motor vehicle sold on credit.
(c) Goods returned to us by credit customers.
(d) Money transferred from bank to the cash till.
(e) Laptop accepted as part payment from debtor.
(f) Cheque received in respect of rent received.

4.3 For each of the following, state in which day book the transaction would be recorded.

(a) Owner's car brought into business for business use.
(b) Van bought by garage on credit for business use.
(c) Sale of goods on credit previously purchased for cash.
(d) Stock for resale sent back to creditor due to its unsuitability.
(e) Office furniture bought for purpose of resale.
(f) Cheque sent to supplier for purchase of fixed asset on credit.

4.4 From the following, construct the two-column cash book for the month of March 2010.

Balances as at 1 March 2010 were as follows:

Bank £560 (Dr)
Cash £45 (Dr)

March 2 Paid rent by cheque £240
March 4 Sold goods for cash £89
March 7 Paid M Harold – a creditor – by cheque £110
March 9 Paid cheque for £430 from own private account into business account
March 12 Paid wages by cheque £135
March 13 Received £76 commission in cash
March 18 Purchased goods for £56 paid immediately by cheque
March 22 Paid electricity by cash £23

4.5 From the following data, construct the cash book for the month of May 2011.

May 1 Balance at bank £430 (overdrawn) and £21 cash in hand
May 3 Sale of equipment for £120 with payment received by cheque
May 5 Cash of £120 withdrawn from bank and placed into cash till
May 9 Purchase of goods for £50 payment by cheque
May 11 Payment received by cheque from K Maher (a debtor) for £42
May 12 Rent paid by cheque £255
May 15 Purchase of office supplies £71 paid with cash
May 21 Sale of goods for cash £99
May 31 Banked all cash held in till – except for £20

4.6 The following transactions relate to the cash book of P Rapley for the month of June 2011. Construct the cash book for that month.

Jun 01 Balance at bank £450 (debit balance) and £198 cash in hand
Jun 02 Paid S Cowling (a supplier) by cheque £276
Jun 03 Received £125 cash from J Blakeley (a debtor)
Jun 05 Bought fixtures for £355, payment made by cheque
Jun 07 Borrowed £800 from bank: money transferred directly into account
Jun 10 Took £50 cash for personal use
Jun 12 Cash sales of £96 paid directly into bank
Jun 15 Rent received £43 cash
Jun 18 Purchases for £176 cash
Jun 20 Cash of £100 banked
Jun 21 Paid insurance by cheque £145
Jun 25 Cheque received for £89 from N Standen (a debtor)
Jun 28 Sold office equipment for £65 cash
Jun 29 Withdrew £50 from bank for personal use

4.7 Write up a two-column cash book from the following data.

May 01 Balances at start of month
      Bank £45.62 (o/d)
      Cash in till £23.92
May 02 Petrol paid £16.23 cash
May 04 Cash sales of £215.00 paid directly into the bank
May 06 Sundry expenses paid £6.11 cash
May 09 A Kanner lent us £800, paid by cheque
May 12 We pay a supplier, A Rogers, by cheque £56
May 14 Rent paid by cheque £67
May 17 Cash withdrawn from bank for business use £30
May 19 Vehicle bought for business use £450 paid by cheque
May 22 Withdrew £90 from bank for private use
May 23 Sold computer for £150 cash
May 24 Commission received in cash £24
May 26 P Cargill, a debtor, pays us £56 cash
May 28 Interest paid on overdraft charged directly to bank account for £11.14
May 29 Cash purchases £89.50
May 30 Money worth £100 transferred from cash till to bank account

4.8 The following data relates to the cash and bank transactions of J Ashmore for the month of October 2013. You are required to construct the cash book for that month.

Oct 1 Balance in cash till £41

Balance at bank £320

Oct 2 The following invoices are settled by cheque with the suppliers each allowing a 5% discount (the invoice total is pre discount)

D Von Geete £420

C Baron £180

Oct 4 Paid heating bill £25 cash

Oct 8 Paid insurance of £87 by cheque

Oct 12 The following paid their accounts by cheque, in each case deducting 5% cash discounts (the amounts are pre discounts)

A Ardley £200

J Thorogood £560

N Goody £80

Oct 13 Bought office equipment by cheque £120

Oct 17 Withdrew £66 from bank to be placed in cash till

Oct 19 Cheque received from S Wilson for £96 in full settlement of Wilson's outstanding balance of £106

Oct 22 Paid office expenses £25 cash

Oct 23 Sold motor vehicle for £280 (received by cheque)

Oct 26 Paid B Rivers £280 by cheque in full settlement of the £300 balance owing to him for credit purchases

Oct 27 Cheque paid out for private expenses of £89

Oct 29 All cash bar £25 deposited into bank

4.9 The following data relates to the cash and bank transactions of S Hickling for the month of November 2012. You are required to construct the cash book for that month.

Nov 01 Balances at the start of the month:

Cash in hand £11

Overdraft of £289

Nov 02 Borrowed £430 from E Allston, money paid directly into bank

Nov 04 The following paid their accounts by cheque, in each case deducting 2.5% cash discounts (the amounts are pre discount):

T Joyner £280

S Platt £160

M Brookes £400

Nov 08 Paid wages £177 by cheque

Nov 10 Paid P Yarrow by cheque £285 (based on an invoice of £300 and a 5% discount)

Nov 12 Bought computer for office use paying by cheque £320

Nov 15 Withdrew £50 from bank for cash till

Nov 17 The following invoices are settled by cheque with the suppliers each allowing a 5% discount (the invoice total is pre discount):

M Skipsey £280

P Muskett £220

Nov 19 Cash purchases for £79

Nov 21 Commission received £48 cash

Nov 24 The following paid their accounts by cheque, in each case deducting 5% cash discounts (the amounts are pre discount):

E Dixon £240

J Shephardson £100

Nov 26 Cash sales £189

Nov 28 Cash of £100 deposited into the bank

Nov 29 J Terry, a debtor, pays Hickling £120 by cheque which is after taking a discount of £8

Nov 30 Equipment bought for £290 payment made by cheque

4.10 From the following data, construct the cash book for the month of February 2015.

Feb 1 Balances at the start of the month: Bank £878, Cash in hand £101

Feb 2 Bought equipment paying by cheque for £325

Feb 3 Purchases of £192 paid for by cheque

Feb 5 Motor repairs paid in cash, £33

Feb 8 The following invoices are settled by cheque with the suppliers each allowing a 5% discount (the invoice total is pre discount):

S Jens £160

S Lee £60

Feb 10 Cash sales for £120 with half paid directly into the bank

Feb 12 D Clough settles his account with us by sending a cheque for £132 which allows him a discount of £12

Feb 14 Cash drawings of £68

Feb 17 Cash of £50 withdrawn from the bank

Feb 20 We settle an account of £280 owing to D West by sending a cheque for £252 in full settlement

Feb 24 The following invoices are settled by cheque with the suppliers each allowing a 2.5% discount (the invoice total is pre discount):

K Hawley £200

A Vincent £160

Feb 25 The following paid their accounts by cheque, in each case deducting 5% cash discounts (the amounts are pre discount):

D Vanian £440

I Astbury £140

Feb 26 Rent received in cash £76

Feb 27 Cash taken out of business for personal use £80

4.11 On 1 August, the financial position of Sarah Bowler's business was:

	£	
Balance at bank	190.67	(o/d)
Cash in hand	54.50	
Debtors:		
C Roberts	475.00	
J Bellwood	125.00	
P Shortland	84.00	
Stock	210.00	
Creditors:		
S Arora	94.00	
E Hawkins	105.00	
J Clover	256.00	

During August:

1 The three debtors settled their accounts by cheque subject to a cash discount of 3%

2 Sundry expenses of £32.80 were paid in cash

3 Arora was paid by cheque less a discount of 5%

4 The accounts of Hawkins and Clover were settled by cheque subject to a 4% discount

5 Rent of £190.00 was paid by cheque.

Construct the three-column cash book for the above data.

4.12 The following items have not been recorded in the cash book of M Robins for the first week of December 2010.

		£	
1 December	Balance in cash till	45.00	
1 December	Balance at bank	231.97	

Information from cheque counterfoils:

2 December	R Wheatcroft (cash discount of £5.00)	126.00	Cheque amount
4 December	P Cocking (cash discount of £12.50)	320.00	Cheque amount
6 December	M Clegg (cash discount of £3.75)	87.00	Cheque amount

Paying-in slips

3 December	R Armitage (discount received of £10.00)	215.00	Cheque banked
5 December	G Gregory (discount received of £8.50)	160.00	Cheque banked

In addition, the following items will need entering into the cash book:

	£
From the bank statement:	
Credit transfer received from A Stroish	111.30
Bank charges	14.50
Interest paid	3.55
Cash till roll:	
Till receipts	327.31
Cash payments:	
Petrol	28.54
Office expenses	18.76

At the end of each month Robins will always ensure that all cash, except a float of £45, is transferred into the bank account.

Construct the cash book for the month of December for M Robins.

4.13 The following is a summary of the petty cash transactions for S Donnelly for August 2005.

2005

Aug 1 Received from petty cashier £100 as petty cash float

		£
Aug 2	Rail fares	17
Aug 4	Petrol	8
Aug 8	Stationery	4
Aug 10	Cleaning	11
Aug 18	Petrol	16
Aug 21	Cleaning	10
Aug 22	Bus fares	4
Aug 25	Cleaning	2
Aug 28	Stationery	5
Aug 30	Petrol	6

(a) Rule up a petty cash book with analysis columns for expenditure on cleaning, travel expenses and stationery.

(b) Enter the month's transactions.

(c) Enter the receipt of the amount necessary to restore the imprest and carry down the balance for the commencement of the following month.

4.14 The petty cash book for Treebound Stories, a small bookshop, operates on a weekly basis using the imprest system. The entries have not yet been completed for the week ending 13 November 2005.

(a) Complete the petty cash book (below) for the week from the following details:

Nov 10	Petrol	£17.80
Nov 11	Envelopes	£4.56
Nov 11	Cleaner	£8.75

(b) Balance the petty cash book and total the analysis columns. Make the necessary entries to restore the imprest to £100.

Received	Date	Details	Voucher number	Total	Travel costs	Stationery	Office expenses
£	2005			£	£	£	£
100.00	Nov 6	Balance b/d					
	Nov 7	Bus fares	31	15.20	15.20		
	Nov 7	Stamps	32	0.40		0.40	
	Nov 8	Printer paper	33	21.20			21.20
	Nov 8	Coffee	34	2.40			2.40

4.15 For the following transactions write up the sales day book and post the details to the relevant accounts in the sales ledger.

2010
Jan 3 A Genn   £45
Jan 8 T Wright   £89
Jan 11 S Gill   £111
Jan 12 J Gillot   £76
Jan 18 A Genn   £21
Jan 27 T Wright   £54

4.16 For the following transactions write up the sales day book and post the details to the relevant accounts in the sales ledger.

2012
October 3 I Sharp   £197
October 6 T Wilson   £224
October 9 J Dolman   £96
October 14 T Wilson   £302
October 19 N Jackson £561
October 24 T Wilson   £177

4.17 For the following transactions write up the purchases day book and post the details to the relevant accounts in the ledgers.

2014
August   4 W Cann   £43
August 11 G Michael £19
August 12 B Currie   £27
August 17 J Taylor   £86
August 21 M King   £24
August 26 G Michael   £91

4.18   For the following transactions write up the purchases day book and post the details to the relevant accounts in the ledgers.

2012
March   2 J Austen   £78
March   6 P Chang   £118
March   9 L Martins   £21
March 18 L Martins   £65
March 21 E Blindefelt   £43
March 31 P Chang   £76

4.19   Enter the following transactions into the appropriate day books and post the entries into the correct accounts.

2010
April   1 Goods sold on credit to E Ram for £125
April   6 Goods sold on credit to B Lomus for £210
April   8 Goods purchased on credit from P Alport for £96
April 12 Goods sold on credit to E Ram for £82
April 19 Goods purchased on credit from J Widmare for £140

4.20   Enter the following transactions into the appropriate day books and post the entries into the correct accounts.

2016
June   2 Goods sold on credit to J Lahr for £76
June   5 Purchased goods on credit from K Oldman for £39
June   8 Purchased further goods on credit from Oldman for £17
June 12 Goods sold on credit to S Aitken for £56
June 16 Goods sold on credit to M Armitage for £87
June 22 Purchased goods on credit from D Nicholls for £41

4.21   Enter the following transactions to the sales and returns inwards day books where relevant. Post the transactions to the personal accounts and show the relevant accounts affected in the general ledger.

2017
November   2 Credit sales made to D Pearce for £49
November   4 Credit sales made to A Haslem for £214
November   9 Credit sales made to R Compton for £76
November 12 Haslem returns goods worth £54
November 15 Credit sales made to Pearce for £181
November 18 Compton returns goods worth £19

4.22   Enter the following transactions to the purchases and returns outwards day books where relevant. Post the transactions to the personal accounts and show the relevant accounts affected in the general ledger.

2019

March   1 Goods purchased from M Swann for £97

March   3 Goods purchased from G Denton for £65

March   4 We return goods worth £12 to Swann

March 11 Goods purchased from L Webster for £114

March 14 Goods purchased from M Swann for £52

March 18 We return goods worth £21 to Swann

March 21 We return goods worth £8 to Denton

4.23 Enter the following transactions to the relevant day books, post each transaction to the personal accounts and transfer the monthly totals to the accounts in the general ledger.

2013

July   1 Credit sales of £87 to S Wilkins

July   3 Credit sales of £118 to J Nesbit

July   4 Goods purchased on credit from S Johnson for £62

July   8 Wilkins returns goods worth £23

July 11 Goods sold on credit to P Jones for £240

July 15 Goods purchased on credit from N James for £88

July 19 We return goods to Johnson worth £25

July 22 Goods purchased from P Wesson on credit for £55

July 28 Jones returns goods worth £24

4.24 Enter the following transactions to the relevant day books, post each transaction to the personal accounts and transfer the monthly totals to the accounts in the general ledger.

2015

May   1 Goods purchased on credit from L Schmidt for £75

May   4 Goods purchased on credit from M Rogers for £54

May   5 Credit sales for £165 to S Luscombe

May   8 We return goods to Schmidt worth £24

May 11 Luscombe returns goods worth £31

May 16 Credit purchases from N Arthur for £81

May 18 Sales made on credit to J Keeble for £101

May 21 Goods returned to Arthur valued at £11

May 22 Goods sold to J Keeble for £145

May 25 Keeble returns goods worth £32

4.25 Show the journal entries necessary to record the following items.

2006

June   1 Bought equipment on credit from B Eden for £900

June   5 A debt owing to us by M Sparks for £38 is written off as a bad debt

June   8 We owe £180 to W Bohanna but the debt is transferred to C Hurford

June 13 Computer taken out of the business for personal use worth £690

June 19 Delivery van bought on credit from Vans R Us Ltd for £1,900

June 25 Furniture accepted in return for outstanding debt owed to us by R Denys £425

4.26 Show the journal entries necessary to record the following items.

2006

August   1 Debt of £15 owing to us by F Grew is written off as bad

August   5 We exchange equipment worth £900 for a van of equivalent value owned by a friend

August   8 We are owed £200 by J Harker; she is declared bankrupt and we received £25 in full settlement

August 13 Commission received of £25 was mistakenly entered into the sales account – we now correct the mistake

August 19 Office equipment bought on credit from Fantastic Drawers Ltd for £670

August 25 Typewriter taken out of business for personal use was valued at £40

4.27 Show the journal entries necessary to record the following items.

2007
May 1 Sold equipment on credit to N Johnston for £500
May 3 H Jagielka owed the firm £30 but the debt is transferred to P Kenny
May 12 Owner's car valued at £1,200 is brought into the firm for business use
May 13 We owe M Burns £189 for credit purchases. This debt is paid for by giving Burns equipment of equivalent value
May 21 Machinery bought on credit from Jacks Ltd for £2,700

4.28 Show the journal entries necessary to record the following items.

2003
April 5 We exchange fixtures worth £1,300 for a machine of equivalent value with a friend
April 8 We are owed £125 by J Large; a settlement of 20p in the £ is accepted when he is declared bankrupt
April 12 Debt of £33 owing to us by N Yarrow is written off as bad
April 22 Fixtures and fittings bought on credit from Magic Fittings Ltd for £450
April 25 Car taken out of business for personal use was valued at £2,300

4.29 Show the journal entries necessary to record the following items (narratives are not required).

(a) Bought van on credit for £800 from P Gray
(b) The owner withdraws goods from the business worth £75 for personal use
(c) The owner brings her own private computer into the business at a valuation of £180
(d) A desk worth £50 is accepted in full settlement of the £50 owing to the business by L Skipsey
(e) Sale of car on credit to J Rowell worth £250
(f) Bought office fixtures on credit from L Palmer for £95

4.30 Show the journal entries necessary to record the following items (narratives are not required).

(a) Motor van sold on credit to K Hodgson for £355
(b) A debt owing to us by T Fairhurst of £27 is written off as a bad debt
(c) Owner introduces personal car into business at a valuation of £295
(d) Office equipment bought on credit for £820 from S Merrills
(e) Some of the office equipment worth £75 purchased from Merrills is found to be faulty and returned to Merrills
(f) Insurance paid by the business is found to contain £25 relating to the owner's private insurance

4.31 Show the journal entries necessary to record the following items (narratives are not required).

(a) A debt owing to us by R Marshall for £60 is partly written off as bad, with a cash payment of 25p in the £ received in full settlement
(b) Owner takes goods out of the business worth £47 for personal use
(c) Machinery bought on credit for £172 from M Wainwright
(d) Machinery returned to Wainwright worth £31
(e) Total amount paid for annual heating is £800; however, it is now discovered that one-fifth of this relates to the owner's personal electricity bill
(f) Plant sold to H17 Ltd on credit for £425

CHAPTER 5

Value added tax

Learning objectives

By the end of this chapter you should be able to:

- Calculate the level of VAT for inclusion on an invoice
- Ascertain the VAT liability of a business through offsetting VAT paid against VAT collected
- Record the accounting entries for VAT in the ledgers
- Calculate the VAT on invoices where VAT has already been included
- Calculate the VAT due when discounts are offered.

Introduction

Value added tax (VAT) is a tax on sales used in the UK. For most goods and services sold in the UK part of the selling price will not contribute to the business's profits but will be passed on to the government in the form of tax revenue.

VAT is administered in the UK by HM Revenue and Customs – a branch of the UK government. It is an *indirect tax*, which means that it is not collected by the government directly but is collected by businesses on behalf of the government.

It is a requirement on EU members to impose a form of VAT. The minimum level allowable by the EU is set at 15% (though some countries impose an equivalent to VAT as high as 25%). Some goods and services are **zero rated** (e.g. food in supermarkets), and UK domestic fuel for heating is subject to VAT at 5%. Most goods and services are subject to VAT at the rate of 17.5% (though this was reduced as a temporary measure for 2009 to 15%). Businesses with a taxable turnover above a certain amount are obliged to register for VAT and then have to make payments to the government on a regular basis.

The administration of VAT

VAT is collected by businesses involved in the production of a good or service who sell this on to another consumer – regardless of whether this is the final consumer, or whether this consumer will, in turn, add something to the good and then sell it on to another consumer.

However, businesses are allowed to claim back the VAT that is paid on the purchase of products and other inputs into the production process. Rather than having to collect VAT on any sales made and also pay VAT on any purchases made, businesses can use the amount paid on purchases to offset (reduce) the amount paid on any sales made. The final consumer of the product has no-one to sell the product to and therefore the final consumer will pay the full 17.5% VAT.

Example 5.1

During May 2007, a business sells £15,000 of goods (before the addition of VAT). During the same period, the business has also purchased goods for £9,000 (also before the addition of VAT).

VAT due on sales   = £15,000 × 17.5%   = £2,625
VAT paid on purchases   = £9,000 × 17.5%   = £1,575

The difference between the two will be the VAT due   = £1,050.

VAT and double-entry bookkeeping

The double-entry system can be modified for the inclusion of VAT with a few simple amendments. It will also need including in day book entries before these are posted to the ledger accounts.

Given that the tax is collected by traders and businesses on behalf of the government, invoice totals will include the VAT. However, we must ensure that only the net amount (excluding VAT) is entered into the sales, purchases and returns accounts.

Credit purchases

Credit purchases are posted to the ledger accounts as follows:

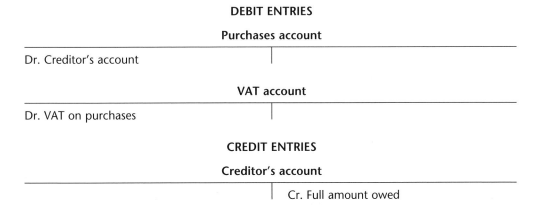

DEBIT ENTRIES

Purchases account

Dr. Creditor's account

VAT account

Dr. VAT on purchases

CREDIT ENTRIES

Creditor's account

Cr. Full amount owed

You will notice that there are two debit entries for the one credit entry. The total of the two debits – the net purchase (without VAT) and the VAT itself – will equal the credit entry – the credit purchase with VAT included (the gross total) which is credited to the supplier's account.

Credit sales

These are treated in the same way.

Credit sales with VAT	
Debit	*Credit*
Debtor's account with *gross* amount	Sales account with *net* sale (no VAT)
	VAT account with VAT on sale

Returns

The same applies to both returns inwards and returns outwards.

Returns inwards with VAT	
Debit	*Credit*
Returns inwards with *net* amount	Debtor's account with *gross* amount
VAT on returns inwards	

Returns outwards with VAT	
Debit	*Credit*
Creditor's account with *gross* amount	Returns outwards with *net* amount
	VAT on returns outwards

As stated earlier, the selling price of a good will include VAT, which means that part of the business's overall sales revenue will not contribute to the business's profits.

A more comprehensive example follows.

Example 5.2

The following example shows how entries are posted from the day books to the ledger accounts, with the monthly totals being transferred to the accounts in the general ledger including the VAT account. Most examination assessment questions will not go into this much detail but the example is useful in showing you how the system works in full.

Sales day book

2008	Net	VAT	Gross
	£	£	£
April 5 G Charman	400.00	70.00	470.00
April 24 H Morris	300.00	52.50	352.50
Transferred to General Ledger	<u>700.00</u>	<u>122.50</u>	<u>822.50</u>

Purchases day book

2008	Net	VAT	Gross
	£	£	£
April 1 H Wilde	200.00	35.00	235.00
April 12 B Dean	50.00	8.75	58.75
April 22 H Wilde	150.00	26.25	176.25
Transferred to General Ledger	400.00	70.00	470.00

Returns inwards day book

2008	Net	VAT	Gross
	£	£	£
April 24 G Charman	40.00	7.00	47.00
Transferred to General Ledger	40.00	7.00	47.00

Returns outwards day book

2008	Net	VAT	Gross
	£	£	£
April 7 H Wilde	20.00	3.50	23.50
April 19 B Dean	10.00	1.75	11.75
Transferred to General Ledger	30.00	5.25	35.25

As covered in Chapter 4, the individual transactions are posted to the personal accounts of the debtors and creditors and the monthly totals are posted to the sales, the purchases, the returns, and the VAT accounts in the general ledger.

For example, when looking at the above sales day book, the individual entries *debited* to the debtors' accounts will total £822.50, while the net amounts *credited* to the VAT and sales accounts combined will also total £822.50 – thus maintaining the integrity of the double-entry system.

The entries in the three ledgers will be as follows:

Sales Ledger:

G Charman

2008	£	2008	£
April 5 Sales	470.00	April 24 Returns inwards	47.00

H Morris

2008	£	2008	£
April 24 Sales	352.50		

Purchases Ledger:

H Wilde

2008	£	2008	£
April 7 Returns outwards	23.50	April 1 Purchases	235.00
		April 22 Purchases	176.25

B Dean

2008		£	2008		£
April 19	Returns outwards	11.75	April 12	Purchases	58.75

General Ledger:

Sales

2008	£	2008		£
		April 30	Total for month	700.00

Purchases

2008		£	2008	£
April 30	Total for month	400.00		

Returns inwards

2008		£	2008	£
April 30	Total for month	40.00		

Returns outwards

2008	£	2008		£
		April 30	Total for month	30.00

VAT

2008		£	2008		£
April 30	VAT on purchases	70.00	April 30	VAT on sales	122.50
April 30	VAT on returns inwards	7.00	April 30	VAT on returns outwards	5.25
April 30	Balance c/d	50.75			
		127.75			127.75
			May 1	Balance b/d	50.75

The outstanding balance on the VAT account represents what the business owes to HM Revenue and Customs. It represents the VAT collected less the VAT that has been paid and can be offset against the VAT owing.

Until the payment is actually made, the amount for VAT owing would appear as a current liability on the statement of financial position. If the amount was paid on 17 May, the entry would appear as follows:

VAT

2008		£	2008		£
May 17	Cash book	50.75	May 1	Balance b/d	50.75

If the balance brought down had been a debit balance, the business could claim back VAT from HM Revenue and Customs as it would have paid more for VAT than the business had collected from VAT on sales. Given that the value of sales normally exceeds purchases this situation is unlikely to be anything other than short-lived, and most businesses would not bother to claim the amount back as in the long run the business will pay more in VAT than it claims back.

You should now attempt review questions 5.1 to 5.4.

Other items in the VAT account

Non-current assets

VAT is likely to be included on the non-current assets that the business purchases as well as other expenses related to the running of operations. Some businesses will be able to reclaim the VAT paid on the purchase of non-current assets by offsetting it against VAT payable on sales, in the same way that VAT paid on purchases is used.

Example 5.3

If a machine costs £5,000 (net of VAT), the VAT added on would total £875 (17.5% of £5,000). If the business can reclaim the VAT back on this purchase the entries in the ledger accounts would be as follows:

Where VAT can be reclaimed on purchases of non-current assets:

Machinery			
	£		£
Bank	5,000		

Cash book			
	£		£
		Machinery (plus VAT)	5,875

VAT			
	£		
VAT on machinery	875		

Where VAT *cannot* be reclaimed on purchases of non-current assets:

Machinery			
	£		£
Bank	5,875		

Cash book			
	£		£
		Machinery (plus VAT)	5,875

We can see that whether the VAT can be reclaimed or not the total of the two debits equals the credit entry.

Instructions will normally be provided as to whether or not the business is allowed to reclaim VAT when purchasing non-current assets.

Cash sales and cash expenses

Especially for smaller businesses, there may be small amounts that may be entered into the VAT account. VAT collected on cash sales should be treated in the same way as the VAT collected from debtors on credit sales. Likewise, VAT that can be reclaimed on expenses (petty cash payments and others) would be debited to the VAT account in the same way as VAT on purchases is accounted for.

One complication that may be encountered is where the VAT has already been added in the amount. The problem here is that simply subtracting 17.5% from the total given will NOT give the correct amount. If this is thought about then it is obvious – if an amount is increased by adding 17.5% VAT on top of the original total, the new total is higher, and 17.5% of this new, higher total, will not be the same.

The correct procedure used would be to multiply the total figure as follows:

$$\text{VAT total} = \frac{17.5}{117.5} \times \text{Gross total}$$

Example 5.4

If cash sales for a period totalled £559.30 and already included VAT, then we can work out how much VAT was due on this as follows:

$$\text{VAT total} = \frac{17.5}{117.5} \times £559.30 = £83.30$$

(The more mathematically minded of you may also notice that 17.5/117.5 can be simplified to 7/47.)

You should now attempt review questions 5.5 to 5.11.

VAT and discounts

Trade discounts do not appear in ledger accounts. However, cash discounts (for prompt payment) will appear and the inclusion of VAT in these invoices with discounts will complicate matters.

VAT will always be calculated on the assumption that the cash discount is taken – i.e. the lowest possible total. Even if the payment arrives too late to qualify for the discount, the VAT will be calculated assuming the discount is taken.

Example 5.5

A business sells goods worth £750 but allows a trade discount of 20%. A cash discount is offered for prompt payment at a rate of 5%.

What would be the invoice total for this sale?

Stage 1: Deduct the trade discount.
£750 less 20% equals £600 (£750 − £150).

Stage 2: Deduct the cash discount.
£600 less 5% equals £570 (£30 being the cash discount).

Stage 3: Calculate the VAT.
£570 × 17.5% equals £99.75.

*Stage 4: Calculate the invoice total (adding the VAT on **before** the cash discount is deducted).*
£600 + £99.75 = £699.75.

If the cash discount is taken then the debtor would pay £699.75 less the £30 discount, i.e. £669.75. The trade discount has no effect as it is not included in the accounting aspect of the sale.

A common mistake is to add the VAT on to the amount after the cash discount is deducted. It is important to remember that the invoice total will be *before* the cash discount is taken.

You should now attempt review questions 5.12 to 5.16.

Chapter review

By now you should understand the following:

- How VAT is calculated
- How to enter VAT in the double-entry system thus calculating the liability for VAT for a business
- How to calculate VAT when the invoice is already inclusive of VAT
- How to calculate VAT on an invoice subject to trade and cash discounts.

Handy hints

The following hints will help you avoid errors.

- Ensure that you are familiar with the rate of VAT to be used in any question.
- VAT is a liability so remember that any VAT a business collects will be credited to the VAT account and any paid will be debited.
- Remember that to calculate VAT when it is inclusive you cannot simply deduct 17.5% – it will not get you back to the pre-tax value.
- When dealing with discounts, remember that when calculating the VAT it is necessary to base it on the assumption that cash discounts will be taken, but the VAT will be added on top of the invoice before the discount is deducted.

Key terms

VAT (Value Added Tax) A tax placed on most goods and services in the UK, currently normally levied at 17.5%

Zero rated goods/services Goods and services which are not subject to VAT, such as children's clothing

REVIEW QUESTIONS

For each question, assume that VAT is levied at the rate of 17.5%.

5.1 From the following day book extracts, construct a VAT account for the month of July 2007.

Net figures (before addition of VAT) for July 2007	£
Sales for month	1,750
Purchases for month	1,125
Returns inwards for month	230
Returns outwards for month	178

5.2 From the following day book extracts, construct a VAT account for the month of October 2008.

Net figures (before addition of VAT) for October 2008	£
Sales for month	12,560
Purchases for month	8,790
Returns inwards for month	456
Returns outwards for month	670

5.3 From the following day book extracts, construct a VAT account for the month of March 2003.

Net figures (before addition of VAT) for March 2003	£
Sales for month	895
Purchases for month	785
Returns inwards for month	18
Returns outwards for month	9

Additional information:

(i) VAT owing as at 1 March 2003 was £26.

(ii) VAT paid on 9 March 2003 was £145.

5.4 Consider the following account:

VAT

2003		£	2003		£
May 31	VAT on purchases	289	May 1	Balance b/d	56
May 31	VAT on returns inwards	12	May 31	VAT on sales	546
May 31	Balance c/d	?	May 31	VAT on returns outwards	7
		609			609
			June 1	Balance b/d	?

(i) What does the balance on May 1 represent?

(ii) Calculate the balance for June 1.

(iii) Where will the balance for June 1 appear in the final accounts?

5.5   Bradleigh Payne's books show the following information for February 2005:

- VAT on sales for the month was £867.54.
- VAT on returns inwards was £12.54.
- VAT on purchases for the month was £342.54.
- Cash expenses paid during the month totalled £108.45 which included reclaimable VAT at 17.5%.

Calculate the amount of VAT due for the month of February 2005.

5.6   From the following day book extracts, construct a VAT account for the month of May 2019.

Net figures (before addition of VAT) for May 2019	£
Sales for month	1,123.50
Purchases for month	765.75
Returns inwards for month	98.00
Returns outwards for month	103.00

Additional information:

Cash sales inclusive of VAT for May totalled £484.10.

5.7   From the following day book extracts, construct a VAT account for the month of June 2007.

Net figures (before addition of VAT) for June 2007	£
Sales for month	7,450
Purchases for month	5,780
Returns inwards for month	874
Returns outwards for month	1,010

Additional information:

(i)   Cash sales inclusive of VAT for June totalled £985.
(ii) Fixed assets were purchased for £2,350 during June which includes VAT of £350 which could be reclaimed.

5.8   From the following day book extracts, construct a VAT account for the month of March 2005.

Net figures (before addition of VAT) for March 2005	£
Sales for month	3,240
Purchases for month	2,850
Returns inwards for month	214
Returns outwards for month	180

Additional information:

(i)   VAT owing as at 1 March 2005 was £320.
(ii) Cash sales inclusive of VAT for March totalled £1,270.
(iii) Petty cash expenses incurred in March totalled £123 inclusive of VAT (which can be reclaimed).

5.9   From the following day book extracts, construct a VAT account for the month of April 2006.

Net figures (before addition of VAT) for April 2006	£
Sales for month	5,240
Purchases for month	3,950
Returns inwards for month	412
Returns outwards for month	380

Additional information:

(i) VAT owing as at 1 April 2006 was £220.73.

(ii) Cash sales inclusive of VAT for April totalled £870.

(iii) Petty cash expenses incurred in April totalled £342 inclusive of VAT (which can be reclaimed).

(iv) Fixed assets were purchased during April which includes VAT of £450 which could be reclaimed.

(v) VAT paid on April 18 totalled £299.

5.10 The following extracts are taken from the day books of David Conlon for the three months ended 30 June 2004.

Sales day book

Details	Net	VAT	Total
Total for period	£785.00	£137.38	£922.38

Purchases day book

Details	Net	VAT	Total
Total for period	£562.00	£98.35	£660.35

Sales returns day book

Details	Net	VAT	Total
Total for period	£68.00	£11.90	£79.90

Purchases returns day book

Details	Net	VAT	Total
Total for period	£44.00	£7.70	£51.70

Additional information:

(i) As at 1 April 2004 there was a debit balance in the VAT account of £117.

(ii) A payment for VAT of £183 was made on 24 May 2004.

(iii) VAT reclaimable on expenses totalled £58 for the three months to 30 June 2004.

From the above information, construct a VAT account for the three months ending 30 June 2004.

5.11 From the following transactions, construct the sales, purchases and both returns day books for the month of May 2001. Transfer the totals for the month to the VAT account.

2001

May 1 Bought goods on credit £300 from A Davidson, £200 from C Platt

May 8 Sold goods on credit to M Cousins worth £800

May 12 Bought goods on credit from G Guy totalling £250

May 15 Sold goods on credit to F Connelly for £550

May 18 Returned goods to Platt for £36

May 22 Sold goods on credit to M Cousins for £280

May 25 Connelly returned goods worth £120

May 28 Granville returned goods worth £82

5.12   For the following sales transactions calculate the following:

(i)   Sales invoice totals with VAT at 17.5%

(ii) Amount due if the cash discount is taken.

(a) Sales of £1,500 with a cash discount of 5%

(b) Sales of £1,000 with a trade discount of 20% and a cash discount of 2.5%

(c) Sales of £2,000 with a trade discount of 10% and a cash discount of 1.25%

(d) Sales of £640 with a trade discount of 25% and a cash discount of 3%

5.13   Calculate the VAT on each of the following transactions:

(a) Cash sales inclusive of VAT totalling £274.95

(b) Net sales totalling £1,345.00

(c) Petty cash expenses inclusive of VAT totalling £38.75.

5.14   Twelve tube alloys are sold to Moir Ltd for £40 each. A trade discount of 20% is allowed on the order and a cash discount of 5% is offered. However, Moir Ltd returns four of these. Calculate the value of the credit note to be issued to Moir Ltd.

5.15   Twenty-five Stembolts are sold for £8 each. A trade discount of 25% is offered on the sale. A discount of 2.5% is allowed for prompt payment. Calculate the value of the invoice for the total transaction.

5.16   Chris Cureton's books show the following information for January 2005:

Cash sales were £413.50 including VAT at 17.5%.

VAT on purchases for the month was £1,898.66.

Equipment purchased on 15 January 2005 included reclaimable VAT of £450.

Calculate the amount of VAT due for the month of January 2005.

CHAPTER 6

Capital and revenue expenditure

Learning objectives

By the end of this chapter you should be able to:

● Distinguish between capital and revenue expenditure
● Distinguish between capital and revenue receipts
● Know how the categories of expenditure are treated in the financial statements
● Understand and account for the incorrect treatment of categories of expenditure.

Introduction

In Chapter 2 you were introduced to the idea that businesses will purchase assets, some for business use, and some for resale. The distinction was that any asset purchased with the intention of resale would be entered into the purchases account whereas any asset purchased to be used within the business would appear in its own asset account according to the type of asset purchased (e.g. vehicles, machinery and equipment).

In Chapter 3, this distinction of asset type started to have an impact on where these items would appear in the financial statement. It should not have been lost on you that the items that were counted as 'assets' were not included as expenses in the statement of comprehensive income for that year. Only assets which were counted as purchases appeared as expenses.

Although there was some rationale for this distinction it has yet remained to be formally defined as to how we should categorise the expenditure on assets. It is time to clarify this area by introducing new terminology in the form of capital and revenue expenditure.

Classifying capital and revenue expenditure

Capital expenditure is where a firm spends money on the purchase of a fixed asset or in the adding of value to an existing fixed asset. Capital expenditure will also include the amounts spent on getting the asset into useable condition, and so would not only include the purchase price of the fixed asset but would also include the transportation costs of the fixed asset to the business, the installation costs of the asset, and any legal costs involved in acquiring the asset.

Revenue expenditure refers to those expenses which do not add value to the fixed assets of the business and are incurred on a day-to-day basis. These costs will normally be attributable to a particular period of time. For example, the wages for a particular month would count as revenue expenditure. The purchase of stock – because it is not to be kept within the business – would also be counted as revenue expenditure.

Example 6.1

DHP Autos has spent the following amounts in the last financial year relating to the purchase and operation of a pick-up truck.

	£
Cost of purchasing pick-up truck	12,000
Painting business logo on side of van	400
Replacing worn-out tyres	360
Road tax for year	150
Fuel costs for year	980
Upgrading of truck with new engine	2,400

The expenditure can be classified into capital and revenue expenditure as shown in Table 6.1.

Table 6.1

Example	Type of expenditure?	Explanation	Capital expenditure	Revenue expenditure
Cost of purchasing pick-up truck	Capital	Buying new asset	£12,000	
Painting business logo on side of van	Capital	Adding value to asset	£400	
Replacing worn-out tyres	Revenue	Not adding value, day-to-day running expense		£360
Road tax for year	Revenue	Regular expense incurred every year		£150
Fuel costs for year	Revenue	Regular, day-to-day expense		£980
Upgrading of truck with new engine	Capital	One-off expense – adding value to asset	£2,400	
Totals			£14,800	£1,490

You should now attempt review questions 6.1 to 6.15.

Joint expenditure

An item of expenditure might be split into both capital and revenue expenditure. This is known as **joint expenditure**. This doesn't mean we are double-counting, but means that part of the total expense would be classified as capital expenditure with the remainder classified as revenue expenditure.

For example, a heating system for a factory might involve expenditure on repairing an existing system but also include some expenditure on improving the system. In this case, we should attempt to allocate the amount belonging to repairs as revenue expenditure with the amount spent on improving the system being allocated as capital expenditure.

In the case of joint expenditure, it is not always clear how to divide up the expenditure between the two classifications. Some degree of estimation may be required.

Payments for finance leases involve joint expenditure; this is discussed later in this chapter.

Capital and revenue receipts

The same reasoning as we use with classifying expenditure can be used in classifying revenues and monies received by the business. The sale of fixed assets would be included as a capital receipt. Other capital receipts would include the issue of shares (for a limited company) and the receipt of money on taking out a business loan.

The sale of inventory (either for cash or on credit) would be counted as a revenue receipt. To summarise, incomes relating to the operations of the business, such as rental income and commission earned, would be countered as revenue receipts.

You should now attempt review questions 6.16 and 6.17.

Areas of debate

Classifying expenditure into capital or revenue is not always easy. The type of output a business produces will determine whether or not an item of expenditure is classified as an asset (i.e. capital expenditure) or an expense (i.e. revenue expenditure). The size of the expenditure will also have an influence on how expenditure is classified.

In Chapter 7, we will deal with accounting concepts. The concept of **materiality** will shape how we classify expenses. For example, a very large firm may consider expenditure on small items of office furniture immaterial and therefore treat these as revenue expenditure (say, 'office expenses', or 'sundries'). However, a small business may consider the same level of expenditure on similar items to be material enough to be classified as capital expenditure (i.e. an asset).

Some items do not fit easily into either category. For example, the purchase of computer software could be considered to be capital expenditure as it is adding value to the fixed assets of the business. However, computer software may be updated so frequently that it comes to be seen as revenue expenditure in that a business purchases software merely to maintain the usefulness of its computers.

Interest paid on any loans taken out by the business and interest received by any loans made by the business would be treated as either revenue expenditure or revenue income. However, in the case of a non-current asset being constructed (e.g. property) then it may be allowable to include the interest charge incurred as capital expenditure.

IAS 17

A lease is an arrangement where a business gains the use of an asset from another business and in return will make payments to the owner of the asset.

IAS 17 (Leases) categorises leases as either operating leases or finance leases. An **operating lease** is usually a short-term lease in which the risks and rewards remain with the lessor (the original supplier of the asset). A **finance lease** is a more long-term arrangement whereby the risks and rewards of the asset are transferred to the lessee (the business which is paying to lease the asset).

In the financial statements of a lessee, operating leases are treated as a revenue expense and will be deducted from the profits. Any payment for a finance lease is treated as joint expenditure where the finance charge for the lease is treated as a revenue expense but the asset will also be treated as an asset on the statement of financial position.

How expenditure on leases is to be treated therefore depends on the type of lease. However, the distinction between operating and finance leases is not always clear-cut. If the asset is likely to be transferred to the lessee at the end of the lease, or if the asset is likely to be leased for a major part of its useful life, then the treatment is more likely to be as a finance lease.

Type of lease	Treatment of expenditure
Operating lease	Treated as revenue expenditure
Finance lease	Treated as revenue* and capital expenditure

* It is the finance charge on the lease which is treated as the revenue expenses in the case of a finance lease.

IAS 38

Businesses will often spend money on research and development. This can be to create new processes or new products.

Research involves theoretical or experimental work to gain new knowledge but development involves this knowledge being used to create new products, systems or services. IAS 38 (Intangible Assets) splits expenditure on research and development thus:

IAS 38 (Intangible Assets) – Treatment of research and development expenditure	
Research expenditure	Treated as revenue expenditure unless the research expenditure involves capital expenditure on non-current assets – e.g. research facilities.
Development expenditure	Treated as an expense or treated as capital expenditure on the statement of financial position if it can be established that the development expenditure will lead to an intangible asset that can be valued reliably and either used or sold.

Incorrect classification of expenditure

Mistakes in classification of expenditure – whether it is capital or revenue expenditure – can be made. If this occurs then the following will occur:

1 The profit calculated will be incorrect – profits will be either higher or lower as a result of the error.
2 The statement of financial position will not be correct – though it may still balance.

For example, if a purchase of furniture which is to be used within the business is treated as revenue expenditure then the business expenses will be higher than their correct level. As a result, reported profits will be lower than they would be if the expense had been correctly classified. In addition, the balance for non-current assets will be lower on the statement of financial position. This type of error would not necessarily show in the financial statements – it would be termed an error of principle and is covered in Chapter 11.

You should now attempt review questions 6.18 to 6.20.

Chapter review

By now you should understand the following:

● How to distinguish between capital and revenue expenditure
● How the categories of expenditure are treated in the financial statements
● How to distinguish between capital and revenue incomes
● How to correct for mistakes in the classification of expenditure.

Relevant accounting standards

IAS 17   Leases
IAS 38   Intangible Assets

Handy hints

The following hints will help you avoid errors.

● Ensure you consider the main activities of the business organisation as they will help in the classification of what is and is not capital and revenue expenditures/incomes.
● If an item relates to a period of time then it is likely to be revenue expenditure.
● Be particularly vigilant with the treatment of loans and loan interest – this often causes confusion, especially with the repayment and taking out of loans.

Key terms

Capital expenditure   Expenditure on the purchase of, and any additional costs involved in the improvement, installation and acquisition of non-current assets

Revenue expenditure   Expenditure involved in the day-to-day running of a business

Capital income   Income generated from one-off sources (e.g. the sale of non-current assets, loans acquired)

Revenue income   Income generated from the sale of goods and services provided by a business

Joint expenditure   Expenditure which contains elements of both capital and revenue expenditure

Finance lease   An arrangement to obtain the right to use an asset where the risks and rewards of ownership are transferred to the lessee (the business paying to lease the asset)

Operating lease   An arrangement to obtain the right to use an asset where the risks and rewards of ownership remain with the lessor (the business supplying the asset)

REVIEW QUESTIONS

6.1   Classify the following expenses either as capital expenditure or revenue expenditure:

(a) Electricity bill for year
(b) Costs of new heating system
(c) Installation costs of new heating system
(d) Carriage inwards on new boiler for heating system
(e) Repair costs of heating system
(f) Upgrade of boiler in three years' time.

6.2   In a fast food outlet divide the following costs according to whether they are capital expenditure or revenue expenditure:

(a) Purchase of deep fat fryer
(b) Painting logo outside new premises
(c) Rental charge for premises
(d) Purchase of buns for burgers
(e) Delivery charge for deep fat fryer
(f) Interest charge on loan taken out to purchase deep fat fryer
(g) Part-time staffing costs
(h) Purchase of drinks machine.

6.3   For the following items, decide in each case whether they are a capital or revenue receipt:

(a) Sales of sofas by furniture retailer
(b) Sale of cash till by a car retailer
(c) Loan taken out by sports retailer
(d) Interest received by clothing shop
(e) Sale of shop counter by fast food shop fitter
(f) Sale of houses by property estate management company.

6.4 For a commercial farm, classify the following expenditure into either capital or revenue:

(a) Delivery costs of pesticide

(b) Insurance of tractors

(c) Installation costs of new machinery for milking cows

(d) Wages paid for casual labour

(e) Petrol for combine harvester

(f) Cost of constructing new extension to farm barn

(g) Repair costs to existing barn door.

6.5 Craig Watson is the ITC manager for a large company. He is responsible for installing a new computer suite. The following costs are associated with this installation. He is unsure whether to classify the costs associated as capital or revenue expenditure. Craig asks for your help in classifying these costs:

(a) Cost of twelve new personal computers

(b) Delivery cost of new computers

(c) New desks and chairs required for suite

(d) Power costs associated with running computers for one year

(e) Annual licence cost for software

(f) Stationery for printers

(g) Cleaning costs of new suite

(h) Installation cost of new wireless system.

6.6 The following costs are associated with running a business van which is now five years old. Classify the costs into either capital or revenue expenditure.

(a) Customising the interior of the van for business purposes

(b) Road insurance for the driver

(c) Road tax

(d) Petrol costs

(e) Obtaining an MOT

(f) Painting the van in the business colours

(g) Installing satellite navigation system for business use

(h) Replacement tyres.

6.7 Ashley Vincent runs an amusement arcade. The following costs arise out of his operations. Classify these costs into either capital or revenue expenditure:

(a) Ground rent for arcade premises

(b) Power costs in running arcade

(c) Part-time staff paid wages in summer months

(d) Purchase of new arcade consoles

(e) Delivery costs of new consoles

(f) Installation costs of new security system

(g) Replacement bulbs for neon sign outside premises

(h) Staff training on how to operate new arcade consoles.

6.8 Classify each of the following into capital or revenue expenditure:

(a) New machinery

(b) Repairs to machinery

(c) Carriage inwards on goods for resale

(d) Installation cost of new machinery

(e) Carriage inwards on new machinery

(f) Salaries to research staff

(g) Fee to architect for design of new plant

(h) Painting new factory.

6.9 From the following information calculate the *capital cost* of the new factory:

	£
Purchase price of land	140,000
Construction charges of factory	85,000
Insurance for plant & equipment	4,800
Installation costs of plant & equipment	3,600
Business rates	8,900
Legal fees	12,000
Total costs	254,300

6.10 For the following data, calculate the amounts to be included for both capital and revenue expenditure:

	£
Buying new machine	4,500
Delivery costs of machine	755
Power costs for machine for financial year	1,120
Installation costs of machine	92
Maintenance of machine	217

6.11 The following costs relate to the purchase and modernisation of new premises. Calculate the amounts to be included in capital and revenue expenditure.

	£
New premises purchased	48,000
Repainting of premises	1,800
Costs of new improved window fittings	4,330
Legal costs associated with purchases of premises	1,600
Business rates on premises	3,100

6.12 The following costs are associated with the purchase of a new food counter for a delicatessen. Calculate the amounts to be included in capital and revenue expenditure.

	£
Purchase of new food counter	5,600
Installation costs of food counter	460
Inventory for food counter	710
Refrigeration costs for first year of food counter	226
Staffing costs of food counter	9,800
Carriage inwards charged on delivery of food for counter	188
Carriage inwards on food counter	250

6.13 The following costs relate to the installation of a new heating boiler in a factory. Calculate the amounts to be included in capital and revenue expenditure.

	£
Installation and purchase price of new heating boiler	2,670
Servicing of boiler	312
Running costs of boiler	661
Breakdown repair costs	431
Delivery charge for new boiler	76

6.14 Keris Emery intends to buy a second-hand car for business use. The car is listed in the local newspaper as costing £2,999 but Keris has been able to negotiate a price of £2,500. However, there are some extra costs associated with the purchase. The car will need new tyres to make it roadworthy, which will cost £400 for a set. Additionally, she will need to install a satellite navigation system at a cost of £250. Road tax for the year is going to total £190 and she estimates the fuel costs for the year will be £2,105. She also wants the car painted at a cost of £120. A local garage has agreed to install the tyres and the satellite navigation system at a joint price of £600 if she pays in cash.

Keris decides to go ahead with the purchase and takes the local garage up on its offer.

What would be the value of the car on the balance sheet?

6.15 The following costs relate to the running of a sports shop that specialises in selling golf clubs. Classify these into either capital or revenue expenditure and provide a total for each category.

	£
Purchase of golf clubs for resale	1,990
Cost of installing fittings in shop	5,488
Wages paid to shop assistant	1,656
Insurance of premises	868
Delivery costs for golf clubs	143
Legal costs of setting up business	870

6.16 Classify the following into expenditure or receipt and whether they are of a capital or revenue nature:

(a) Sales of mushy peas by a fish and chip shop
(b) Purchase of potato chipping machine by fish and chip shop
(c) Delivery charge on purchase of shower units by a bathroom retailer
(d) Repainting logo on side of existing business van
(e) Painting premises newly finished
(f) Payment to staff installing new machine in factory
(g) Payment to staff repairing existing machine in factory
(h) Purchase of a car by a second-hand car dealer
(i) Sale of van by home delivery business
(j) Rental income earned by dry cleaning business.

6.17 A local community sports club is run as a not-for-profit organisation. Classify the following amounts as either capital expenditure, revenue expenditure, capital income or revenue income, and provide a total for each category.

	£
Sale of club house equipment	560
Purchase of supplies for club snack bar	312
Wages paid to cleaner of club house	89
Purchase of new snooker table for club house	750
Heating and lighting expenses for club house	221
Annual subscription fees received from club members	408
Loan received from local council	1,200
Delivery costs for snooker table	109

6.18 If an item of expenditure is mistakenly classified as capital rather than revenue expenditure, explain the effect of this error on the reported net profit of the business.

6.19 Petra Gadd has produced an income statement for her first year of business. However, she has made errors in classifying some of her expenditure.

	£	£
Gross profit		5,453
Less expenses		
Insurance	423	
Wages	3,123	
Carriage outwards on goods sold	123	
New office fixtures	950	
Marketing costs	765	
Installation costs of new fixtures	99	5,483
Net loss		(30)

The gross profit includes income from the sale of a fixed asset amounting to £320.

Produce a corrected statement of comprehensive income for Petra.

6.20 The following trading account relates to the business of Chappell Ltd.

Chappell Ltd: Trading Account

	£	£
Sales		9,800
Less cost of goods sold:		
Opening inventory	590	
Add Purchases	4,563	
	5,153	
Add Carriage inwards	454	
	5,607	
Less Closing inventory	667	4,940
Gross profit		4,860

However, the following issues were later discovered:

1 A motor vehicle used within the business was sold and the £725 revenue earned was included within the sales figure.
2 Furniture for the office was included within the purchases figure. The cost of this furniture was £1,160.
3 The figure for carriage inwards included carriage inwards on goods purchased of £279. The remainder of the carriage expense related to the delivery charge for the office furniture.

Based on the above information produce a redrafted trading account.

CHAPTER 7

Accounting concepts and standards

Learning objectives

By the end of this chapter you should be able to:

- Understand the principles that underlie the presentation of the financial statements of a business
- Understand the accounting concepts that are relevant to the business and how to apply these to various situations
- Recognise how changing accounting standards affect UK businesses.

Introduction

Throughout this book we refer to **accounting concepts**. These concepts act as a guide to the 'proper' way of recording and presenting accounting transactions and statements. Accounting concepts are not laws in the traditional sense of the word but are meant to provide a framework of informal rules and guidance for those who are meant to construct the financial statements of business entities.

For limited companies, these concepts are integrated into a range of **Accounting standards**. Accounting standards are a series of continually evolving statements and guidelines as to how the accounts of limited companies are constructed. These standards have evolved over time and are gradually being more closely integrated into a common set of international standards. Over the last thirty years the International Accounting Standards Board (IASB) (until 2001 this was known as the International Accounting Standards Committee) has sought to develop a set of accounting standards which can be applied by an increasing number of countries. Some countries still operate under their own **GAAP** rules and regulations. It is believed that the development of the IASB and the standards that they publish will gradually supersede the national standards and frameworks produced by individual countries.

Financial statements – the underlying principles

The Framework for the Preparation and Presentation of Financial Statements was issued by the IASB. Its main objective was to provide guidance to assist businesses both in how their financial statements were to be prepared (i.e. what rules were to be applied) and in how to present them (i.e. how the financial statements would appear).

The main objective of the financial statements is to provide a true and fair view of the financial position of the business for the **user groups** of the business. To ensure that this takes place, the framework sets out four principal requirements for financial statements: understandability, relevance, reliability and comparability.

Understandability

Financial statements should be accessible enough to be understood by the users of the information. The framework sets out the main users of the financial statements as follows:

- Investors
- Employees
- Lenders
- Suppliers
- Customers
- Government
- The public

Relevance

Financial statements should provide relevant information. Information would be judged as relevant if it enables users of the information, such as investors, to make judgements as to the past, present and hopefully future performance of the business.

Reliability

Financial statements must reliably show the effects of financial transactions on the firm's financial position. The information must be free from bias.

Comparability

The financial statements must be prepared in such a manner as to ensure that comparisons can be made with earlier time periods. This requires accounting policies to be consistently applied and an outline of what policies have been used and any changes that are made to such policies.

Given that this textbook is primarily aimed at the accounting procedures and financial statements of the sole trader, the formal accounting standards may only have a limited amount of importance. However, we are going to refer to standards where they capture the essence of an accounting concept. In addition, there is a chapter on the accounts of limited companies, for which accounting standards are definitely relevant.

You should now attempt review questions 7.1 to 7.4.

Accounting concepts

These concepts are used in the construction of financial statements and the recording of accounting transactions. Knowledge of these concepts is likely to be assessed through the use of scenarios whereby you will be given a particular situation which you would give appropriate advice by applying particular concepts.

Business entity

The accounting records of a business should be for the business alone. All items that relate to the owner's personal dealings should remain separate from those of the business. In this way the business is said to exist as a separate business entity (though legally the business of the sole trader does not exist separately from the owner). Implications of this concept are that expenses incurred by the business are the only ones that appear in the business records. This distinction can be blurred when an asset is used for both business and personal use by the owner. For example, a vehicle may be used for both business and private purposes. In this case, the financial statements must only show the true business expenses. Any use of business resources for private matters should be recorded in the accounts as drawings.

Going concern

The assumption is made that the business will continue trading into the future, and that the business and its assets are not expected to be sold off in the near future. As a result, the valuations of the assets of the business should not be based on potential resale value but on more objective, verifiable means, such as cost.

Accruals

The accruals concept means that the financial statements are constructed on the basis that incomes and expenses are linked to the period in which they are incurred rather than when the money for the income or expense changes hands. For example, the sales made in one period of time would appear as income for that period even if the receipt of money for the sales was received in a later period of time.

Prudence

To be prudent is to be careful. The concept of prudence requires the accounts to be constructed with a fair degree of caution. The implications of this are that profits should not be anticipated before they are reasonably certain. Similarly, the valuation of assets should not be based on optimistic overvaluations. For example, it is common practice (and is stated in IAS 2) that inventory should always be valued at the lower of cost or net realisable value (where the net realisable value is the estimated selling price less any costs involved in getting the asset into saleable condition). The prudence concept links with the requirement of reliability for the financial statements. This concept is sometimes known as conservatism.

Consistency

Any accounting methods that are selected should be used in a consistent manner. For example, depreciation policy for non-current assets should be maintained consistently so as to ensure fair comparisons to be made with earlier accounting periods. This can be linked with the requirement of comparability for the financial statements in order to provide a true and fair view of the financial position of the business.

Materiality

A 'material' amount refers to a monetary amount that is significant enough to be recorded separately. For instance, many businesses will group together small items of expenditure as either 'general' or 'sundry' expenses. More importantly, expenditure on some items could be classified as either an asset or an expense – this will depend on the side of the business. For example, a business may consider expenditure on office furniture as not 'material' and this would be treated as an expense. However, a smaller business may consider some of the office furniture to be material enough to be recorded as a non-current asset.

Duality

This concept ties in with the accounting equation which was covered in the Chapter 1. Each transaction can be viewed and considered to have two effects on the business – one on the assets of the business and one on the financing of the business. These effects will always be equal to one another.

Historical cost

Where possible assets (non-current and current) should be valued at the original cost of the asset – known as historical cost. Historical cost is chosen as it is objective and verifiable which means it is superior to subjective valuations which may be lacking in prudence. Even if historical cost is applied there are exceptions to this rule, such as when a business provides for depreciation on non-current assets.

Realisation

A sale should not be recognised until the legal title of the goods sold passes from supplier to customer. This is not necessarily the moment when money is received from the sale. For credit sales it could be when the goods are issued to the customer.

Introduction to accounting standards

This section deals with the accounting standards for limited companies. Financial statements for sole traders and partnerships are not expected to comply with these standards. Given that these standards apply to limited companies, and many of the standards are built on some of the accounting concepts, it is worth a brief exploration of some of these standards.

Accounting standards are not laws in their own right. The legal position of a business and its financial records is set out in the Companies Acts. However, accounting standards are still important and it is part of company law for company accounts to have been prepared on the basis of the accounting standards. If a business decides to ignore the guidance given in a particular accounting standard then this would need to be stated in the notes to the accounts in the published annual report with reasoning provided as to why the standards have not been followed.

Accounting standards in the UK

Historically, the development of accounting standards saw the development of SSAPs – Statements of Standard Accounting Practice – between 1971 and 1990. These were gradually updated and replaced by the Financial Reporting Standards (FRSs). Since 2005 it is required that all EU listed companies must produce financial statements that comply with international accounting standards which consist of the following:

● International Accounting Standards (IASs)
● International Financial Reproofing Standards (IFRSs).

Even companies which are not EU listed companies are likely to move towards the use of the international standards as, where required, it is more likely to attract investment from investors not exclusively located in the UK. The following international standards are currently in issue as at 2009. Some of the IASs have been superseded by IFRSs and these are listed here in addition.

International Accounting Standards

IAS   1   Presentation of Financial Statements
IAS   2   Inventories
IAS   7   Statement of Cash Flows
IAS   8   Accounting Policies, Changes in Accounting Estimates and Errors
IAS 10   Events after the Reporting Period
IAS 11   Construction Contracts
IAS 12   Income Taxes
IAS 16   Property, Plant and Equipment
IAS 17   Leases
IAS 18   Revenue
IAS 19   Employee Benefits
IAS 20   Accounting for Government Grants and Disclosure of Government Assistance
IAS 21   The Effects of Changes in Foreign Exchange Rates
IAS 23   Borrowing Costs
IAS 24   Related Party Disclosures
IAS 26   Accounting and Reporting by Retirement Benefit Plans
IAS 27   Consolidated and Separate Financial Statements
IAS 28   Investments in Associates
IAS 29   Financial Reporting in Hyperinflationary Economies
IAS 31   Interests in Joint Ventures
IAS 32   Financial Instruments: Presentation
IAS 33   Earnings Per Share

IAS 34   Interim Financial Reporting
IAS 36   Impairment of Assets
IAS 37   Provisions, Contingent Liabilities and Contingent Assets
IAS 38   Intangible Assets
IAS 39   Financial Instruments: Recognition and Measurement
IAS 40   Investment Property
IAS 41   Agriculture

As stated earlier, over time these are being superseded by IFRSs. The IFRSs in issue are listed below.

International Financial Reporting Standards

IFRS 1   First-time Adoption of International Financial Reporting Standards
IFRS 2   Share-based Payment
IFRS 3   Business Combinations
IFRS 4   Insurance Contracts
IFRS 5   Non-current Assets Held for Sale and Discontinued Operations
IFRS 6   Exploration for and Evaluation of Mineral Resources
IFRS 7   Financial Instruments: Disclosures
IFRS 8   Operating Segments

In the UK some businesses will still be constructing and presenting accounts and the respective financial statements based on the SSAPs and FRSs. However, it is believed that most businesses will adopt the international standards outlined above.

In this book we will refer to the appropriate international standard where relevant.

You should now attempt review questions 7.5 to 7.10.

Chapter review

By now you should understand the following:

- The principles that are used in the construction of financial accounts
- How accounting concepts are applied within the construction and presentation of financial accounts
- How to resolve any conflicts between accounting concepts
- The use of accounting standards in the construction and presentation of financial accounts
- How accounting standards have evolved over time.

Handy hints

The following hints will help you avoid errors.

- Questions are likely to be set which assess your ability to apply the relevant concepts or accounting standards to a given scenario – learning the concepts and standards by rote will only be part of the job.
- Check carefully if you need to have knowledge of all the standards – not all examination boards require working knowledge of all standards. Some may only refer to a small number of them.
- For sole traders it is the concepts that are applicable – the standards are for the accounts of limited companies.

Key terms

Accounting concept   A guide as to how to deal with a certain type of transaction when preparing the accounts of a business

Accounting standards   A series of statements which act as guides for a variety of particular issues when preparing the accounts of a limited company

GAAP   Generally Accepted Accounting Principles: the framework of accounting regulations and standards in a particular country or common area of harmonised accounting systems (e.g. UK GAAP, US GAAP)

User group   A distinct group of people and/or organisations with a shared characteristic and a common interest in the financial statements of a business (e.g. shareholders or suppliers)

REVIEW QUESTIONS

7.1   If accounting standards are not legal requirements, why would a business bother complying with these standards?

7.2   Why would a business still use UK GAAP instead of adopting international standards?

7.3   What is meant by the term 'understandability' with respect to the characteristics of financial statements?

7.4   State four user groups as stipulated by the characteristic of 'understandabilty'.

7.5   What would be the effect on reported profits of a business of not applying the accruals concept?

7.6   Which concepts are being ignored in each of the following scenarios?

(a) Inventory is valued at selling price given that the business has never failed to sell its inventory.

(b) A sole trader decides to include the petrol costs in full as business expenses despite some of the mileage being for personal use.

(c) A similar business has recently been sold for £80,000 more than the book value of the net assets. As a result, the owner of a business wishes to include goodwill in the non-current assets at a similar value to reflect the belief that the business is worth more than its net assets.

(d) Including a sale to a regular customer before the order is received.

7.7   In each case state which concept or concepts are relevant to the situation given.

(a) Subtracting an amount paid for insurance because it belongs to the next year
(b) Maintain the same percentage rate of the provision for doubtful debts despite it not being always accurate in predicting future bad debts
(c) Valuing inventory at likely selling price for a successful business
(d) Valuing a non-current asset at its likely market value.

7.8   Alec Powell runs a small shop selling sports equipment. He has run this business as a sole trader for a number of years and has built up a small niche market by offering a specialist service for local sports teams. This has enabled him to continue trading with a high level of sales even though larger 'chains' have undercut his prices. He wants your advice on a number of issues relating to drawing up the financial accounts for the year ended 31 December 2010:

(a) A similar business at the other side of the city has been recently sold as a going concern to a larger chain of sports shops. The selling price of the business was £50,000 higher than the book value of the assets. Mr Powell believes that his own sports shop would generate similar amounts of goodwill and would like to include a value for goodwill on the statement of financial position.
(b) Each of the last four years he has sold football boots to one of the local football teams every February. He has been informed that next year the club would probably continue in this manner. In anticipation Powell has produced the set ready for sale. He would like to include these in the 2010 sales figures due it being 'almost certain' that these will be sold.
(c) One of the machines that are used to print the team shirts has been depreciated using the straight line method for the last five years. However, the machine will need replacing five years before Powell expected. With this in mind, he would like to increase the amount of depreciation that he charges each year to show a more realistic valuation for the machine. (This part of the question may require that you have studied Chapter 10.)
(d) On March 30 this year Powell received £4,000 relating to sales made in the previous year. He would like to include this £4,000 as income for this year as this is the period in which it was received.

Using your knowledge of accounting and the concepts outlined in this chapter advise Mr Powell in each point on what would be the appropriate action to take.

7.9   Ollie Varadi recently valued his end-of-year stock at £10,000. The following items have not been included in his stock valuation.

Items	Cost	Net realisable value	Replacement cost
	£	£	£
Proton A	600	950	750
Lepton XV	350	440	290
Mellor 7	800	700	480

(a) Calculate the total value of Varadi's stock.
(b) Name one concept used in the valuation of stock.
(c) Explain the term net realisable value.

7.10 Which accounting standards deal with the following issues?

(a) Depreciation of non-current assets

(b) How goods bought for resale should be treated in the financial statements

(c) How to adjust the statement of financial position when a mistake is noticed and how it is to be corrected

(d) How to treat the hiring of an asset for business use.

CHAPTER 8

Adjustments to the financial statements

Learning objectives

By the end of this chapter you should be able to:

- Construct ledger accounts which contain balances outstanding both at the start and the end of the current account period
- Apply the accruals concept to the construction of the statement of comprehensive income
- Make appropriate adjustments to the statement of financial position for outstanding balances.

Introduction

In all the previous examples of financial statements (statements of comprehensive income and statements of financial position) that we have dealt with so far we have always assumed that all the expenses were paid exactly when they were due. This is unrealistic. As you are probably aware, most households and businesses will not pay expenses at the exact moment they are due (for example, many bills for services such as electricity will require part payment in advance, while some payments are made after the electricity has been consumed). This divergence between the date an expense is due and the date it is paid will be dealt with in this chapter. This will apply to both expenses that are incurred by the business and to income received.

The **accruals concept** is applied in determining how much should appear in the statement of comprehensive income as an expense or income for any particular accounting period. All incomes and expenses that are incurred in a particular period of time should appear in the statement of comprehensive income of that particular period of time – regardless of whether they have actually been paid or received by the business. In other words, even if a bill remains unpaid at the end of the period the statement of comprehensive income will still show this as a full expense.

Accruals

The term 'accruals' refers to expenses that remain unpaid. They are, in effect, expenses owing. This can be displayed in the following example.

Example 8.1

A business with a financial year-end of December 31 incurs a regular insurance charge for business activities totalling £600. In years where the expense is paid on time, the ledger account for insurance would appear as follows:

Insurance

		£				£
Dec 31	Bank	600	Dec 31	Statement of Comprehensive Income		600

It is perfectly possible that the annual total was actually broken up into several smaller payments throughout the year. The single entry used in the above example is merely used to keep the entries down to a minimum.

So far, so good: the annual charge of £600 is transferred to the Statement of Comprehensive Income as the ledger account is, in effect, 'emptied' at the end of the financial year.

However, if we imagine that one year, the business doesn't pay the full amount – let us say that it only pays £520 of the total – then the ledger account would appear as follows:

Insurance

		£				£
Dec 31	Bank	520	Dec 31	Statement of Comprehensive Income		600

Applying the accruals concept means that we have a discrepancy in the above ledger account – the amount to be transferred to the statement of comprehensive income must be the full amount that belongs to the year (i.e. the £600 due), whereas the amount debited to the ledger account (representing the amount actually paid) is only £520.

We deal with this issue by referring to the outstanding balance on the account (£80) as an accrual (an amount owing). This will be carried forward to the next accounting period. Hence, the ledger account will appear as follows:

Insurance

		£				£
Dec 31	Bank	520	Dec 31	Statement of Comprehensive Income		600
Dec 31	Balance c/d	80				
		600				600
			Jan 1	Balance b/d		80

The accrual will remain on the account as an outstanding balance. How do we know that it relates to an amount owing? Easy: The outstanding balance is a credit balance – meaning it is a liability.

Accruals
are also known as
accrued expenses, expenses owing *and* **expenses in arrears.**

Prepayments

It is perfectly possible that a business pays some of its expenses before the date required. These amounts paid in advance are known as **prepayments**.

Example 8.2

The business in example 8.1 also incurs an annual charge for rent of £5,000. However, if we imagine that on one year it will pay £500 in advance of the following year's rent (and has kept up to date with the rest of the current year's payments) then the ledger account for rent would appear as follows:

Rent

		£				£
Dec 31	Bank	5,500	Dec 31	Statement of Comprehensive Income		5,000
			Dec 31	Balance c/d		500
		5,500				5,500
Jan 1	Balance b/d	500				

In this example, the outstanding balance is the result of overpayment. This is brought down to the next year's account as a debit balance. It represents the amount paid this year for the next year's charge. Note that the rental charge for the year (as transferred to the statement of comprehensive income) is unaltered by the prepayment. The closing debit balance represents the prepaid amount.

Prepayments
are also known as
prepaid expenses *and* **amounts paid in advance.**

Revenue

The application of prepayments and accruals can also be extended to revenue accounts. If a business has other sources of income, then it is perfectly possible that some of this income will be received in advance of its due date, or not received on time.

Example 8.3

The same business receives commission each year totalling £780. However, by the end of the year the business is still owed £100 (i.e. it has only received £680 so far).

This would be shown in the ledger account as follows:

Commission received

		£			£
Dec 31	Statement of		Dec 31	Bank	680
	Comprehensive Income	780	Dec 31	Balance c/d	100
		780			780
Jan 1	Balance b/d	100			

The outstanding balance would be referred to as **revenue owing** or **accrued revenue** and would be represented by a debit balance (in the same way that trade receivables are a debit balance).

Example 8.4

Continuing from the previous example, imagine that in the following year (assuming the total due is still £780) the business actually received £50 in excess of the amount due in respect of the following year's amount.

This would appear in the ledger account as follows:

Commission received

		£			£
Dec 31	Statement of		Dec 31	Bank	830
	Comprehensive Income	780			
Dec 31	Balance c/d	50			
		830			830
			Jan 1	Balance b/d	50

The amount paid to the business in advance is known as **prepaid revenue**.

You should now attempt review questions 8.1 to 8.3.

Accruals and prepayments and the statement of financial position

If we are always to include the full amount due for incomes and expenses regardless of whether they have been paid or received then surely the statement of financial position would not balance? Your initial reasoning might be as follows:

If an expense remains owing then the balance at the bank would be higher than if the expenses had been paid in full. This would suggest that the statement of financial position would not balance.

However, this can be dealt with by the inclusion of the outstanding balances on the statement of financial position as either a current asset or a current liability.

Type of balance:	Balance on account:	Appears on statement of financial position as:
Accrual	Credit	Current liability
Prepayment	Debit	Current asset
Accrued revenue	Debit	Current asset
Prepaid revenue	Credit	Current liability

Dealing with trial balances when outstanding balances exist

Many assessment style questions will require the completion of the financial statements from a given trial balance. In this situation, the amounts appearing within the trial balances for incomes and expenses will represent the amounts actually paid or received. Any adjustments needed for outstanding balances will be presented outside the trial balances – usually underneath. A worked example appears below.

Example 8.5

The following trial balance relates to H Speller as at 31 December 2014:

	Dr £	Cr £
Inventory at 1 Jan 2014	6,105	
Sales		56,193
Purchases	30,010	
Office expenses	3,980	
Rent	1,750	
Wages	11,325	
Premises	26,500	
Equipment	4,990	
Trade receivables	2,655	
Trade payables		3,156
Bank	1,074	
Capital		34,500
Drawings	5,460	
	93,849	93,849

Additional information:

1 Inventory as at 31 December 2014 was valued at £7,230.
2 Office expenses still owing as at 31 December 2014 amounted to £510.
3 Rent accrued at 31 December 2014 was £230.
4 Wages paid in advance for 2015 totalled £995.

Each of the expenses is adjusted as for the outstanding balance; amounts accrued are added on to the amount paid to reflect the amount that 'belongs' to the time period shown. Similarly, the amount prepaid 'belongs' to the next year and therefore will be subtracted from the amount paid.

Showing your workings in brackets by the side of any adjustment is a good habit to get into – if you make a mistake then, with workings, you may still gain marks for some of your workings.

H Speller
Statement of comprehensive income for the year ended 31 December 2014

	£	£
Sales		56,193
Less Cost of goods sold:		
Opening inventory	6,105	
Add Purchases	30,010	
	36,115	
Less Closing inventory	7,230	28,885
Gross profit		27,308
Less: Expenses		
Office expenses (£3,980 + £510)	4,490	
Rent (£1,750 + £230)	1,980	
Wages (£11,325 – £995)	10,330	16,800
Net profit		10,508

The outstanding balances for accruals and prepayments would appear on the statement of financial position as follows:

Current Assets

Prepayments £995

Current Liabilities

Accruals £510 + £230

You should now attempt review questions 8.4 to 8.7.

Dealing with balances from more than one year

It is possible that you will have to produce ledger accounts and calculate amounts to be entered into the statement of comprehensive income for income and expense accounts where balances are outstanding from *both* the previous year and also the year following the current year.

The accruals concept still applies, which means that the amount due for a particular year will need to have adjustments made for any outstanding balances from any time other than the current year.

Example 8.6

Let us consider the account for the expense of electricity over the year of 2012.

	£
Electricity owing from 2011 as at 31 December 2011	37
Amounts paid for electricity during 2012	421
Electricity prepaid for 2012 as at 31 December 2012	56

The ledger account for electricity will appear as follows:

Electricity

2012		£	2012		£
Dec 31	Bank	421	Jan 1	Balance b/d	37
			Dec 31	**Statement of**	
				Comprehensive Income	**328**
			Dec 31	Balance c/d	56
		421			421
2013			2013		
Jan 1	Balance b/d	56			

On a practical level, when completing a ledger account it is often the case that what is entered into the account last is not the last item to be entered by the date on the calendar. In the above example, the closing balance at the ends of the year is entered 'before' the amount to be transferred to the statement of comprehensive income – which is entered as the amount needed to ensure that the account totals the same for both sides of the account. Obviously the dates for entries would still need to follow chronological order.

Example 8.7

The following data relates to the account of rent received for 2012:

	£
Amount still owing from tenants for 2011 as at 1 January 2012	265
Amounts received during 2012	1,890
Amounts still owing from tenants as at 31 December 2012	118

Rent received

2012		£	2012		£
Jan 1	Balance b/d	265	Dec 31	Bank	1,890
Dec 31	**Statement of**		Dec 31	Balance c/d	118
	Comprehensive Income	1,743			
		2,008			2,008
2013			2013		
Jan 1	Balance b/d	118			

As in the previous example, the amount to be transferred to the statement of comprehensive income can be calculated once all the information already known has been entered.

You should now attempt review questions 8.8 to 8.15.

Links with other topics

Completion of a set of financial statements (usually just the statement of comprehensive income and the statement of financial position) is a very popular topic for examination assessment. However, it is likely that this topic will be integrated with other topics which require adjustments to the financial statements.

To answer the last few review questions in this chapter, you need to know about bad debts and provision for doubtful debts, and about depreciation. These topics are covered in Chapters 9 and 10.

You should now attempt review questions 8.16 to 8.19.

Chapter review

By now you should understand the following:

- How to maintain ledger accounts with outstanding balances at the end of the current period
- How to produce financial statements with outstanding balances
- How to maintain ledger accounts with outstanding balances both at the end and at the start of the year.

Handy hints

The following hints will help you avoid errors.

- Try to think of what belongs to the year or period in question – only the expenses or incomes belonging to this period will appear in the statement of comprehensive income.
- Show your workings and adjustments when constructing the financial statements. Many marks are awarded for the process of calculating the amounts to appear in the financial statements. An answer which is incorrect and has no workings will get no marks, whereas an incorrect answer with partially correct workings will probably gain some marks.

Key terms

Accruals concept The accounting concept whereby all incomes and expenses are matched to the period in which they are incurred

Accruals Any expenses still owing at the end of the accounting period

Prepayments Any expenses which are paid in advance of the accounting period in which they are due to be paid

Accrued revenue Any revenue owing to a business which has not been received by the end of the period in which it was due

Prepaid revenue Any revenue which is received by a business in advance of the period in which it is due

REVIEW QUESTIONS

8.1   The following transactions took place during the financial year ended 31 December 2010. In each case construct the ledger account.

   (a) Advertising paid during 2010 totalled £712 but as at 31 December 2010 there was £45 still owing.
   (b) Insurance paid during 2010 totalled £556. Out of the total paid, £21 was for January 2011.
   (c) Heating and lighting expenses paid during 2010 amounted to £650 of which £250 was for 2011.
   (d) Cheques received for rent during the year totalled £1,100. However, by the end of the year the firm was still owed £180.

8.2   The following transactions took place during the financial year ended 31 December 2012. In each case construct the appropriate ledger account.

   (a) Cheques cashed by the firm for commission received amounted to £560, of which one quarter of this amount related to the following year.
   (b) Wages paid during the year totalled £3,200. Accrued wages at the end of the year were £470.
   (c) Money received for rental income totalled £1,600. However, this was paid for the period 1 January 2012 to 30 April 2013.
   (d) Insurance was paid during 2012 as follows:

Date payment made:	Amount paid:	Period payment made for:
Jan 1	£400	Jan 1 to May 31
May 14	£400	Jun 1 to Oct 31
Nov 10	£400	Nov 1 to Mar 31

8.3   The following information relates to the accounts of A Vincent, who finished her first year of business as at 31 March 2013:

   (a) An insurance charge of £930 was incurred although only £725 was paid in respect of this amount.
   (b) Heating and lighting due for the year was £1,340. Cheques were sent out on 1 April and every following three months for £400 each.
   (c) Property is sub-let to a tenant at a charge of £5,800 per annum. Cheques had been received for £4,750 by the end of the year.
   (d) Cheques had been paid out for motor expenses totalling £750. This was to cover the fifteen-month period starting 1 July 2012.

   Show the ledger accounts for each of the above.

8.4   The following trial balance was extracted from the books of J Churchard at the close of business on 31 July 2005.

	£	£
Inventory at 1 Aug 2004	6,105	
Sales		56,193
Purchases	30,010	
Office expenses	3,980	
Rent	1,750	
Wages	11,325	
Premises	26,500	
Equipment	4,990	
Trade receivables	2,655	
Trade payables		3,156
Bank	1,074	
Capital		34,500
Drawings	5,460	
	93,849	93,849

Additional information:

1 Inventory 31 July 2005 £7,230
2 Office expenses owing at 31 July 2005 £510
3 Rent accrued at 31 July 2005 £230
4 Wages paid in advance 31 July 2005 £995.

Construct a statement of comprehensive income for the year ended 31 July 2005 and a statement of financial position at that date.

8.5 The following trial balance was extracted from the accounts of B Wright as at 31 December 2014. From this, construct a statement of comprehensive income for the year ended 31 December 2014 and a statement of financial position as at the year-end date.

	£	£
Equipment	11,400	
Machinery	5,340	
Sales		45,312
Purchases	31,980	
Insurance	1,013	
Salaries	6,409	
Rent	3,870	
Opening inventory	3,231	
Trade receivables	4,231	
Trade payables		5,436
Bank	891	
Capital		24,500
Drawings	6,883	
	75,248	75,248

Additional information:

(i)   Inventory in trade as at 31 December 2014 was valued at £5,670.
(ii) Salaries accrued as at 31 December amount to £703.
(iii) Rent owing at the year-end was £540.

8.6 The following trial balance was extracted from the accounts of C Wattison as at 31 December 2013. From this, construct a statement of comprehensive income for the year ended 31 December 2013 and a statement of financial position as at the year-end date.

	Dr	Cr
	£	£
Opening inventory	12,560	
Sales		119,000
Purchases	71,500	
Insurance	8,930	
Heating and lighting	2,360	
Wages and salaries	23,400	
Property	74,000	
Plant	7,560	
Trade receivables	8,340	
Trade payables		7,431
Bank	2,210	
Capital		91,312
Drawings	6,883	
	217,743	217,743

Additional information:

1 Inventory in trade as at 31 December 2013 was valued at £13,420.
2 Wages and salaries accrued as at 31 December amounted to £799.
3 Insurance prepaid as at the year-end totalled £190.
4 Heating and lighting prepaid as at the year-end totalled £312.

8.7 The following trial balance has been extracted from the ledger of M Krause:

	Dr	Cr
	£	£
Sales and Purchases	256,000	379,000
Premises	220,000	
Plant, machinery and equipment	31,500	
Administration expenses	4,720	
Salaries	28,900	
Insurance	2,890	
Sundry expenses	990	
Selling expenses	6,725	
Power costs	3,780	
Vehicles	18,900	
Trade receivables and payables	12,772	9,995
Inventory as at 1 January 2012	23,450	
Bank		3,132
Capital		242,000
Drawings	23,500	
	634,127	634,127

Additional information as at 31 December 2012:

1 Inventory in trade was valued at £16,740.
2 Power costs accrued were £235.
3 Sundry expenses owing were £90.
4 Salaries prepaid were £1,150.
5 Insurance prepaid was £312.

From this, construct a statement of comprehensive income for the year ended 31 December 2012 and a statement of financial position as at the year-end date.

8.8 Construct the ledger accounts for S Yates based on the following data:

(a) Heating and lighting owing as at 1 Jan 2016 £32. Amounts paid during 2016 £453. Heating and lighting owing as at 31 December 2016 £56.

(b) Insurance owing at 1 Jan 2016 £187. Amount paid during 2016 £955. Insurance prepaid as at 31 December 2016 £42.

(c) Wages paid in advance in 2015 for the year 2016 £211. Wages paid during 2016 £6,980. Wages owing as at 31 December 2016 £544.

(d) Telephone paid in 2016 £378. Prepaid as at 1 January 2016 £17. Prepaid as at 31 December £61.

8.9 Construct the relevant ledger accounts for T Ritzema from the following information for the year ended 31 December 2017.

(a) Commission received during 2017 £750. Amount owing to the business as at 1 January 2017 £50. Amount owing to the business as at 31 December 2017 £88.

(b) Rent received during 2017 £2,800. Amount prepaid in 2016 for the following year £195. Amount owing to the business as at 31 December 2017 £362.

(c) Royalties owing to the business as at 1 January 2017 £94. Royalties received in 2017 £899 of which £21 related to royalties due in 2018.

8.10 The following details relate to the heating costs for the year ended 31 December 2015:

(i) Gas bill unpaid as at 1 Jan 2015 £45
(ii) Electricity prepaid as at 1 Jan 2015 £12
(iii) Gas paid by standing order £35 per month
(iv) Electricity paid on Jan 1 £250
(v) Electricity paid on Jun 15 £460
(vi) Gas unpaid as at 31 Dec £81
(vii) Electricity unpaid as at 31 Dec £33.

Show the ledger account for heating (assuming gas and electricity are combined).

8.11 The following details relate to the rent received for the year ended 31 December 2016. The business lets two properties (A and B) to two other businesses.

(i) Rent received in advance as at 1 Jan 2016 in respect of property A £130
(ii) Rent received still owing as at 1 Jan 2016 in respect of property B £240
(iii) Rent received by cheque on 23 Jan in respect of property A £780
(iv) Rent received by cheque on 12 Mar in respect of property B £1,430
(v) Rent received by cheque on 15 Jun £2,810 in respect of property A
(vi) Rent received by cheque on 30 Sep £4,520 in respect of property B
(vii) Rent received by cheque on 28 Nov in respect of property A £1,575
(viii) Rent received still owing in respect of property A as at 31 Dec 2016 £382
(ix) Rent received in advance in respect of property B as at 31 Dec 2016 £76.

Construct the ledger amount for rent received for the year ending 31 December 2016. When constructing the account, show all opening and closing balances individually.

8.12 The following data relates to the accounts of L Katz for the year ended 31 December 2013. Calculate the amounts to be deducted from the year's gross profit.

Amounts paid	£
Rent	500
Insurance	245
Wages	1,280

Additional information:

	As at 31 Dec 2012	**As at 31 Dec 2013**
Rent	Balance owing £74	Balance owing £56
Insurance	Balance prepaid £18	Balance owing £11
Wages	Balance owing £94	Balance prepaid £130

8.13 The following data relates to the accounts of M Lyne for the year ended 31 December 2015. Calculate the amounts to be deducted from or added to the year's gross profit.

Amounts paid and received	£
Salaries	5,600
Rent received	2,750
Motor expenses	843

Additional information:

	As at 31 Dec 2014	**As at 31 Dec 2015**
Salaries	Balance owing £439	Balance prepaid £280
Rent received	Balance owing £117	Balance owing £265
Motor expenses	Balance prepaid £42	Balance prepaid £55

8.14 The financial year of G Norfolk ended on 31 December 2003. From the following information, ascertain the amounts to be included in the statement of comprehensive income for the year ended 31 December 2003, through use of ledger accounts or otherwise.

1 Advertising: paid during 2003 £190, prepaid for 2004 £25.
2 Heating costs: owing as at 1 January 2003 £54, paid during 2003 £340, still owing at end of the year £31.
3 Rent received: received during 2003 for period covering 1 March 2003 to 29 February 2004 was £1,200 (no rent was receivable for January or February 2003).
4 Insurance: prepaid at 1 January 2003 £44; paid in 2003 £501.

8.15 The financial year of Liz King ended on 31 December 2011. From the following information, ascertain the amounts to be included in the statement of comprehensive income for the year ended 31 December 2001, through use of ledger accounts or otherwise.

1 Rent: owing at 1 January 2011 £110; paid in 2011 £540.
2 Marketing costs: paid in 2011 £111; owing at 31 December 2011 £34.
3 Royalties earned: received in 2011 £200; still owed at 31 December 2011 £40.
4 Insurance: prepaid at 1 January 2011 £32; paid in 2011 £865.
5 Wages and salaries: paid during 2011 £470; owing at 1 January 2011 £25; owing at 31 December 2011 £87.

8.16 From the following trial balance of A Westwood, you are asked to draw up a statement of comprehensive income for the year ended 30 June 2003.

	Dr £	Cr £
Sales		52,000
Purchases	23,000	
Inventory as at 1 July 2002	8,550	
Premises	75,000	
Equipment	18,000	
Returns inwards	340	
Bank	1,280	
Wages	6,950	
Insurance	390	
Rent	1,350	
Advertising	260	
Capital		94,660
Drawings	10,450	
Returns outwards		450
Trade receivables	6,500	
Trade creditors		4,960
	152,070	152,070

Additional information:

1 Inventory as at 30 June 2003 was valued at £10,660.
2 Depreciation is to be provided as follows: Premises 10%, Equipment 20% (both on cost).
3 A provision for doubtful debts is to be created at 5% of trade receivables at the year-end.
4 Accrued rent was £211 as at 30 June 2003.
5 Insurance paid in advance was £120 as at 30 June 2003.

8.17 The following trial balance has been extracted from the ledger of I Mellor.

	£	£
Buildings	32,000	
Equipment	9,060	
Sales		143,750
Purchases	99,600	
Electricity	1,231	
Wages and salaries	18,721	
Rent	3,233	
Inventory as at 1 April 2010	9,875	
Trade receivables	7,861	
Trade payables		6,546
Bank	3,132	
Insurance	787	
Office expenses	5,345	
Bad debts	280	
Capital		52,440
Drawings	11,611	
	202,736	202,736

Additional information as at 31 March 2011:

(i) Inventory in trade was valued at £8,760.
(ii) Electricity is accrued by £67.
(iii) Wages and salaries owing were £540.
(iv) Rent has been prepaid by £119.
(v) Insurance paid in advance was £53.

Prepare a statement of comprehensive income for the year ending 31 March 2011 and a statement of financial position as at that date.

8.18   The following trial balance of N Dorritt was extracted as at 31 March 2018.

	Dr	Cr
	£	£
Inventory as at 1 April 2017	11,423	
Sales		98,787
Purchases	79,121	
Heating and lighting	893	
Wages	7,121	
Distribution costs	2,321	
Machine repairs	989	
Discounts allowed	864	
Machinery	25,400	
Vehicles	9,250	
Provision for doubtful debts		280
Bad debts	187	
Trade receivables	6,000	
Trade payables		5,402
Bank	1,400	
Loan (repayable in 2022)		10,000
Capital		39,000
Drawings	8,500	
	153,469	153,469

Additional information as at 31 March 2018:

(i) Inventory in trade was valued at £13,490.
(ii) Accruals were as follows:
    (a) Wages £1,120
    (b) Distribution costs £435
    (c) Machine repairs £87.
(iii) Heating and lighting prepaid was £134.
(iv) The provision for doubtful debts is to be maintained at 4% of trade receivables.

Prepare a statement of comprehensive income for the year ending 31 March 2018 and a statement of financial position as at that date.

8.19 The following trial balance was extracted from the books of R Booth at the close of business on 31 December 2009.

	£	£
Opening inventory	20,672	
Sales		449,000
Purchases	312,000	
General expenses	8,881	
Salaries	54,535	
Administration costs	13,123	
Insurance	4,535	
Rent	9,789	
Bad debts	545	
Plant	62,000	
Equipment	18,000	
Provision for depreciation: Plant		9,500
Provision for depreciation: Equipment		5,200
Provision for doubtful debts		280
Trade receivables	10,200	
Trade payables		7,800
Bank	8,500	
Capital		72,000
Drawings	21,000	
	543,780	543,780

Additional information:

1 Inventory at 31 December 2009 £19,122
2 Salaries accrued at 31 December 2009 £5,435
3 Administration costs owing at 31 December 2009 £312
4 Insurance paid in advance at 31 December 2009 £765
5 The provision for doubtful debts is to be maintained at 5% of trade receivables
6 Depreciation is to be provided as follows: Plant: 20% on cost; Equipment: 20% reducing balance.

Prepare a statement of comprehensive income for the year ending 31 December 2009 and a statement of financial position as at that date.

CHAPTER 9

Bad debts and provision for doubtful debts

Learning objectives

By the end of this chapter you should be able to:

- Account for bad debts in the ledger accounts of the business
- Understand the steps a business may take to avoid the incidence of bad debts
- Construct and update the account for the provision for doubtful debts
- Show the effect of the provision for doubtful debts on the statement of financial position
- Account for bad debts recovered
- Understand the effects of creating a provision for discounts on debtors.

Introduction

When drawing up a statement of financial position one should be prudent in the values placed on asset values. Any business that allows sales on credit terms runs the risk of a debtor not settling the amount owing in full, meaning the business will incur what is known as a **bad debt**. Bad debts are a normal, if unfortunate, consequence and will need to be accounted for if we are not to overstate the value of total assets for a business.

Similarly, if we are aiming to show realistic values for the assets of the business, then we would need to anticipate the likelihood of future bad debts. This can be dealt with through the creation of a provision for doubtful debts.

*Remember: Debtors may appear on the statement of financial position as **trade receivables**.*

Accounting for bad debts

Even in a successful economy, business failure will be commonplace and businesses will be unable to pay the amounts that they owe. In difficult trading conditions, such as during a recession, bad debts will become even more frequent. Obviously we need some way of accounting for bad debts.

Example 9.1

During 2008, the following credit sales were made:

- On 15 January, sales of £750 were made to I Fraser.
- On 11 March, sales of £480 were made to M Flower.

On 31 December 2008, the following was decided:

- The amount owing by Fraser would be written off as a bad debt.
- Flower had declared himself bankrupt and a payment of 25 pence in the £ was all that would be received in full settlement.

The individual debtor accounts would appear as follows:

I Fraser

2008		£	2008		£
Jan 15	Sales	750	Dec 31	Bad debts	750

M Flower

2008		£	2008		£
Mar 11	Sales	480	Dec 31	Bank	120
			Dec 31	Bad debts	360
		480			480

The credit entry for the bad debt in the debtor's account will, in effect, 'close down' the debtor's account by balancing it off. However, it is possible that the debtor will be able to pay part of the outstanding balance (as in Flower's account in the above example). In this case the credit entries will include the amount received in settlement and the remainder which is written off by the bad debt being entered to balance off the account.

To complete the entries, the amounts are transferred to the debit side of the bad debts account.

Bad debts

2008		£	2008		£
Dec 31	I Fraser	750	Dec 31	Statement of comprehensive income	1,110
Dec 31	M Flower	360			
		1,110			1,110

At the end of the trading period, the total amounts will be transferred to the statement of comprehensive income – as a revenue expense. In other words, bad debts are expenses for the period in which they are written off. Even if a debt is outstanding from an earlier period of time, the bad debt belongs to the trading period in which the debt is written off.

Within the trial balance, the balance for debtors (which may appear as trade receivables) should be assumed to be after the bad debts have been subtracted – therefore no further adjustment for bad debts is needed on this figure. However, if the information came to light after the trial balance had been presented, then the bad debts should be deducted from the debtors figure.

How can a business minimise the risk of bad debts?

Bad debts can be avoided by not allowing sales to be made on credit. However, this risks alienating potential customers. In addition, although a business will bear risks by allowing sales on credit it will benefit from being able to purchase inventory on credit. Minimising the risk of bad debts will involve implementing a system of **credit control**. Steps in a reliable system of credit control could involve the following:

● Asking for references from a business before allowing credit
● Offering sufficient cash discounts to encourage prompt payment
● Chasing up outstanding debts when credit periods are exceeded
● Using a **debt factor** (a debt factoring business specialises in collecting debts and will purchase outstanding debts at a discounted price from some businesses if there is a chance the debts can be collected)
● Only allowing a certain credit limit
● Only allowing regular customers credit.

You should now attempt review questions 9.1 to 9.3.

Provision for doubtful debts

Given that bad debts are commonplace the amount for total debtors is likely to over-state the amount that we will actually receive in settlement (i.e. we are assuming that we will never collect all that we are owed) which means it would not be prudent to place the debtors at their full value on the statement of financial position. As a result, it is prudent to calculate an estimate for the future size of any bad debts. This is known as the **provision for doubtful debts**.

What is a provision?

According to IAS 37 a provision is 'a liability of uncertain timing or amount'.
  Four types of provisions are covered in this book:

● **Provision for doubtful debts**
● **Provision for discounts on debtors**
● **Provision for depreciation**
● **Provision for unrealised profit on unsold inventory**.

The provision for doubtful debts figure will be deducted from the debtors figure on the statement of financial position to represent a more realistic figure that will be collected from debtors. The size of the provision will depend on a number of factors. Ideally it should reflect the size of future bad debts.

Calculating the size of the provision for doubtful debts

As this is an estimate and cannot be known with certainty, the following factors are likely to influence the size of any provision:

- The length of time debts have been outstanding – this can be achieved through an **aged debtors schedule** which 'ages' each debt owing to the firm
- Historical trends for bad debts in a particular industry
- Economic factors – i.e. what are the prevailing macroeconomic conditions – in times of economic decline we would expect the incidence of bad debts to rise as business failure is more common.

Although a realistic estimate for the size of the provision is important, we will mostly use a simple method for calculating the size of the provision, based on a simple percentage of the total debtors figure at the end of the trading period.

Accounting entries for the provision for doubtful debts

All provision accounts exhibit credit balances. Although provisions can be treated in a similar manner to expenses in the statement of comprehensive income, unlike expense accounts, the outstanding balance on the provision account is carried forward to the next period. The balance on a provision account will remain the same until it is adjusted by either increasing or decreasing the provision.

The adjustment for the provision will be entered into the statement of comprehensive income in the period in which the adjustment is made:

Accounting entries for provision for doubtful debts:			
Increasing the provision		Decreasing the provision	
Debit	Credit	Debit	Credit
Statement of comprehensive income	Provision for doubtful debts	Provision for doubtful debts	Statement of comprehensive income

From the above table it should be clear that the increase in the provision will be treated as an expense in the statement of comprehensive income, whilst the reduction in the provision will be treated as an income in the statement of comprehensive income.

Adjustments for provisions for doubtful debts in statement of comprehensive income	
Increasing the provision	Decreasing the provision
Debit profit and loss with increase only (i.e. the increase is treated as an 'expense')	Credit profit and loss with decrease only (i.e. treated as an 'income')

Example 9.2

A business discovers that bad debts, on average, are 5% of the value of total debtors and therefore would like to create a provision for doubtful debts equivalent to 5% of the year-end debtor balances.

Year	Debtors (£) at 31 December	Required size of provision (5%)
2002	£5,000	£250
2003	£6,000	£300
2004	£6,000	£300
2005	£4,500	£225

The ledger account for provision for doubtful debts would appear as follows:

Provision for doubtful debts

		£			£
2002			2002		
Dec 31	Balance c/d	250	Dec 31	Statement of comp. income	250
2003			2003		
Dec 31	Balance c/d	300	Jan 1	Balance b/d	250
			Dec 31	Statement of comp. income	50
		300			300
2004			2004		
Dec 31	Balance b/d	300	Jan 1	Balance b/d	300
2005			2005		
Dec 31	Statement of comp. income	75	Jan 1	Balance b/d	300
Dec 31	Balance c/d	225			
		300			300
			2006		
			Jan 1	Balance b/d	225

In 2002, the *full* amount of the provision has to be debited to the statement of comprehensive income as an expense as no previous provision exists and the balance is carried forward to the next period.

In 2003, the provision is increased (due to an increase in the size of the debtors figure), but it is only the increase in the provision that is debited to the statement of comprehensive income.

In 2004, the provision remains unaltered as the size of the debtors figure remains unchanged. Therefore, no entry is needed for the statement of comprehensive income – the balance brought forward from the previous year is simply carried forward to the following year.

In 2005, a decrease in the overall debtors figure leads to the provision being reduced in size. Therefore we need to debit the provision account to reduce the overall balance and we will credit the statement of comprehensive income with the size of the decrease. This will be treated as revenue income in the 2005 statement of comprehensive income.

Provision for doubtful debts and the statement of financial position

As with all provision accounts, it is the *full* amount (i.e. the end-of-year balance) that will appear on the statement of financial position and this will be deducted from the relevant asset. In the example above, the relevant section of the statements of financial position would appear as follows:

Statement of financial position extracts at 31 December

	£	£
Current assets (for 2002)		
Debtors	5,000	
Less Provision for doubtful debts	250	4,750
Current assets (for 2003)		
Debtors	6,000	
Less Provision for doubtful debts	300	5,700
Current assets (for 2004)		
Debtors	6,000	
Less Provision for doubtful debts	300	5,700
Current assets (for 2005)		
Debtors	4,500	
Less Provision for doubtful debts	225	4,275

You should now attempt review questions 9.4 to 9.15.

Bad debts recovered

Occasionally a debt that has been written off as a bad debt will be recovered and we receive the money we were due. The accounting treatment of bad debts recovered is shown in the following example.

Example 9.3

A debt of £220 owing to the business from A Marcou had previously been written off as bad. Some months later the debt is recovered.

The double-entry adjustments would appear as follows:

1 We reinstate the original debt in the personal account of the debtor:

A Marcou

	£		£
Bad debts recovered	220		

Bad debts recovered

	£		£
		A Marcou	220

2 We account for the payment received as we would when any debtors settles their account:

A Marcou

	£		£
Bad debts recovered	220	Bank	220

Bank

	£		£
A Marcou	220		

The balance on the bad debts recovered account would be treated as revenue income for the period in which the debt is recovered, i.e. it will contribute to the profits for that period.

Alternatively, some businesses may offset the balance on the bad debts recovered against any bad debts for that period – thus reducing the bad debts for that period.

Provision for discounts on debtors

A much less common type of provision exists when creating a **provision for discounts on debtors**. The reasoning behind this is that the total debtors figure will overstate the amount to be collected as cash discounts given to debtors will inevitably reduce the amounts actually received. It is prudent, therefore, to create the provision for discounts on debtors.

If this provision is created and utilised then the value should be based on the likely rate of cash discounts given, and should be deducted from the debtors figure after the provision for doubtful debts has been deducted (because the full debtors figure would include the estimate for future bad debts which certainly don't qualify for discounts).

For example, if debtors at the year-end were valued at £12,000 and the provision for doubtful debts at the same period was £600 (5%) and the provision for discounts on debtors was to be set at 2%, then the provision for discounts on debtors would be set at (£12,000 − £600) × 2% = £228. On the statement of financial position of this firm, the net value of debtors after all provisions have been deducted would be £11,172 (£12,000 − £600 − £228).

The accounting treatment of provision for discounts on debtors is exactly the same as any other provision account - whereby the credit balance for the provision is maintained and adjusted through profit and loss amendments.

You should now attempt review questions 9.16 to 9.20.

Chapter review

By now you should understand the following:

- How to account for bad debts
- What credit control polices might consist of
- How to calculate the value of the provision for doubtful debts
- The provision for doubtful debts account
- How to account for bad debts received
- The principles of provisions for discounts on debtors.

Handy hints

The following hints will help you avoid errors.

- Do not treat bad debts and the provision for doubtful debts as the same thing – the former is an event which has occurred, the latter is something which may or may not occur in the future.
- It is only the change in the size of the provision for doubtful debts that appears in the statement of comprehensive income.
- It is the full value of the provision which is deducted from the value of debtors on the statement of financial position.

Key terms

Bad debts   Debts for which payment is not expected to be received which are therefore written off against profits

Credit control   Systems used by a business to control and manage its trade receivables

Debt factoring   The process of selling a debt of the business to a factor that specialises in debt collection

Aged debtors schedule   A system used to calculate the size of the provision for doubtful debts whereby trade receivables are classified according to age in order to estimate the likelihood of their becoming bad debts

Provision   A future liability or future expectation of expenditure of uncertain value or timing

Provision for doubtful debts   An estimate of the likely size of future debts – this is only an estimate in order to show a more realistic (and prudent) value of debts likely to be collected on the statement of financial position

Bad debts recovered   Debts previously written off as bad for which payment is eventually received

Provision for discounts on debtors   A provision created which estimates the likely size of cash discounts to be given to debtors in order to show a more realistic size for the debtors figure on the statement of financial position

REVIEW QUESTIONS

9.1 A new business which started trading on 1 January 2009 wrote the following debts off as shown below:

15 April	D Hirst	£65
31 May	M Bright	£24
19 August	P Williams	£110

Construct the bad debts account for the year to 31 December 2009.

9.2 Goods were sold on credit to L Farthing on 19 October 2008 for £950. On 15 December Farthing was declared bankrupt. A payment of 30 p in the £ was received in full settlement and the remainder was written off as a bad debt.

Show the ledger account of L Farthing to record the above details.

9.3 During the financial year ended 31 March 2011, it was found that S Peck – a debtor – was declared bankrupt. She owed the firm £860, but it was found that a payment of 20 pence in the pound was to be received in full and final settlement.

Show the account for S Peck after all adjustments have been made.

9.4 From the following data ascertain the size of the provision for doubtful debts for each year, stating the entry needed in the respective year's statement of comprehensive income. In each case, the provision should be based on 3% of outstanding debtors at the year end.

Year	Debtors as at 31 December (£)
2009	10,000
2010	12,000
2011	13,000
2012	11,000

9.5 From the following data ascertain the size of the provision for doubtful debts for each year, stating the entry needed in the respective year's statement of comprehensive income. In each case, the provision should be based on 4% of outstanding debtors at the year-end.

Year	Debtors as at 31 December (£)
2009	155,000
2010	180,200
2011	184,500
2012	183,100

9.6 From the following data ascertain the size of the provision for doubtful debts for each year, stating the entry needed in the respective year's statement of comprehensive income. In each case the provision should be based on 5% of outstanding debtors at the year end. The balance on the provision account as at 1 January 2005 stood at £505.

Year	Debtors as at 31 December (£)
2005	7,800
2006	7,300
2007	8,650
2008	8,990

9.7 P Brothers decides to increase his current provision for doubtful debts from £650 to £890 for the financial year ended 30 June 2009. His debtors at the year-end are valued at £13,450.

Show the provision for doubtful debts account for the year ended 30 June 2009 and provide an extract from the end-of-year statement of financial position.

9.8 For the year ended 31 December 2006, L Cornelius decides to create a provision for doubtful debts equal to 5% of debtors at the year-ends. The debtors figure before bad debts were subtracted was £18,800. Bad debts for the year were £560.

Show the provision for doubtful debts account for the year ended 31 December 2006 and provide an extract from the statement of financial position for the end-of-year statement of financial position.

9.9 At 31 December 2006, M Fowler decides to reduce his provision from 4% of debtors, which was used for 2005, to 2% of debtors. Debtors were £25,000 as at 31 December 2005 and were exactly 25% lower one year later.

Show the provision for doubtful debts account for Fowler for the years ended 31 December 2005 and 2006. The provision for doubtful debts as at 31 December 2004 was £850.

9.10 A firm's provision for doubtful debts was set at the following levels for the following years.

Year	Size of provision
2009	£800
2010	£900
2011	£950
2012	£750

Show the provision for doubtful debts accounts for the four-year period ending 31 December 2012 – assuming that no existing provision existed.

9.11 A firm's provision for doubtful debts was set at the following levels for the following years:

Year	Size of provision
2004	£1,045
2005	£912
2006	£1,008
2007	£1,560

Show the provision for doubtful debts accounts for the four-year period ending 31 December 2007 – assuming that no existing provision existed.

9.12 A firm decides to create a provision for doubtful debts equivalent to 4% of debtors at the year-end. The debtors figures for the years ended 31 December are as follows:

Year	Debtors
2010	£12,500
2011	£9,800
2012	£11,650
2013	£13,490

Show the provision for doubtful debts account for the years 2010–2013.

9.13 A firm decides to create a provision for doubtful debts equivalent to 6% of debtors at the year-end. The debtors figures for the years ended 31 December are as follows:

Year	Debtors
2010	£11,900
2011	£12,800
2012	£12,800
2013	£11,650

Show the provision for doubtful debts account for the years 2010–2013.

9.14 The following balances were extracted from the trial balance as at 31 December 2007:

	Dr £	Cr £
Trade receivables	8,500	
Provision for doubtful debts		420

The provision is to be maintained at 4% of debtors.
Show the provision for doubtful debts account for the year ended 31 December 2007.

9.15 The following balances were extracted from the trial balance as at 31 December 2009:

	Dr £	Cr £
Trade receivables	18,400	
Provision for doubtful debts		250

The provision is to be maintained at 3% of debtors.
Show the provision for doubtful debts account for the year ended 31 December 2009.

9.16 The following table contains balances extracted from the trial balance at the years ended 31 December:

	2004 £	2005 £	2006 £	2007 £
Bad debts	500	650	475	380
Provision for doubtful debts	400	200	300	350
Bad debts recovered	300	0	100	50

Calculate the effect on each year's profit from the above data – you can assume that no provision for doubtful debtors existed prior to 2004.

9.17 The following table contains balances extracted from the trial balance at the year ended 31 December:

	2007 £	2008 £	2009 £	2010 £
Bad debts	1,150	1,430	960	635
Provision for doubtful debts	600	720	840	470
Bad debts recovered	0	95	170	300

Calculate the effect on each year's profit from the above. The provision for doubtful debts stood at £425 as at 31 December 2006.

9.18 The following table contains balances extracted from the trial balance at the year ended 31 December:

	2002 £	2003 £	2004 £	2005 £
Bad debts	745	656	810	452
Provision for doubtful debts	556	454	564	776
Bad debts recovered	0	0	100	50

Calculate the effect on each year's profit from the above. The provision for doubtful debts stood at £457 as at 31 December 2001.

9.19 Data relating to debtors over a four-year period is as follows:

	Debtors at 31 December (£)	Provision for doubtful debts
2003	5,000	4%
2004	6,500	5%
2005	8,750	6%
2006	7,780	5%

Show the provision for doubtful debts account for the years 2003–2006 assuming no provision existed prior to 2003.

9.20 The following balances were extracted from the trial balance as at 31 December 2009:

	Dr £	Cr £
Debtors	15,000	
Provision for doubtful debts		580
Provision for discounts on debtors		112

The provision is to be maintained at 4% of debtors and the provision for discounts on debtors is to be maintained at 2%.

Prepare a statement of financial position extract showing debtors as at 31 December 2009 and calculate the effect on the net profit for the year ended 31 December 2009.

CHAPTER 10

Depreciation of non-current assets

Learning objectives

By the end of this chapter you should be able to:

- Calculate depreciation for non-current assets using straight-line and reducing balance methods
- Record the accounting entries needed for depreciation
- Show the effect of depreciation in the financial statements
- Calculate the profit or loss on the disposal of a non-current asset.

Introduction

Non-current assets are those assets that will generate future benefits to the business and whose costs can be reliably measured. They are listed together on the statement of financial position. The purchase of a non-current asset is classified as capital expenditure and therefore does not appear as an expense in the financial statements. However, the method by which we account for the 'cost' of non-current assets is through the process of **depreciation** which will appear in the statement of comprehensive income. As an application of the accruals concept, we match the cost of the asset to the time period in which the firm benefits from the use of the asset.

According to IAS 16 (Property, Plant and Equipment), depreciation is the systematic allocation of the **depreciable amount** of an asset over its useful life where the depreciable amount refers to the cost of the asset less any expected **residual value**.

The depreciation 'charge' will be deducted against the profit for each year in which the firm benefits from the use of the asset. However, although this depreciation charge appears as an expense it is actually a **provision**. This means that, although the firm may pay for the asset in one particular period of time, the 'charge' for the asset in the financial statements will appear for the years in which the business benefits from the use of the asset.

Why do assets lose value?

Depreciation is charged to reflect the benefits gained from the use of the asset for a particular period of time. The (non-current) assets that are subject to depreciation are assumed to have a finite life. Factors determining the useful life of a non-current asset would include wear and tear, obsolescence, and depletion.

Wear and tear

Assets will gradually 'wear out' over time. This is particularly the case when an asset is used on a frequent basis. Repair and maintenance expenditure can keep the asset in use, but it will still eventually wear out.

Obsolescence

Obsolescence is the process of an asset becoming obsolete. An asset becomes obsolete when it becomes outdated or is superseded by other types of assets. The two main types of obsolescence are as follows:

(i) *Technical obsolescence* occurs when an asset becomes technically out of date. For example, computers will lose value because they quickly become superseded by faster and more powerful models – even if the original computer still functions as well as it did when it was purchased.

(ii) *Market obsolescence* refers to the situation where an asset becomes outdated mainly because the goods produced by the asset become old-fashioned. For example, in the early 1980s, when video cassette recorders (VCRs) were first adopted by households on a mass scale, there were two main types of VCR system: VHS and Betamax. Though the Betamax system appeared technically superior, it was the VHS system which proved far more popular. Therefore, the production facilities for Betamax VCRs would have lost value through the product being outmoded. Examples of this type of obsolescence are harder to find.

Depletion

Some assets, particularly natural resources (e.g. gold mines, oil reserves), will only hold value while the asset can be exploited. As the asset is depleted – 'used up' – the asset will lose value until the asset is exhausted and contains no more value.

Do all assets lose value?

Although most non-current assets will lose value over time, land and property (freehold property) will generally hold or even increase its value. Based on IAS 16 it is allowable for a business to include a non-current asset on the statement of financial position at a revalued amount. For example, although freehold property should be subject to depreciation it is actually more likely that the property will appreciate in value (certainly the trend is for property prices to increase in the UK).

Freehold land would not normally be subject to depreciation as it has an unlimited useful life. Leasehold land would normally be depreciated over the period of the lease.

Remember, the historical cost concept generally gives us more objective and reliable values of these assets than any subjective market valuation which is prone to change and speculation. As a result any revaluations should be carried out frequently so as to ensure fair values.

Methods of depreciation

There are a variety of methods of depreciation but the main focus will be on two methods, straight line and reducing balance.

Straight line method

This method of depreciation is widespread and is the easiest method to use. The ease of use arises out of the simplicity of the method. The depreciation charge, once calculated, remains the same for every year of the asset's life.

The depreciation is calculated as follows:

$$\text{Depreciation charge (per year)} = \frac{(\text{Cost of asset} - \text{residual value})}{\text{Number of years of asset's life}}$$

The **residual value** is often known as the scrap value and is the estimated value of the asset at the end of its life. It is usually prudent to assign a value of zero for the residual value.

Example 10.1

A firm purchases a motor van for business use on 1 January 2016 at a cost of £12,000. The van is expected to last for five years and the firm believes that the van will have a residual value of £3,000.

The depreciation charge would be as follows:

$$\text{Depreciation charge (per year)} = \frac{£12,000 - £3,000}{5} = £1,800 \text{ per year}$$

The £1,800 depreciation charge will appear in each statement of comprehensive income for the following five years or until the van is sold.

If we had assumed no scrap value then the charge would have been:

$$\text{Depreciation charge (per year)} = \frac{£12,000}{5} = £2,400 \text{ per year}$$

A zero scrap value is commonly used. As a result, straight line depreciation is often quoted as a percentage of cost. For example, if depreciation is to be provided at 10% on cost then we would depreciate the asset by 10% of its cost each year – for ten years. The percentage merely shows how many years the asset is expected to last.

Reducing balance method

This method of depreciation, also known as **diminishing balance**, will charge more in the earlier years of an asset's life than in the later years. This arises out of the depreciation being based on a percentage of the asset's net book value – that is the cost value of the asset less all previous depreciation.

Net Book Value (NBV) = Cost of asset – accumulated depreciation

As the asset ages, the depreciation charged in previous years will accumulate and so the book value will decline. If the percentage is fixed then a smaller net book value will inevitably mean that less depreciation is charged the older the asset gets. This method may be more appropriate when the business expects to benefit from the asset less as the asset ages.

Example 10.2

A machine costs £25,000 and is to be depreciated using reducing balance at a rate of 20%. The depreciation charged each year would be as follows:

	£
Cost of asset	25,000
Year 1 depreciation (20% of £20,000)	5,000
Net book value after year 1	20,000
Year 2 depreciation (20% of £15,000)	4,000
Net book value after year 2	16,000
Year 3 depreciation (20% of £12,000)	3,200
Net book value after year 3	12,800

There is no need to know the residual value with this method. However, it can be factored into the percentage rate chosen for this method. The percentage rate is based on a complex formula which takes into account the cost, expected lifetime, and residual value and would normally result in a percentage rate to be used which is not a whole figure. Therefore, as far as examination assessment goes, it is normal for the percentage rate for reducing balance to be given to you already calculated and normally as a whole number.

You should now attempt review questions 10.1 to 10.5.

Depreciation and the statement of financial position

On the statement of financial position we normally value non-current assets at historical cost. With the introduction of depreciation, this is modified and the value for non-current assets on the statement will now be based on historical cost less the provision for depreciation. This is sometimes known as the **carrying amount** or **net book value**.

It is the full balance on the provision for depreciation account that is deducted from the cost value on the statement of financial position, i.e. we use the net book value. Using the example above, the non-current asset would appear as follows:

Statement of financial position extract (end of year 3)

	Cost (£)	Depreciation (£)	Net book value (£)
Machinery	25,000	12,200	12,800

When completing assessment questions that are based on trial balances, it is important to remember that the accumulated provision for depreciation will consist of the current year's depreciation (as found in the profit and loss account) plus the existing provision which will normally be listed as a credit balance in the trial balance. Look out for this as it is a common source of confusion for students.

A comparison of the two methods

Example 10.3

A delivery vehicle costs £25,000 and is expected to last five years. At the end of the five years it is expected to have a scrap value of £2,000. Calculate the depreciation for each year using

(a) Straight line method
(b) Reducing balance method (using a rate of 40%).

The straight line depreciation would be (£25,000 − £2,000)/5 = £4,600.

| | Straight line | | Reducing balance | |
| | Depreciation | NBV at year-end | Depreciation | NBV at year-end |
	£	£	£	£
Cost		25,000		25,000
Year 1	4,600	20,400	10,000	15,000
Year 2	4,600	15,800	6,000	9,000
Year 3	4,600	11,200	3,600	5,400
Year 4	4,600	6,600	2,160	3,240
Year 5	4,600	2,000	1,296	1,944

Which method is chosen will depend on which method is most appropriate. This will, in turn, depend on the type of asset and how it is to be used within the business. However, straight line is the most common method of depreciation in the UK. This is mainly due to both the ease of use and the fact that, in practical terms, it is often difficult to make an accurate assessment of the benefits the business gains from the use of the asset (straight line makes the assumption that benefits from usage are the same each year).

Changing methods of depreciation

The method chosen should ideally reflect the pattern of how the business benefits from the consumption of the non-current asset. The depreciation method should be reviewed each year, and if it is found inappropriate then a change in method is allowable. According to IAS 8 (Accounting Policies, Changes in Accounting Estimates and Errors), any change in depreciation policy should be applied retrospectively to previous financial statements where this is practical.

In the long term, whatever method is selected the profits of the business will remain the same in the long run. If more depreciation charge is allocated in the earlier years of an asset's life then lower amounts will be charged in later years. The depreciation method has no impact on the cash balances of the business as depreciation is a provision not an expense.

However, in the short term it has appeared that some high profile businesses have attempted to manipulate profits by the under-recording of depreciation. For example, if a business decides that the useful life of an asset needs extending then the depreciable amount will be 'spread' over a greater period of time thus lowering each year's depreciation charge. Although this makes no difference over the long run, short-term profits would be higher. This practice of course is completely against the principle of providing a true and fair view of the business.

Mid-year purchases and sales

In many examples, assets are bought and sold either on the first day of the firm's financial year, or the very last day. This makes the calculation of depreciation very straightforward. However, this is unrealistic as assets will be bought and sold almost certainly at some intermediate point within the year. This will make the calculation of depreciation more complicated. As a result there are two approaches used.

1 Depreciation can be calculated on a proportionate basis. For example if an asset is purchased some way within a year then the proportion of the year would be used in the depreciation provision.

Example 10.4

A business whose financial year ends on 31 December purchases equipment for £8,000 on 1 October. It is to be depreciated at 20% on cost.

Firstly, calculate the annual depreciation: 20% of £8,000 = £1,600.
Secondly, calculate the proportion of year that the asset is owned: 3 months out of 12 months, i.e. one quarter of a year.
Hence, the depreciation will be $^{1}/_{4} \times$ £1,600 = £400.

This method is often known as calculating depreciation on a *time or monthly basis*. This method is only realistic for assets bought and sold at convenient dates within the year, e.g. half-way, or one-third of the way into a year.

2 Many firms will charge a full year's depreciation in the year of purchase regardless of when, within the year, the asset is purchased. Additionally, many firms will charge no depreciation for the year if the asset is sold.

You will always be informed in any question which option is to be used. Out of the two options, the second one is the easiest. If the firm uses the reducing balance method then it will normally use the second option.

Depreciation and double-entry bookkeeping

Depreciation entries are kept in the double-entry accounts. The full title for these depreciation accounts is the *provision for depreciation* of whatever asset is being depreciated. There should be a separate provision for depreciation account for each class of non-current asset.

All provision accounts are credit balances and the balance on each account will remain as long as the firm has that particular non-current asset. This is unlike expenditure accounts which are 'emptied' and transferred to the final accounts at the year-end.

Example 10.5

A firm with a financial year-end of 31 December purchases a piece of equipment for business use on 1 January 2016 for £24,000. It is to be depreciated at 25% on cost (i.e. the asset will be deprecated by four equal amounts of £6,000).

The accounts would appear as follows:

Equipment at cost

2016		£	2016		£
Jan 1	Bank	24,000	Dec 31	Balance c/d	24,000

This balance will remain on the equipment account as long as the firm has this equipment as an asset – regardless of its net book value.

Provision for depreciation on equipment

2016		£	2016		£
Dec 31	Balance c/d	6,000	Dec 31	Statement of comprehensive income	6,000
2017			2017		
Dec 31	Balance c/d	12,000	Jan 1	Balance b/d	6,000
			Dec 31	Statement of comprehensive income	6,000
		12,000			12,000
2018			2018		
Dec 31	Balance c/d	18,000	Jan 1	Balance b/d	12,000
			Dec 31	Statement of comprehensive income	6,000
		18,000			18,000
2019			2019		
Dec 31	Balance c/d	24,000	Jan 1	Balance b/d	18,000
			Dec 31	Statement of comprehensive income	6,000
		24,000			24,000

It is the closing balance on the account which would be transferred to the statement of financial position. This represents the accumulated depreciation on that particular asset.

If an asset ever reaches zero net book value then the asset would have been said to be 'fully depreciated'.

You should now attempt review questions 10.6 to 10.9.

Asset disposal

Firms will often sell or scrap a non-current asset before the end of its useful life. Given that the revenue received from selling an asset would be classified as a capital receipt it cannot be included as revenue towards the profit. However, the profit or loss *on the sale* would be included as either revenue income or a revenue expense depending on whether a profit or loss was made.

In either case, we will need to open up an *'asset disposal account'* which helps to ascertain the profit or loss that is made on the disposal of the asset.

When an asset is sold, the entries that currently exist for the asset in the accounts must be removed and these balances on both the asset account and the provision for depreciation account would be transferred to the disposal account.

Example 10.6

A machine which cost £20,000 on 1 January 2012 is sold on 31 December 2014 for £3,700. The asset has been depreciated at 25% on cost.

Given that the asset has been possessed for three years, the accumulated depreciation would have been $3 \times 25\% \times £20,000 = £15,000$.

The accounts for the year of disposal would appear as follows:

Machinery at cost

2014		£	2014		£
Jan 1	Balance b/d	20,000	Dec 31	Machinery disposal	20,000

Provision for depreciation of machinery

2014		£	2014		£
Dec 31	Machinery disposal	15,000	Dec 31	Balance b/d	15,000

The above two entries for machinery disposal both 'cancel' the records of the asset and its accumulated depreciation from the firm's accounts as the balances are transferred to the asset disposal account shown as follows:

Machinery disposal

2014		£	2014		£
Dec 31	Machinery at cost	20,000	Dec 31	Provision for depreciation of machinery	15,000
			Dec 31	Bank	3,700

If the disposal account balanced now then this would mean that we had sold the asset for exactly the same amount as the net book value. This is unlikely, so the account will normally need to be balanced off with the profit or loss on the disposal.

Machinery disposal

2014		£	2014		£
Dec 31	Machinery at cost	20,000	Dec 31	Provision for depreciation of machinery	15,000
			Dec 31	Bank	3,700
			Dec 31	Statement of comprehensive income	1,300
		20,000			20,000

In this case it is £1,300 which is needed to balance off the account. This is a £1,300 loss. We can tell this is a loss as the other half of the double-entry for the profit or loss would be on the debit side of the statement of comprehensive income which always implies expenses or losses.

Another method for calculating the profit or loss on disposal

If the profit or loss on an asset disposal is required as part of a larger question, then it may not be necessary to construct a disposal account. The calculation can be done manually.

The profit or loss on disposal is always calculated as follows:

Profit (Loss) on disposal = Selling price of asset − Net book value of asset

The profit or loss can be calculated as follows:

1 Calculate the accumulated depreciation for the asset.
2 Calculate the net book value of the asset.
3 Calculate the profit or loss on disposal by subtracting the NBV from the selling price.

You should now attempt review questions 10.10 to 10.16.

Example 10.7 – a more complicated example

A business makes the following purchases of machinery:

2013	Jan 1	Machine 001	£4,000
2013	Oct 1	Machine 002	£2,000
2014	Jun 30	Machine 003	£5,000

Depreciation is to be provided at a rate of 20% on cost on a monthly basis.

On 31 March 2015, Machine 001 was sold for £2,150. No other purchases or sales of machinery take place in 2015. We will show the following:

(i)   Machinery at cost account for 2013–2015
(ii) Provision for depreciation of machinery account for 2013–2015

(iii) Machinery disposal account

(iv) Statement of financial position extract for years ended 31 December 2013–2015.

Machinery at cost

2013		£	2013		£
Jan 1	Bank	4,000	Dec 31	Balance c/d	6,000
Oct 1	Bank	2,000			
		6,000			6,000
2014			2014		
Jan 1	Balance b/d	6,000	Dec 31	Balance c/d	11,000
Jun 30	Bank	5,000			
		11,000			11,000
2015			2015		
Jan 1	Balance b/d	11,000	Mar 31	Machinery disposal	4,000
			Dec 31	Balance c/d	7,000
		11,000			11,000

Provision for depreciation of machinery

2013		£	2013		£
Dec 31	Balance c/d	900	Dec 31	Statement of comprehensive income	900
2014			2014		
Dec 31	Balance c/d	2,600	Jan 1	Balance b/d	900
			Dec 31	Statement of comprehensive income	1,700
		2,600			2,600
2015			2015		
Mar 31	Machinery disposal	1,800	Jan 1	Balance b/d	2,600
Dec 31	Balance c/d	2,400	Dec 31	Statement of comprehensive income	1,600
		4,200			4,200

Workings for depreciation:

		£	£
2013:	$20\% \times £4,000$	800	
	$20\% \times £2,000 \times \frac{1}{4}$	100	900
2014:	$20\% \times £4,000$	800	
	$20\% \times £2,000$	400	
	$20\% \times £5,000 \times \frac{1}{2}$	500	1,700
2015:	$20\% \times £4,000 \times \frac{1}{4}$	200	
	$20\% \times £2,000$	400	
	$20\% \times £5,000$	1,000	1,600
Disposal	$20\% \times £4,000 \times 2.25$	1,800	

Machinery disposal

2015		£	2015		£
Mar 31	Machinery at cost	4,000	Mar 31	Provision for depreciation of machinery	1,800
			Mar 31	Bank	2,150
			Mar 31	Statement of comprehensive income	50
		4,000			4,000

Statement of financial position extract as at 31 December 2013

	Cost (£)	Depreciation (£)	Net book value (£)
Machinery	6,000	900	5,100

Statement of financial position extract as at 31 December 2014

	Cost (£)	Depreciation (£)	Net book value (£)
Machinery	11,000	2,600	8,400

Statement of financial position extract as at 31 December 2015

	Cost (£)	Depreciation (£)	Net book value (£)
Machinery	7,000	2,400	4,600

Depreciation of intangible assets

Intangible assets are defined by IAS 38 (Intangible Assets) as 'identifiable non-monetary assets without physical substance'. These assets will generate future benefits to the business and common examples of intangible assets would include computer software, copyrights and patents. Intangible assets are measured on the statement of financial position at either cost or a revalued amount. The same requirements as for tangible non-current assets (IAS 16) broadly apply to intangible assets. As a result intangible assets would be subject to depreciation. However, it is normal to refer to the depreciation of intangible assets as **amortisation**.

You should now attempt review questions 10.17 to 10.20.

Chapter review

By now you should understand the following:

● How to calculate depreciation for both straight line and reducing balance methods
● How to adjust the financial statements so as to account for depreciation
● How to maintain the ledger accounts for the depreciation for non-current assets
● How to calculate and account for the profit or loss on asset disposal.

Relevant accounting standards

IAS 16   Property, Plant and Equipment
IAS 8   Accounting Policies, Changes in Accounting Estimates and Errors
IAS 38   Intangible Assets

Handy hints

The following hints will help you avoid errors.

- Remember that although depreciation appears as a deduction against profit it does not involve cash – it is a provision.
- The value for the statement of financial position is the cost of the asset less all depreciation – including the current year's amount.
- Ensure you read the depreciation policy carefully – what does it say about purchases and disposal of assets mid-year?
- For ledger accounts it is beneficial to calculate the annual charge for depreciation before you enter this in the ledger account – especially when the business has multiple entries for a class of asset.

Key terms

Depreciation   The allocation of the depreciable amount (cost less residual value) of a non-current asset over its useful life

Depreciable amount   The cost of a non-current asset less any expected residual (scrap) value

Residual value   The value a business expects to receive for a non-current asset at the end of its useful life – often assumed to be zero

Straight line   A method of depreciation which allocates the same depreciation charge each year

Reducing balance   A method of depreciation which charges more in earlier years due to the depreciation charge being based on the declining net book value of the asset

Intangible asset   An asset without physical presence, such as goodwill

Carrying amount   The cost of an asset less accumulated depreciation to date (also known as the *net book value*).

Amortisation   Depreciation provided for intangible assets

REVIEW QUESTIONS

10.1   A firm buys machinery for business use which costs £50,000 and is expected to last four years with no residual value.

Produce a table comparing the depreciation and net book values for each year of the asset's life using the straight line and reducing balance methods of depreciation (take the rate of 50% for reducing balance).

10.2   A firm buys a delivery van for business use. The van costs £16,000 and is expected to last five years with an estimated scrap value of £500.

Produce a table comparing the depreciation and net book values for each year of the asset's life using the straight line and reducing balance methods of depreciation (take the rate of 50% for reducing balance).

10.3   A firm buys equipment for business use. The equipment costs £2,500 and is expected to last four years with an estimated scrap value of £200.

Produce a table comparing the depreciation and net book values for each year of the asset's life using the straight line and reducing balance methods of depreciation (take the rate of 30% for reducing balance).

10.4   A firm buys a truck for business use. The truck costs £14,000 and is expected to last three years with an estimated scrap value of £3,000.

Produce a table comparing the depreciation and net book values for each year of the asset's life using the straight line and reducing balance methods of depreciation (take the rate of 40% for reducing balance).

10.5   A firm purchases a delivery van for business use at a cost of £36,000. The van is expected to have a three-year lifespan with no scrap value. Depreciation for the van will be charged by using either the straight line method or the reducing balance method (using a rate of 70% per annum).

Calculate the depreciation for each of the three years, using both methods.

10.6   A vehicle is purchased on 13 February 2017 for £30,000. It is to be depreciated using the reducing balance method at a rate of 20%.

Show the provision for depreciation account for the years 2017–2019 (assuming a full year's depreciation is provided in the year of purchase).

10.7   A machine is purchased on 1 January 2015 for £20,000 and is to be depreciated using the reducing balance method at a rate of 20%.

Show the provision for depreciation of machinery account for the years 2015, 2016 and 2017.

10.8   Equipment is purchased on 30 June 2013 for £15,000 and is to be depreciated at 25% on cost on a monthly basis.

Show the provision for depreciation of equipment account for the years 2013, 2014 and 2015.

10.9   The following non-current assets are purchased:

2012	May 1	Equipment	£3,000
2013	Jan 1	Equipment	£2,000
2014	Mar 31	Equipment	£4,000

Depreciation is to be charged on equipment at the rate of 25% on cost and is provided on a proportionate basis.

Show the provision for depreciation of equipment account for the years ended 31 December 2012–2014.

10.10   Pierce Ltd makes the following purchases of machinery:

1 January 2013	£25,000
1 July 2013	£50,000
31 March 2014	£10,000

All machinery is to be depreciated at 10% on cost on a monthly basis.

Show the provision for depreciation of equipment account for the years 2013, 2014 and 2015.

10.11   A lorry is purchased on 30 June 2014 for £10,000. It is to be depreciated using one of the following two methods of depreciation:

(a) Straight line, on a monthly basis, with an expected scrap value of £2,000 and a lifespan of five years.

(b) Reducing balance, using 30%, with a full year's depreciation charged in the year of purchase but none in the year of sale.

If the lorry is sold for £3,900, on 31 December 2017, calculate the profit or loss on disposal using both of the above options for depreciation.

10.12   A computer system is purchased for £5,400 on 1 Jan 2016. Installation costs amount to £400. Running costs for the year are estimated to be £600. Depreciation is to be provided on the system using reducing balance at a rate of 20%. A full year's depreciation is provided in both year of purchase and year of sale. On 26 April 2017, the system is sold for £3,250.

Produce an asset disposal account to record the sale of the asset. The financial year of the business ends on 31 December.

10.13   A delivery van cost £32,000 and was purchased on 28 March 2016. It was depreciated at a rate of 25% using the reducing balance method. A full year's depreciation was charged in the year of purchase but no depreciation was to be charged in the year of sale. The van was sold for £13,000 on 4 April 2019.

Produce an asset disposal account to record the sale of the asset. The business's financial year ends on 31 December.

10.14   Equipment is purchased for £14,000 on 30 September 2015. It is depreciated using the straight line method, with no residual value and an expected lifespan of seven years. Depreciation is to be based on a monthly basis. On 1 April 2017, the equipment was sold for £8,800.

Produce an asset disposal account to record the sale of the asset. The business's financial year ends on 31 December.

10.15   A delivery truck is bought on 30 June 2014 for £50,000. It is depreciated using reducing balance at a rate of 20% per annum, with no depreciation provided in the year of purchase or in the year of sale. On 23 May 2018, the truck is sold for £21,500.

Produce an asset disposal account to record the sale of the truck. The business's financial year ends on 31 December.

10.16   Vehicle HG56, which had cost £12,000, has been depreciated at 20% on cost. It was purchased on 30 June 2015 and depreciation is provided for on a monthly basis. On 30 October 2017 it is traded in for a new vehicle which costs £19,000. A cheque for £12,000 is paid in full settlement of the outstanding balance.

Calculate the profit or loss on the trade-in.

10.17   The following is an extract taken from the statement of financial position of Gerken Ltd as at 31 December 2006:

Gerken Ltd
Statement of financial position extract as at 31 Dec 2006

	£
Non-current assets	
Equipment	200,000
Less: Depreciation	125,000
	75,000

On 31 December 2007, new equipment, costing £40,000, was purchased. The purchase price is settled partly through the trade-in of old equipment. The old equipment was traded in at a value of £7,500. The old equipment had cost £70,000 in 2002, but had been depreciated by £59,000 as at 31 December 2007. Depreciation is normally provided for equipment at 25% on cost – no depreciation is to be provided for the new equipment.

(a) Calculate the profit or loss on disposal of the old equipment.
(b) Produce a statement of financial position extract showing equipment after all the above transactions have been completed on 31 December 2007.

10.18   Yeates Ltd has the following balances on its accounts in respect of machinery and its depreciation: 31 December 2011: Machinery £21,000, Provision for depreciation of machinery £8,600. The firm then makes the following purchases of machinery:

2012 Jan 1	£10,000
2012 Jun 30	£12,000
2013 Mar 31	£16,000
2014 Sep 30	£20,000

Machinery is depreciated using straight line at a rate of 25% on cost and is provided on a monthly basis. On 31 March 2015, machinery purchased for £6,000 on 1 July 2011 is sold for £300.
   Show the following:

(a) Machinery at cost account for the years ended 31 December 2012 to 2015
(b) Provision for depreciation of machinery account for the years ended 31 December 2012 to 2015
(c) Machinery disposal account for the year ended 31 December 2015
(d) Statement of financial position extract for machinery as at 31 December 2015.

10.19   Lisbie plc makes the following acquisitions during 2016.

1 January	Machinery	£5,200
31 March	Fixtures	£3,800
30 April	Machinery	£4,200
30 June	Machinery	£6,000
31 August	Fixtures	£2,400
30 September	Fixtures	£1,500

Fixtures are depreciated at 20% using reducing balance. A full year's depreciation is provided in the year of purchase. Machinery is depreciated at 10% on cost based on a monthly basis.
   The balance on the machinery account as at 1 Jan 2016 was £14,800, and the balance on the provision for depreciation of machinery was £7,600. On 31 December, the machinery purchased on 1 Jan 2016 was sold for £2,500.

Construct the following:

(a) Machinery at cost account for year ended 31 December 2016
(b) Provision for depreciation of machinery for year ended 31 December 2016
(c) Machinery disposal account for year ended 31 December 2016
(d) Fixtures at cost account for year ended 31 December 2016
(e) Provision for depreciation of fixtures for year ended 31 December 2016
(f) Statement of financial position extracts as at 31 December 2016 for fixed assets.

10.20 For Morris Ltd, the following machinery is purchased:

Machine A	1 January 2014	£25,000
Machine B	31 March 2014	£30,000
Machine C	30 June 2016	£20,000
Machine D	1 October 2017	£12,000

Depreciation is to be charged at 20% on cost based on the value of machinery at the end of year. No depreciation is provided in the year of disposal of any asset.
    On 27 July 2017, machine B was sold for £7,000.

(a) Construct the following accounts:
    (i) Machinery at cost for the years ended 31 December 2014 to 2017
    (ii) Provision for depreciation of machinery for the years ended 31 December 2014 to 2017
    (iii) Machinery disposal for the year ended 31 December 2017.
(b) Produce a statement of financial position extract showing the machinery as at 31 December 2017.

CHAPTER 11

Errors and suspense accounts

Learning objectives

By the end of this chapter you should be able to:

- Correct for errors in the double-entry accounts that don't affect the trial balance's ability to agree
- Use a suspense account when the trial balance fails to agree
- Produce a statement of corrected profit when errors have occurred.

Introduction

Within the accounting information system there are a number of checks that can be used to locate errors that have taken place. In this and the following two chapters we will look at how we can check the double-entry system and how to correct this when errors occur. Ideally, these checks will help to prevent errors occurring in the first place.

However, errors will take place and it is important that, once located, these are corrected quickly and accurately. The final accounts will be inaccurate and misleading to varying degrees until the corrections take place. Errors can be classified in various ways, but a common distinction is made between those that would and those that would not affect the trial balance agreement.

Errors that don't affect the trial balance agreement

A trial balance that agrees would normally confirm that the double-entry bookkeeping has been carried out accurately. However, there are still types of errors that occur that would not prevent the trial balance from agreeing. These errors are defined as follows:

Name of error	Description of error
Error of omission	The transaction was missed out completely – no debit or credit entry was made in any account.
Error of commission	The correct totals are entered on the correct sides of the accounts but the entry is made in the wrong personal account. This often occurs when names of either customers or suppliers are similar.
Error of principle	As above, the correct totals are made on to the correct sides of the account, but one half of the transaction is entered into the wrong type of account. For example, classifying expenditure on assets as an expense would fall under this heading.
Error of original entry	The transaction is recorded in the correct accounts and on the correct sides of the account but the amount entered is incorrect for the transaction – the accounts are either under or overcast.
Reversal of entries	The transaction is entered with the correct amounts in the correct accounts but the debits and credits are reversed. For example, a credit sale would be debited to sales and the debtor's account would be credited.
Compensating error	More than one error combines to have the same effect on each side of the trial balance and gives the impression that it has cancelled out the effect on each side. For example, if both purchases and sales were overcast by £100 then the trial balance would still agree.

Correction of the errors

The procedure to follow when correcting errors is as follows:

1 Enter the correction into the Journal.
2 Correct the entries in the double-entry accounts.

All errors are corrected in the Journal regardless of what day book they would normally have been entered into. This is so a narrative can be included to explain the error and its correction.

We will consider one example of each type of error and see how it would be corrected.

Example 11.1: error of omission

A credit purchase of goods of £112 from E Cole was missed out completely.

Correction:
The correction in the ledger accounts here is very straightforward – just enter them as per normal.

Journal extract

	Dr	Cr
	£	£
Purchases	112	
E Cole		112

Correction to error of omission – credit purchase now included

Purchases

	£		£
E Cole	112		

E Cole

	£		£
		Purchases	112

Example 11.2: error of commission

A credit sale of £76 to A Salmon was mistakenly debited to the account of A Sandon.

Correction:
For any error of commission, the double-entry correction will involve one entry cancelling out the original mistake (by entering it on the opposite side of the account where the entry was mistakenly placed), and one entry in the account where it should have been entered in the first place.

Journal extract

	Dr	Cr
	£	£
A Salmon	76	
A Sandon		76

Correction to error of commission – personal accounts corrected

A Sandon

	£		£
Sales	76	A Salmon	76

A Salmon

	£		£
A Sandon (Sales)	76		

The entry in blue represents the mistaken entry – debiting that account by the same amount has the effect of 'cancelling out' this mistake.

Example 11.3: error of principle

Motor expenses paid of £230 were mistakenly debited to the motor vehicles account.

Correction:
As with the correction for an error of commission, the correction will involve one half of the entry cancelling out the mistaken entry (by entering it on to the opposite side of the account where the entry was mistakenly placed), and by entering the other half of the entry into the account where it should be have been entered in the first place.

Journal extract

	Dr	Cr
	£	£
Motor expenses	230	
Motor vehicles		230
Error of principle – now corrected		

Motor expenses

	£		£
Motor vehicles	230		

Motor vehicles

	£		£
Bank	230	Motor expenses	230

The entry in blue represents the mistaken entry – crediting that account by the same amount has the effect of 'cancelling' this mistake.

Example 11.4: error of original entry

A cash payment of £45 for advertising was mistakenly entered in both accounts as £54.

Correction:
Although this is an error of original entry, when the numbers are back-to-front it is often referred to as an **error of transposition** – due to the numbers being transposed. The correction of this is the same as that for errors of original entry.

The correction will mean that the accounts need adjusting by the discrepancy. In this case we need to adjust the accounts by the £9 difference. As the accounts were overcast by £9, we need to enter this £9 adjustment on the opposite of each original entry so as to reduce the overall effect of the transaction.

Journal extract

	Dr	Cr
	£	£
Cash book (cash column)	9	
Advertising		9
Error of principle – now corrected		

The narrative is particularly useful here as the above entry could otherwise be interpreted as a different transaction, such as £9 cash received as advertising income.

Cash book (Cash column)

	£		£
Advertising	9	Advertising	54

Advertising

	£		£
Cash	54	Cash	9

The blue type represents the original entry. The £9 entry has the effect of reducing the balance down to the correct £45.

In this example, the account was overcast. If the account had been undercast, then we would have to 'add' adjustments to the same side of the accounts as the original transaction had been entered.

Example 11.5: reversal of entries

Goods of £28 returned by the firm to C Rowlands was debited to the returns account and credited to the account of Rowlands.

Correction:
For all errors of reversal, the correction will involve entering double the original amount on the opposite side from the original entry. Simply entering the same amount as the original transaction would only cancel out the effect of the error. That is why we need double the original amount.

Journal extract

	Dr	Cr
	£	£
C Rowlands	56	
Returns outwards		56
Error of principle – now corrected		

C Rowlands

	£		£
Returns outwards	56	Returns outwards	28

Returns outwards

	£		£
C Rowlands	28	C Rowlands	56

The blue type represents the original (mistaken) entry.

Example 11.6: compensating error

The account for insurance was **overcast** by £250, as was the account for rent received.

Correction:
It is safest to think of this as two separate errors that require correcting. In each case, the account has been overcast and this means we need to enter, on the opposite side of the account, the amount we wish to reduce the balance by (i.e. the excess).

Journal extract

	Dr £	Cr £
Rent received	250	
Insurance		250

Two accounts overcast compensating for each other – now corrected

Rent received

	£		£
Insurance	250		

Insurance

	£		£
		Rent received	250

You should now attempt review questions 11.1 to 11.8.

Errors that do affect the trial balance agreement

If the trial balance totals fail to agree then it is likely that one or more of the following errors have been made:

1 Only entering one half of transaction in the accounts (not completing the double-entry)
2 Entering different amounts for the debit and credit entries
3 Entering two debits or two credits for a transaction.

When faced with trial balance totals that do not agree then it is important to find these errors as quickly as possible. This should be the priority. However, if they cannot be found immediately then a firm can ensure that the trial balance totals do agree by opening up a **suspense account**.

Example 11.7

Trial balance as at 31 December 2007

	Dr £	Cr £
Totals of each column	55,400	56,000
Suspense	600	
	56,000	56,000

The suspense entry in the trial balance means that we need to open up a suspense account in the general ledger with a debit balance of £600. This implies that errors (or an error) have been made that combine to give the effect of a £600 shortage on the debit column of the trial balance. This does not necessarily mean that we have missed out debit entries somewhere in our bookkeeping, as it is possible that the errors have actually artificially increased the total of the credit column and that the debit column is correct.

This can only be ascertained once the errors have been located and corrected.

Suspense

2007		£	2007	£
Dec 31	Trial balance difference	600		

This balance will remain here until the errors are found. Each time an error is located which would affect the trial balance agreement, an entry would be made in the suspense account as part of the correction procedure.

When the errors have been located and corrected we will find that the balance on the suspense account disappears. However, until that occurs, the suspense balance would appear in the final accounts on the firm's statement of financial position.

Suspense account balance	Appears on statement of financial position as:
Debit	Asset
Credit	Liability

Example 11.8

Let us continue the example above – where there is a £600 shortage in the debit column.

In January 2008, the firm discovered that the following errors had been made:

A The wages account had been undercast by £120

B A credit sale of goods for £250 to S Butler had been credited to both accounts

C The returns inwards account had been overcast by £70

D The purchases account was undercast by £50.

Correction:

For each correction, a journal entry must be made. However, if the error does affect the trial balance agreement, then one half of the double-entry transaction needed to correct the error will involve an entry into the suspense account, and the other half will be the entry which corrects the error in the appropriate account.

In this example, each of the four errors *does* affect the trial balance agreement. Therefore each correction will require a suspense entry.

Journal extracts

	Dr £	Cr £
A Wages	120	
Suspense		120
Wages originally undercast – now corrected		
B S Butler	500	
Suspense		500
Entry on wrong side of personal account – now corrected		
C Suspense	70	
Returns inwards		70
Account overcast – now corrected		
D Purchases	50	
Suspense		50
Account undercast – now corrected		

Suspense

2008		£	2008		£
Jan 1	Balance b/f	600	Jan 31	**A** Wages	120
Jan 31	**C** Returns inwards	70	Jan 31	**B** S Butler	500
			Jan 31	**D** Purchases	50
		670			670

As we can see, the suspense account now has no outstanding balance. This means that all the errors which affect the trial balance have been located and corrected. However, there may still be errors present that don't affect the trial balance agreement.

Be aware that in assessed questions, it is possible that you will not be given the opening balance in the suspense account. This is because if you are aware of the opening balance then as you reach the last error to correct, the outstanding balance on the suspense account would give you a strong clue as to whether or not it affects the trial balance. For example, if the suspense account had already balanced off, then you would know without using any accounting knowledge that the last error did not affect the suspense account.

You should now attempt review questions 11.9 to 11.14.

Errors and profits

Once we have corrected the errors in the journal and in the ledger accounts, we should then start to consider whether or not the errors have affected the net profit for the period. If they have, then a statement of corrected net profit will need producing.

There is no distinction between whether an error affects the trial balance agreement or not and whether it affects profits. Whether an error affects profits will depend on the following:

1 Does the error affect items that would appear in the statement of comprehensive income?

If the answer is yes, then it is likely that profits would be affected.

2 Does correcting the error mean that total expenses or incomes will be higher or lower as a result?

If so, then profits are likely to be affected. If the error was simply a misallocation of one expense from another, then overall profits may be unaffected, but if the totals change then profits will also change.

Example 11.9

Steve Blay's net profit is calculated for the year ended 31 December 2013 as £354. However, in January 2014 he discovers the following errors have been made:

1 The purchases daybook was undercast by £32.
2 A credit sale of £43 to B Patterson was mistakenly debited to the account of B Pattinson.
3 Heating paid by cheque of £18 was credited to both accounts.
4 A sale of equipment of £56 was credited to the sales account by mistake.
5 Insurance paid for the private house of the owner of £98 was debited to the business insurance account.

Let us take each error in turn.

1 Purchases appear in the trading account as an expense, this means profits will be £32 lower when we correct for this undercasting.
2 This is an error of commission and will not affect the profit as it only affects the personal accounts of the firm's debtors.
3 As heating is an expense we should debit that account. Given that we have credited this account by mistake we need to debit heating (once to cancel out the credit and once again to reinstate the expense) which will reduce profits by £36.
4 A sale of equipment would not count towards the firm's sales because it is a capital receipt. Therefore we will need to reduce sales and this will reduce profit by the £56.
5 Drawings are not an expense, so the inclusion of these drawings in insurance has overcast the expenses. The correction will reduce expenses and increase profit by £98.

This can be presented as a statement of corrected net profit as follows:

Steve Blay
Statement of corrected net profit for year ended 31 Dec 2013

		£	£
Net profit			354
Add:	Insurance overcast		98
			452
Less:	Purchases undercast	32	
	Heating undercast	36	
	Sale of equipment	56	124
Corrected net profit			328

You should now attempt review questions 11.15 to 11.20.

Chapter review

By now you should understand the following:

● How to record entries in the ledger to correct for errors made
● How to open up and make entries in a suspense account
● How to recalculate profit in the light of discovered errors.

Handy hints

The following hints will help you avoid errors.

- Correcting an error will always involve a debit and a credit entry.
- When incorrect amounts have been entered it is the difference between the correct and incorrect amount that needs entering in the ledger account.
- Only use the suspense account if the error prevents the trial balance agreeing.

Key terms

Error of omission   The missing out of a transaction from the double-entry accounts

Error of commission   Recording an entry in the wrong personal account

Error of principle   Recording an entry in the wrong type or class of account

Error of original entry   Recording the wrong amounts on both the debit and credit entries of a transaction

Error of transposition   Recording a number entered in an account with the numerals in the wrong order

Reversal of entries   Recording a transaction on the opposite side of both accounts

Compensating errors   Two errors which combine to ensure that the trial balance still agrees even though errors exist

Overcasting   Entering an amount in excess of the correct amount in an account

Undercasting   Entering an amount less than the correct amount in an account

Suspense account   A temporary account used when the trial balance disagrees so as to facilitate the construction of the financial statements

REVIEW QUESTIONS

11.1 For each of the following transactions, state the type of error being made.

(a) Carriage inwards of £45 entered in both accounts as £67.
(b) Purchases on credit of £32 from S Nutt was debited to Nutt's account and credited to purchases.
(c) Business insurance of £32 was actually a payment made for the owner's private insurance.
(d) Sales on credit for £89 to J Morrissey were debited to the account of J Munson.
(e) Purchases of goods for resale was entered into a fixed asset account.

11.2 For each of the following transactions, state the type of error being made.

(a) Payment to A Johnson for £45 missed out of accounts.
(b) Returns inwards from F Ressmeyer of £43 entered in both accounts as £34.
(c) Sale of equipment which was bought for resale entered in equipment account.
(d) Cash contributed by owner to business was debited to capital and credited to cash.
(e) Discounts received of £43 credited to sales.

11.3 Identify the type of error made in each of the following transactions.

(a) Motor expenses of £45 was mistakenly entered into the motor vehicles account.

(b) Purchase of equipment on credit for £340 was entered into the purchases account.

(c) Goods returned to C Morley worth £32 was debited to the account of C Morton.

(d) A payment of £18 made to creditor, P Infanti, was not entered in the accounts.

(e) Sales of £18 on credit to P Currie was debited to sales and credited to Currie's account.

11.4 For the following transactions, produce journal entries to correct the errors that have been made. No narratives are required.

(a) Sales of goods for £200 have been credited to the motor vehicles account.

(b) Purchases of goods for cash £100 has not been entered in the ledger accounts.

(c) Sales of goods on credit of £82 to T White were entered by mistake in W Thite accounts.

(d) Returns outwards of £117 to M Chase were entered in both accounts as £171.

(e) A cash withdrawal from the bank of £32 was debited to the bank and credited to the cash account.

11.5 For the following transactions, produce journal entries to correct the errors that have been made. No narratives are required.

(a) Wages were overstated by £18 as were discounts received, coincidentally by the same amount.

(b) Drawings of £47 were entered in the sundry expenses account by mistake.

(c) A motor vehicle purchased by cheque for £300 was debited to motor expenses.

(d) Returns inwards of £32 from C Howe were mistakenly entered in the account of H Cowe.

(e) Purchases on credit from S Prince for £214 was undercast in both accounts by £29.

11.6 For the following transactions, produce journal entries to correct the errors that have been made. No narratives are required.

(a) Business wages of £280 was entered in the machinery account by mistake.

(b) Sales on credit to S Painter for £89 were entered in both accounts as £98.

(c) Capital contributed from the owner of a machine worth £500 was credited to the sales account by mistake.

(d) Returns inwards of £32 from C Throup were entered on the wrong side of both accounts.

(e) Cash and cheques paid for insurance totalling £76 were treated as business expenses but it later transpired that half of this amount was for the owner's private insurance.

11.7 For the following transactions, produce journal entries to correct the errors that have been made. No narratives are required.

(a) Purchases of goods on credit for £38 from S Barnes were entered by mistake in the account of S Baines.

(b) Cheque received from M Brassington for £46 was entered in both accounts as £64.

(c) Motor repairs of £32 were treated as Motor vehicles.

(d) A payment by cheque to A Stacey, a creditor, of £97 was completely missed out.

(e) A sale on credit to J Spillane for £32 was entered as £43.

11.8 For the following transactions, produce journal entries to correct the errors that have been made. No narratives are required.

(a) Repairs paid in cash for £97 was entered in both accounts as £79.

(b) A sale on credit to C Quinn for £32 was debited to Sales and credited to Quinn's account.

(c) Commission received of £156 by cheque was missed out from the ledgers.

(d) Rent paid by cheque for £760 included rent of the owner's private residence for £420.

(e) Advertising paid of £34 cash was entered in both accounts as £43.

11.9 For the following errors state whether or not the correction of the error would require an entry to be made in a suspense account.

(a) Sales account overcast by £30.

(b) Drawings entered in the credit side of the account.

(c) Insurance of £56 paid in cash was entered in both accounts as £156.

(d) Returns inwards of £42 was entered into returns outwards by mistake.

(e) Purchases of goods on credit for £198 from G Bannister was missed out completely.

(f) Capital contributed into the firm by the owner was credited to sales in error.

(g) Payment received from a debtor was credited to the bank account.

(h) Discounts received of £50 was entered in commission received by mistake.

11.10 The following totals of Peter Yarrow's trial balance on 30 April 2009 did not agree and were as follows:

Debit £18,312   Credit £17,482

An accountant friend checked though the accounts and found the following mistakes:

(a) Discounts allowed have been entered as a credit entry of £470. However, the true figure for this entry of discounts allowed should have been £280.

(b) Rent received by cheque of £630 was only entered into the cash book.

(c) The sales day book was undercast by £950.

(d) Yarrow withdrew £810 from the bank for his own use. He had entered this as a sundry expense.

Produce the journal entries required to correct these errors and the suspense account showing the corrections.

11.11 A trial balance was extracted on 31 March 2011 and the totals did not agree with there being a £422 shortage on the credit column. As a result, a suspense account was opened. In April 2011, the following errors were discovered.

(a) Insurance paid by cheque for £120 was entered on the debit sides of both accounts.

(b) We paid T Curran £18 cash but it was entered in both accounts as £81.

(c) Goods returned from G Oliver worth £34 were entered in Oliver's account as a debit entry.

(d) Purchases were overstated by £114.

Produce the journal entries needed to correct the errors and make corresponding entries, where appropriate, in the suspense account.

11.12 A trial balance was extracted on 31 December 2008 and the totals did not agree, there being a £90 shortage on the debit column. As a result, a suspense account was opened. In January 2009, the following errors were discovered. Produce the journal entries needed to correct the errors and make corresponding entries, where appropriate, in the suspense account.

(a) The sales day book was overcast by £150.

(b) Wages paid in cash of £80 was entered correctly in the cash account but in the wages account was entered as £180.

(c) Machinery purchased on credit for £240 from I Fraser was credited to machinery and debited in Fraser's account.

(d) Returns inwards of £40 were only entered in the debtor's account.

11.13   A trial balance was extracted on 31 December 2008 and the totals did not agree, there being a £54 shortage on the credit column. As a result, a suspense account was opened. In January 2009, the following errors were discovered.

(a) Cash paid into the bank of £44 was entered on the credit side of both accounts.
(b) Insurance paid by cheque was entered as £87 when it should have been £78.
(c) Returns outwards of £90 was treated correctly in the creditor's account but was then debited to returns inwards.
(d) A sale of £158 on credit to J Saunders was only entered into the sales account.
(e) Extra capital contributed in the form of £320 cash was entered correctly in cash but as £230 in the capital account.

Produce the journal entries needed to correct the errors and make corresponding entries, where appropriate, in the suspense account.

11.14   A trial balance was extracted on 31 March 2012 and the totals did not agree. As a result, a suspense account was opened. During April 2012, the following errors were discovered.

(a) Discounts received of £50 were treated in the general ledger account as though it were discounts allowed.
(b) Carriage inwards of £78 was mistaken as carriage outwards.
(c) Wages paid by cheque of £97 was entered in the wages account correctly but in the bank account as an income of £79.
(d) Returns inwards of £17 from F Grew were credited to the personal account of F Glue by mistake.
(e) A credit sale to Silly Sausage Ltd for £76 was debited to sales and credited to the personal account.
(f) Purchases of £64 on credit from A Bell were only entered in the personal account.

Produce the journal entries needed to correct the errors and make corresponding entries, where appropriate, in the suspense account and calculate the initial discrepancy from the trial balance.

11.15   Net profit for the year was calculated as £1,340. However, shortly afterwards the following errors were found. Calculate the net profit once all the errors have been corrected.

(a) Sales of £560 were undercast by £96.
(b) Insurance of £76 was missed out of the income statement.
(c) Repairs to the vehicle for £42 were treated as revenue income.
(d) Purchases of £118 were entered into the accounts as £181.
(e) A sale of goods to J Bond for £120 was credited to the account of J Brand.

11.16   Net profit for the year was calculated as £2,510. However, shortly afterwards the following errors were found. Calculate the net profit once all the errors have been corrected.

(a) Returns inwards of £240 were treated as returns outwards.
(b) Discounts received of £89 were entered in the accounts as £98.
(c) A purchase of equipment for £3,200 was treated as revenue expenditure.
(d) A return of goods from G Moreton for £64 was entered as a further sale for the same amount.
(e) A bad debt written off for £112 was missed out of the income statement.

11.17   A net loss for the year was calculated as £130. However, shortly afterwards the following errors were found. Calculate the net profit (or loss) once all the errors have been corrected.

(a) Wages were overcast by £235.
(b) Stock taken by the owner of the business for private use valued at £76 was not recorded.
(c) A sale of a vehicle previously in use within the business for £750 was treated as a sale of stock.
(d) Motor expenses of £39 were omitted from the accounts.
(e) Rent received of £40 was treated as a sale.

11.18 The net profit for M Jeffs for the year ended 31 March 2007 had been calculated as £390. However, the following errors were discovered in April 2007:

(i) The returns inwards day book had been undercast by £82.
(ii) Insurance paid by cheque for £27 included a payment for private insurance of £12.
(iii) Discounts allowed of £25 were credited to the account by mistake.
(iv) A purchase of goods on credit for £45 from A Wood was entered in both accounts as £54.
(v) Carriage outwards paid in cash of £28 was entered in the cash account as £18.

(a) Show the corrections needed for the above errors in the Journal.
(b) Open up a suspense account and make entries as appropriate in correcting the errors thus showing the correct opening balance on the suspense account.
(c) Produce a statement of corrected net profit.

11.19 D Madgett is a sole trader. He has just completed his accounts for the year ended 31 May 2010. His net profit for the year was calculated as £1,760. However, during the following month these errors were discovered:

(i) Sales of goods on credit for £430 to B Street were credited to both accounts.
(ii) Returns inwards of £65 were credited to returns outwards as £95.
(iii) Motor expenses of £145 were debited to motor expenses as £154.
(iv) A sale of an old motor van for £580 was treated as a sale of stock by mistake.
(v) Wages of £760 paid by cash was entered in the wrong side of both accounts.

(a) Show the corrections needed for the above errors in the Journal.
(b) Open up a suspense account and make entries as appropriate in correcting the errors thus showing the correct opening balance on the suspense account.
(c) Produce a statement of corrected net profit.

11.20 B Bolder is a sole trader. She has just completed her accounts for the year ended 31 December 2017. Her net profit for the year was calculated as £3,897. However, during the following month these errors were discovered:

(i) The returns inwards day book was overcast by £320.
(ii) Sales of £430 on credit to I Mellor were entered in the sales account as £240.
(iii) Bolder introduced her own computer into the business at a valuation of £295. However, this was credited to sales by mistake.
(iv) Sundry expenses of £76 cash was entered in both accounts as a credit entry.
(v) A payment by cheque of £25 to M Smith was entered in both accounts as £252.

(a) Show the corrections needed for the above errors in the Journal.
(b) Open up a suspense account and make entries as appropriate in correcting the errors thus showing the correct opening balance on the suspense account.
(c) Produce a statement of corrected net profit.

CHAPTER 12

Control accounts

Learning objectives

By the end of this chapter you should be able to:

- Select items to appear in each of the control accounts
- Construct the sales ledger and purchases ledger control accounts
- Set off balances that appear in both the sales and purchases ledger against each other
- Explain the uses of maintaining control accounts
- Explain the difference between control accounts appearing as part of the double-entry system and as memorandum accounts
- Reconcile balances where discrepancies exist.

Introduction

The chances of errors occurring in the double-entry accounting are, unfortunately, too likely. Given the need for producing accurate and up-to-date information it is important that if errors are made in the books they can be located quickly.

A trial balance will show the existence of arithmetical errors in the ledger accounts. However, locating these errors may still be very time-consuming once the business has passed beyond a certain size. Therefore it is useful to have other methods of locating errors. One such method is through the construction of **control accounts**. Control accounts are used to provide a check on the personal ledger accounts; the sales ledger control account monitors the sales ledger (accounts of trade receivables) and the purchases ledger control account monitors the purchases ledger (accounts of trade payables).

Information used in the control accounts

To check the accuracy of the personal ledgers we can construct control accounts as follows:

- **Sales ledger control account** – for checking the accuracy of the sales ledger
- **Purchases ledger control account** – for checking the accuracy of the purchases ledger.

A control account is constructed from the data found within both day books and ledgers of the business. If we use these total amounts that we can construct a control account which represents the total entries for a period of time relating to items either in the sales ledger or in the purchases ledger. In effect, this control account would appear as an overall account for trade receivables or trade payables.

Location of information for control accounts

The information to construct the control accounts would be found as follows:

Sales ledger control account

Item in account	Location of item
Opening balance	Sales ledger accounts
Credit sales	Sales day book
Money received	Cash book
Returns inwards	Returns inwards day book
Bad debts	General ledger
Discounts allowed	Cash book/General ledger
Closing balance	Sales ledger accounts

Purchases ledger control account

Item in account	Location of item
Opening balance	Purchases ledger accounts
Credit purchases	Purchases day book
Money paid	Cash book
Returns outwards	Returns outwards day book
Discounts received	Cash book/General ledger
Closing balance	Purchase ledger accounts

The closing balance on each control account should be equal to the total of all the closing balances from the relevant ledger. This is because they are using the same data – they are simply taking the data from different places (either the individual accounts or the day books and ledger totals).

Memorandum accounts

Control accounts appear to follow the rules of double-entry bookkeeping. A sales ledger control account would appear similar to the account of a debtor of the business – with amounts owing to the business, further credit sales, and other adjustments that arise out of credit sale transactions between the business and its debtors. Similarly, the purchases ledger control account will appear as though it is the account of a creditor of the business.

However, the control accounts are not necessarily part of the double-entry system. If they are not part of the double-entry system they will act as **memorandum accounts**. A memorandum account is separate from the double-entry system. The memorandum control accounts would act as a device for monitoring the sales and purchases ledgers.

One further twist is that some firms actually use the control accounts as part of the double-entry system. For these businesses, transactions dealing with credit sales and credit purchases would be dealt within the sales ledger and purchases ledger control account respectively. The individual accounts of each debtor and each creditor would then act as the memorandum account and would merely provide information for the business and not act as part of the double-entry system.

Given the prevalence of computerised account systems, it is just as easy to maintain control accounts either as memorandum accounts or as an integrated part of the double-entry system. In any examination questions, you would always be informed which system was in use if this was to affect how you would answer the question.

Layout of control accounts

It will help you to construct control accounts with confidence if you think of each control account as simply the individual accounts for trade receivables and trade payables. The control accounts represent all the individual personal accounts totalled up and will still obey the basic principles of accounts for debtors and creditors. Therefore, if you can commit to memory the basic layout of the individual accounts, then it will greatly increase your chances of being able to construct the control accounts. The typical layouts for trade payables and trade receivables are presented below.

Sales Ledger Control Account

Balances b/d	Receipts
Credit sales	Returns inwards
	Discounts allowed
	Bad debts
	Balances c/d

Purchases Ledger Control Account

Payments	Balances b/d
Returns outwards	Credit purchases
Discounts received	
Balances c/d	

Many assessment questions will focus on the construction of control accounts. In this case it is crucial that you know not only where in the account the data should appear, but also in which control account the data belongs. Most items will appear in only one of the control accounts. However, there are exceptions to this rule. Exceptions will be explored later.

Example 12.1: a sales ledger control account

The following data relates to the credit sales transactions for the month of May 2009.

Information from the sales ledger	£
Balances of trade receivables as at 1 May 2009	3,124
Balances of trade receivables as at 31 May 2009	4,324

Information from other day books and ledgers for month of May	£
Credit sales	23,130
Cash book entries representing receipts from trade receivables	20,855
Discounts allowed	432
Returns inwards	531
Bad debts	112

The control account would appear as follows:

Sales ledger control account

2009		£	2009		£
1 May	Balances b/d	3,124	31 May	Cash book	20,855
31 May	Credit sales	23,130	31 May	Discounts allowed	432
			31 May	Returns inwards	531
			31 May	Bad debts	112
			31 May	Balances c/d	4,324
		26,254			26,254

In this example the control account balances which implies that there are no arithmetical errors in the sales ledger (there could be other errors though).

Example 12.2: a purchases ledger control account

The following data relates to the credit sales transactions for the month of June 2009.

Information from the purchases ledger	£
Balances of creditors as at 1 June 2009	1,897
Balances of creditors as at 30 June 2009	1,676

Information from other day books and ledgers for month of June	£
Credit purchases	8,790
Cash book entries representing payments to creditors	8,328
Discounts received	424
Returns outwards	259

The control account would appear as follows:

Purchases ledger control account

2009		£	2009		£
Jun 30	Cash book	8,328	Jun 1	Balances b/d	1,897
Jun 30	Discount received	424	Jun 30	Credit purchases	8,790
Jun 30	Returns outwards	259			
Jun 30	Balances c/d	1,676			
		10,687			10,687

You should now attempt review questions 12.1 to 12.6.

Another way to ensure that you remember the layout of the control account is to take a refresher on basic double-entry.

Double-entry and control accounts

Trade receivables is an asset account, and trade payables a liability account. Each control account will therefore follow the basic rules of double-entry for assets and liabilities.

In the case of the sales ledger control account, anything that increases what we owed (e.g. more credit sales) will require a debit entry. At the same time, anything that reduces what we are owed (e.g. money received in respect of debt settlement, or goods returned to us) will require a credit entry.

The same principles can be applied to the purchases ledger control account. The following may help you to decide where things belong in the control account.

Sales ledger control account

What we are owed by debtors and increases in these amounts	Amounts reducing what we are owed by our debtors

Purchases ledger control account

Amounts reducing what we owe our creditors	What we owe to our creditors and increases in these amounts

Other items found in control accounts

The earlier examples show very simple control accounts. There are other items that can appear in the control account.

Contra entries

It is possible that a business can be both a debtor and a creditor at the same time. If we have both bought from and sold to the same business then they would have an account in both the sales ledger and the purchases ledger. However, it will usually make more sense to partially set off the debt rather than allow both amounts to be settled in full. For example, if you owe someone £10 and they, at the same time, owe you £5 then it would be sensible for you to simply pay them £5. What you have done here is set off a debt of £5. The entries for these are known as contra entries as they affect the same account (well, the account of the same person) in the ledgers.

Contra entries will therefore reduce both the amount owing and the amount owed. They will appear in *both* the sales ledger and purchases ledger control accounts.

Example 12.3

We owe £56 to J Evans, who at the same time owes us £29. The set-off would be completed as follows:

J Evans (in sales ledger)

	£		£
Balance b/d	29	Amount set off	29

J Evans (in purchases ledger)

	£		£
Amount set off	29	Balance b/d	56

The result of the **set-off** is that the amount owed to Evans is reduced to £27 (£56 – £29) and the amount owed to us by Evans is wiped out.

The set-offs would appear on *both* the credit side of the sales ledger control account and the debit side of the purchases ledger control account.

Set-offs are often known as contra entries as they, in effect, only affect the same account.

Dishonoured cheques

Occasionally we will receive a cheque that our bank will fail to honour. This means that the money we thought we had received will not actually be added to our bank balance. This will be because the payee has insufficient funds (or insufficient overdraft arrangements) in their account and their bank will not pay out on the cheque.

In this case, we need to ensure that the entry we had made for receiving money is, in effect, cancelled out. Given that the money received would be credited to the sales ledger control account, it should make sense to debit the control account with any dishonoured cheques. A rationale for this is that a dishonoured cheque increases what we are owed and therefore we would debit any debtor's account to reflect this.

Other balances

It is possible that we will have unusual balances in each control account. For example, we may have an opening credit balance in the sales ledger account. Why is this unusual? The credit entry implies an amount owing and this would mean that we owed money to one or more of our debtors which appears unusual. However, the explanation for this could be that we received payment from a debtor shortly before the goods were then returned. Perhaps a fault with them was found after payment was made. In this case we would owe the debtor the amount they had paid – hence the credit balance. Similar reasoning can also be applied to the purchases ledger control account.

Use of control accounts

Detection of errors

One of the main benefits of constructing control accounts as memorandum accounts is that it can help to localise errors. This saves time as the location of an error would normally take considerably more time if it were left until after the construction of the trial balance.

The total of closing balances on all trade receivables should match the closing balance in the control account for the sales ledger as they both show the same data (the total amount owed to the firm by its credit customers). If they are not the same then this would indicate that an error has been made.

Errors which would not be detected by constructing control accounts *alone* would include the following:

(i)   A transaction is missed out entirely.
(ii) The amounts in a transaction are incorrectly recorded in all records.
(iii) Transactions entered in the wrong personal account (but otherwise recorded correctly).

The inability to detect these errors is the main limitation on the usefulness of control accounts.

Prevention of fraud

If the maintenance of the double-entry accounts is conducted by someone different from the person who oversees the construction of control accounts then this will also act to make fraud by employees more difficult. This is because the control account will act as a check on the records and will highlight any discrepancies (e.g. under-recording receipts on a personal account).

Incomplete records

If a business does not have a complete set of financial data available, the construction of control accounts can help to determine the missing data. For example, if no data existed for the amount for credit sales, then this could be ascertained by constructing the control account in full and the missing figure would be whatever amount was needed for the account to balance. This technique is a fairly common topic for examination questions.

Example 12.4

The following sales ledger control account was constructed for the month of June 2012:

Sales ledger control account

2012		£	2012		£
1 Jun	Balances b/d	876	30 Jun	Cash book	5,550
30 Jun	Credit sales	6,754	30 Jun	Discounts allowed	722
			30 Jun	Returns inwards	231
			30 Jun	Balances c/d	1,127
		7,630			7,630

However, the total of balances from the sales ledger as at 30 June 2012 was £1,006.
   The following errors were discovered:

1 A bad debt of £65 was recorded in the sales ledger but missed out of the journal.
2 A sales invoice received from D Jack for £120 was missed out completely.
3 The total of balances from trade receivables was overcast by £50.
4 Returns inwards of £31 were entered in all records as £13.

There are a number of steps needed to be completed to ensure that we find the correct totals for balances on the accounts of trade receivables.

Firstly, we need to establish whether or not the errors made affect the control account, the individual accounts in the sales ledger or both.

Adjustment 1   *By being included in the sales ledger it would have been included in the individual accounts, but by missing the entry out of the journal for bad debts we would need to include this in the control account.*

Adjustment 2   *The credit sales of £120 would need to be added both to the control account total and to the totals of the individual accounts.*

Adjustment 3   *The total for the balances on the individual accounts will need reducing by £50.*

Adjustment 4   *The error made here will need adjusting both in the control account and in the individual accounts (an increase is needed of £18).*

The control account can now be updated and would appear as follows:

Updated sales ledger control account

2012		£	2012		£
1 Jun	Balances b/d	876	30 Jun	Cash book	5,550
30 Jun	Credit sales	6,874	30 Jun	Discounts allowed	722
	(Adjustment 2)		30 Jun	Bad debts **(Adjustment 1)**	65
			30 Jun	Returns inwards	249
				(Adjustment 4)	
			30 Jun	Balances c/d	1,164
		7,750			7,750

We would then reconcile the balances for trade receivables from the control account and also the total of the individual balances as follows:

Reconciliation of trade receivables

	£
Balance as per sales ledger	1,006
Add missing sale	120
Add undercast item	50
Less overcast returns	(18)
Balance as per updated control account	1,164

The reconciliation illustrates the differences in the two balances. However, given that the reconciliation is completed successfully we can infer that the errors have now been located and corrected (there could be some other errors but these would not be located through this process).

Example 12.5: a more comprehensive example

The following example shows construction of both the sales ledger and the purchases ledger control account. It also contains items which may not actually belong in the control accounts.

From the following data we will construct the sales ledger and purchases ledger control accounts.

	£
Sales ledger balances as at 1 March 2016	1,001
Purchases ledger balances as at 1 March 2016	666
Credit sales for March	8,305
Credit purchases for March	3,825
Cash sales	2,434
Cash purchases	4,535
Cash and bank receipts in respect of credit sales	8,640
Dishonoured cheques	280
Credit balances in sales ledger as at 1 March 2016	41
Set-offs from sales ledger against purchase ledger balances	66
Returns inwards	101
Bad debts	105
Payments made for credit purchases	3,888
Discounts allowed	265
Discounts received	210
Returns outwards	95
Sales ledger balances as at 31 March 2016	368
Purchases ledger balances as at 31 March 2016	232

The sales ledger control account will be as follows:

Sales ledger control account

2016		£	2016		£
1 Mar	Balances b/d	1,001	31 Mar	Balances b/d	41
31 Mar	Credit sales	8,305	31 Mar	Cash book	8,640
31 Mar	Dishonoured cheques	280	31 Mar	Discounts allowed	265
			31 Mar	Bad debts	105
			31 Mar	Returns inwards	101
			31 Mar	Set-offs	66
			31 Mar	Balances c/d	368
		9,586			9,586

The purchases ledger control account will be as follows:

Purchases ledger control account

2016		£	2016		£
Mar 31	Cash book	3,888	Mar 1	Balances b/d	666
Mar 31	Discount received	210	Mar 31	Credit purchases	3,825
Mar 31	Returns outwards	95			
Mar 31	Set-offs	66			
Mar 31	Balances c/d	232			
		4,491			4,491

Note that the data for cash sales and purchases should not appear in the control account – we are only interested in the items which generate entries into the sales and purchases ledgers.

You should now attempt review questions 12.7 to 12.12.

Chapter review

By now you should understand the following:

- How to classify items into the control account that they belong in
- How to construct the control accounts for the sales and purchases ledgers
- The uses of control accounts
- How to reconcile balances where discrepancies exist.

Handy hints

The following hints will help you avoid errors.

- If you are to construct control accounts, just think of each control account as if it were the individual account of either a debtor or creditor of the business.
- Set-offs appear in both the sales ledger and purchases ledger control accounts – in both cases set-offs reduce the outstanding balances.
- All other items in control accounts can only appear in one of the control accounts.

Key terms

Control account   An account which checks the accuracy of a designated ledger

Sales ledger control account   An account used to verify that the sales ledger has been correctly maintained

Purchases ledger control account   An account used to verify that the purchases ledger has been correctly maintained

Memorandum accounts   Accounts which are not part of the double-entry system and are used as a guide

Setting off   Reducing an outstanding balance owed by one party to another by an amount owed the other way round

REVIEW QUESTIONS

In all the questions for this chapter, the control accounts will act as memorandum accounts unless you are told otherwise.

12.1   From the following data, construct the sales ledger control account for the month of November 2018.

	£
Balances of trade receivables at 1 Nov 2018	1,142
Balances of trade receivables at 30 Nov 2018	698
For the month of November 2018:	
Credit sales	8,899
Cash book entries representing receipts from trade receivables	9,201
Discounts allowed	54
Returns inwards	88

12.2   From the following data, construct the sales ledger control account for the month of January 2017.

	£
Balances of trade receivables at 1 Jan 2017	21,787
Balances of trade receivables at 31 Jan 2017	15,343

For the month of January 2017:

	£
Credit sales	77,520
Cash book entries representing receipts from trade receivables	81,312
Discounts allowed	2,211
Returns inwards	342
Bad debts	99

12.3   From the following data, construct the sales ledger control account for the month of June 2012.

	£
Balances of trade receivables as at 1 June	22,323
Balances of trade receivables as at 30 June	13,123

For the month of June 2012:

	£
Credit sales	213,753
Cash book entries representing receipts from trade receivables	199,131
Discounts allowed	15,435
Returns inwards	7,887
Bad debts	500

12.4   From the following data, construct the purchases ledger control account for the month of July 2018.

	£
Balances of trade payables at 1 July 2018	997
Balances of trade payables at 31 July 2018	123

For the month of July 2018:

	£
Credit purchases for month	4,113
Cash book entries for payments of trade payables	4,898
Discounts received	89

12.5   From the following data, construct the purchases ledger control account for the month of November 2013.

	£
Balances of trade payables at 1 November 2013	5,111
Balances of trade payables at 30 November 2013	8,887

For the month of November 2013:

	£
Credit purchases for month	50,909
Cash book entries for payments of trade payables	45,767
Discounts received	555
Returns outwards	811

12.6 From the following data, construct the purchases ledger control account for the month of May 2014.

	£
Balances of trade payables at 1 May 2014	4,324
Balances of trade payables at 31 May 2014	5,345
For the month of May 2014:	
Credit purchases for month	72,313
Cash book entries for payments of trade payables	69,998
Returns outwards	1,294

12.7 From the following data, construct the sales ledger and purchases ledger control accounts for the month of March 2016.

	£
Sales ledger balances as at 1 March 2016	6,646
Purchases ledger balances as at 1 March 2016	3,424
Credit sales for March	34,530
Credit purchases for March	27,671
Cash and bank receipts in respect of credit sales	35,559
Set-offs from sales ledger against purchase ledger balances	190
Returns inwards	2,090
Bad debts	760
Payments made for credit purchases	24,043
Discounts allowed	755
Discounts received	543
Returns outwards	1,785
Sales ledger balances as at 31 March 2016	1,822
Purchases ledger balances as at 31 March 2016	4,534

12.8 From the following data, construct the sales ledger and purchases ledger control accounts for the month of June 2019.

	£
Sales ledger balances as at 1 June 2019	19,048
Purchases ledger balances as at 1 June 2019	21,343
Credit sales for March	87,870
Credit purchases for March	53,535
Cash and bank receipts in respect of credit sales	83,499
Set-offs from sales ledger against purchases ledger balances	994
Returns inwards	342
Bad debts	659
Payments made for credit purchases	56,312
Discounts allowed	334
Discounts received	213
Returns outwards	876
Sales ledger balances as at 30 June 2019	21,090
Purchases ledger balances as at 30 June 2019	16,483

12.9   From the following data, construct the sales ledger and purchases ledger control accounts for the month of April 2011.

	£
Purchases ledger balances as at 1 April 2011	1,767
Credit sales for April	53,299
Credit purchases for April	27,777
Cash and bank receipts in respect of credit sales	48,912
Credit balances in sales ledger as at 1 April 2011	190
Debit balances in purchases ledgers as at 1 April 2011	223
Set-offs from sales ledger against purchases ledger balances	423
Returns inwards	756
Bad debts	534
Payments made for credit purchases	25,660
Discounts allowed	455
Discounts received	433
Returns outwards	765
Sales ledger balances as at 30 April 2011	4,342
Purchases ledger balances as at 30 April 2011	2,040

12.10   From the following data, construct the sales ledger and purchases ledger control accounts for the month of September 2010.

	£
Sales ledger balances as at 1 September 2010	10,321
Purchases ledger balances as at 1 September 2010	11,233
Credit sales for September	70,213
Credit purchases for September	64,565
Cash sales	5,435
Cash purchases	9,879
Cash and bank receipts in respect of credit sales	59,977
Dishonoured cheques	765
Set-offs from sales ledger against purchases ledger balances	756
Returns inwards	1,123
Bad debts	10,121
Payments made for credit purchases	59,808
Discounts allowed	1,432
Discounts received	433
Returns outwards	765
Sales ledger balances as at 30 September 2010	7,890
Purchases ledger balances as at 30 September 2010	14,036

12.11 From the following data, construct the sales ledger and purchases ledger control accounts for the month of July 2010.

	£
Sales ledger balances as at 1 July 2010	785
Purchases ledger balances as at 1 July 2010	1,010
Credit sales for July	4,342
Credit purchases for July	2,390
Payments made for credit purchases	2,761
Cash sales	890
Cash purchases	1,121
Cash and bank receipts in respect of credit sales	3,989
Dishonoured cheques	115
Set-offs from sales ledger against purchase ledger balances	52
Returns inwards	78
Returns outwards	290
Bad debts	65
Discounts allowed	99
Discounts received	82
Sales ledger balances as at 31 July 2010	959
Purchases ledger balances as at 31 July 2010	215

12.12 From the following data, construct the sales ledger and purchases ledger control accounts for the month of January 2012:

	£
Sales ledger balances as at 1 January 2012	54,255
Purchases ledger balances as at 1 January 2012	42,331
Credit sales for January	509,483
Credit purchases for January	324,324
Cash sales	86,786
Cash purchases	408,850
Cash and bank receipts in respect of credit sales	490,790
Dishonoured cheques	867
Credit balances in sales ledger as at 1 January 2012	913
Set-offs from sales ledger against purchases ledger balances	3,210
Returns inwards	767
Bad debts	2,111
Payments made for credit purchases	398,080
Discounts allowed	5,353
Discounts received	6,438
Returns outwards	1,109
Sales ledger balances as at 31 January 2012	64,564
Purchases ledger balances as at 31 January 2012	42,344
Credit balances in sales ledger at 31 January 2012	2,190

CHAPTER 13

Bank reconciliation statements

Learning objectives

By the end of this chapter you should be able to:

- Update a cash book based on a bank statement containing items not yet posted to the cash book
- Understand the different items appearing on the bank statement of the business
- Produce a bank reconciliation statement based on the cash book and a bank statement
- Ascertain if a differing balance for the cash book and the bank statement is the result of an error.

Introduction

The cash book shows us the cash and bank transactions undertaken by the business. From the business's bank, a bank statement will also be received on a fairly regular basis. This bank statement details all transactions into and out of the bank account. In effect, the bank statement should replicate the bank column of the cash book as they show exactly the same information.

One difference between the businesses cash book and the bank statement will be the types of balances that appear. If the business has money in the bank then this will show as a credit balance on the bank statement. This is not a mistake. It is simply from the bank's viewpoint – i.e. the bank owes us our money. Similarly, if we have a credit balance on the bank column of the cash book then this would appear as a debit balance on the bank statement (we are overdrawn and owe the bank money – meaning we appear as an asset from the bank's viewpoint – a debit balance).

However, although the bank column of the cash book and the bank statement balance should always be the same it is likely that the balances – even if taken on exactly the same date – will not be the same. This discrepancy could be because of any of the following:

1 Items appearing on the bank statement but not in the cash book
2 Items appearing in the cash book but not on the bank statement
3 Errors made by the business or by the bank

So as to ascertain the cause of the discrepancy – and in particular to detect if errors have occurred – a business will draw up a **bank reconciliation statement** which will highlight the cause of any discrepancy between the two balances.

Procedure for bank reconciliation

To illustrate the procedure of bank reconciliation we will use a bank statement and a cash book page both from the month of October 2015 for J Lyne. The bank statement appears as in Exhibit 13.1.

Exhibit 13.1

Bank Statement

Eastern Bank

Statement No. 45   Mr J Lyne   Sort Code 76 45 87
31 October 2015   Account No. 01243487
IBAN GB44HGJUDHD43487

Date 2015	Details	Payment (£)	Receipts (£)	Balance (£)
01 Oct	Opening balance			589
04 Oct	Credit transfer Bellwood Ltd		240	829
06 Oct	Cheque 101450	684		145
12 Oct	Direct Debit Southeast Electricity	86		59
15 Oct	Cheque deposited		298	357
19 Oct	Cheque deposited		76	433
21 Oct	Interest received		4	437
24 Oct	Standing order to 017643	350		87
25 Oct	Direct Debit Eastern Insurance	92		(5) OD*
27 Oct	Dishonoured cheque 19 Oct	76		(81) OD
29 Oct	Cheque deposited		223	142
30 Oct	Cheque 101451	115		27
31 Oct	Closing balance			27

* OD refers to the account being overdrawn – i.e. the amount withdrawn temporarily exceeds the amount in the bank account.

The cash book for the same period appears as in Exhibit 13.2.

Exhibit 13.2

Cash book (bank only)

2015		£	2015		£
01 Oct	Balance b/d	589	04 Oct	B Welsh	684
12 Oct	F Brown	298	26 Oct	R Lewis	115
15 Oct	N Renshaw	76	27 Oct	R Wakeling	99
24 Oct	J Denton	223	29 Oct	D Doyle	204
28 Oct	L Webster	430	31 Oct	Balance c/d	514
		1,616			1,616
01 Nov	Balance b/d	514			

As we can see, although the opening balances for the period agree, the closing balances disagree. In order to verify whether or not this disagreement is caused by error we can begin the process of bank reconciliation.

The following is not the only method of completing the bank reconciliation but it is the one that gives a clear procedure to follow. To complete the bank reconciliation, the following steps should be taken:

1 We need to identify the items that do not appear both in the cash book and on the bank statement, as these could be the reason for the discrepancy.
2 The cash book will need to be brought up to date by entering items found only on the bank statement and not in the cash book.
3 Draw up a reconciliation statement using the updated cash book balance and items appearing in the cash book that were not on the bank statement.

Let us take each step separately.

Identifying items not appearing both in the cash book and on the bank statement

Firstly, we have to locate the items which do not appear both in the cash book and on the bank statement as this may be the reason for any discrepancy – if the items appear both in the cash book and on the bank statement then this would not give the reason for any discrepancy. We ignore the balances and focus on the money paid in and out of the business bank account. The items we are interested in are italicised on the bank statement as shown in Exhibit 13.3 and in the cash book extract shown in Exhibit 13.4.

Exhibit 13.3

Bank Statement

Eastern Bank

Statement No. 45	Mr J Lyne	Sort Code 76 45 87
31 October 2015		Account No. 01243487
		IBAN GB44HGJUDHD43487

Date	Details	Payment (£)	Receipts (£)	Balance (£)
2015				
01 Oct	Opening balance			589
04 Oct	*Credit transfer Bellwood Ltd*		*240*	*829*
06 Oct	Cheque 101450	684		145
12 Oct	*Direct Debit Southeast Electricity*	*86*		*59*
15 Oct	Cheque deposited		298	357
19 Oct	Cheque deposited		76	433
21 Oct	*Interest received*		*4*	*437*
24 Oct	*Standing order to 017643*	*350*		*87*
25 Oct	*Direct Debit Eastern Insurance*	*92*		*(5) OD*
27 Oct	*Dishonoured cheque 19 Oct*	*76*		*(81) OD*
29 Oct	Cheque deposited		223	142
30 Oct	Cheque 101451	115		27
31 Oct	Closing balance			27

The cash book for the same period appears as follows:

Exhibit 13.4

Cash book (bank only)

2015		£	2015		£
01 Oct	Balance b/d	589	04 Oct	B Welsh	684
12 Oct	F Brown	298	26 Oct	R Lewis	115
15 Oct	N Renshaw	76	*27 Oct*	*R Wakeling*	*99*
24 Oct	J Denton	223	*29 Oct*	*D Doyle*	*204*
28 Oct	*L Webster*	*430*	31 Oct	Balance c/d	514
		1,616			1,616
01 Nov	Balance b/d	514			

You may have noticed that the cheque received from N Renshaw which is debited to the cash book does also appear on the bank statement. However, a few days later the bank classifies this as a dishonoured cheque and cancels the receipt into our bank account which means that it really only appears in the cash book.

Bringing the cash book up to date

Increasingly many transactions will appear on a business's bank statement without the business owner(s) taking any direct action. This is because these transactions are largely automated. Common types of transactions which fall into this category are direct debits, standing orders, credit transfers, interest payments and bank charges.

Direct debits

These occur when the business gives permission for a third party to withdraw money from the bank account. Usually this will be to settle a bill. Most utility providers (e.g. gas and electricity suppliers) encourage payment of bills to be made through a direct debit arrangement. They are often paid at the same point each month but the amount paid will vary.

Standing orders

A business can arrange for a regular payment of a fixed amount to be made out of its account. This could be to another business or to a person. Standing orders are similar to direct debits except that the arrangement is made by the business itself and not the recipient of the money.

Credit transfers

These refer to money paid directly into our bank account. Whereas direct debits and standing orders usually refer to payments, these refer to receipts.

Interest/bank charges

Banks themselves will make entries into our bank account automatically. Interest – both paid and received – will usually appear on a bank statement. Charges made by the banks, e.g. for the use of an overdraft, will also appear.

Dishonoured cheques

Although not an automated transaction it is possible that this will appear on our bank statement. If we receive and deposit a cheque then once the cheque is cleared (normally within around three working days) the money is credited (from the bank's viewpoint) to our account. If the payee of the cheque does not have sufficient funds in their account to make the payment, then the cheque may be dishonoured and the money that was added to the account balance would be cancelled. The business would not know about this immediately but a bank would normally write to a customer to inform them of this (and may also charge them for this).

Updated cash book

Once we have located all the items on the bank statement but not in the cash book it is time to bring the cash book up to date with these items. Sometimes this is called a corrected cash book but it basically is the same thing.

The original cash book appeared as follows:

Cash book (bank only)

2015		£	2015		£
01 Oct	Balance b/d	589	04 Oct	B Welsh	684
12 Oct	F Brown	298	26 Oct	R Lewis	115
15 Oct	N Renshaw	76	27 Oct	R Wakeling	99
24 Oct	J Denton	223	29 Oct	D Doyle	204
28 Oct	L Webster	430	31 Oct	Balance c/d	514
		1,616			1,616
01 Nov	Balance b/d	514			

However, with the addition of the extra items, the cash book would now appear as follows:

Updated cash book (bank only)

2015		£	2015		£
01 Oct	Balance b/d	589	04 Oct	B Welsh	684
12 Oct	F Brown	298	26 Oct	R Lewis	115
15 Oct	N Renshaw	76	27 Oct	R Wakeling	99
24 Oct	J Denton	223	29 Oct	D Doyle	204
28 Oct	L Webster	430	31 Oct	Southeast Electricity	86
31 Oct	Credit transfer – Bellwood Ltd	240	31 Oct	Standing order	350
31 Oct	Interest	4	31 Oct	Eastern Insurance	92
			31 Oct	Dishonoured cheque	76
			31 Oct	Balance c/d	154
		1,860			1,860
01 Nov	Balance b/d	154			

(In this example we have 'undone' the closing balance and added the new items in. An alternative way of updating the cash book would be to start with the closing balance and add the items to arrive at the updated closing balance.)

You should now attempt review questions 13.1 to 13.4.

It is now time to complete the third stage – the bank reconciliation.

Producing the bank reconciliation statement

There are likely to be entries in the cashbook which do not appear on the bank statement. This is likely to arise out of the following situation. When a business makes or receives payment by cheque then although this can be written immediately into the cash book it will take time before it appears in the bank account. This is largely because of the time taken by the bank to **'clear'** each cheque. Normally clearing takes around three working days to complete. Therefore any cheques deposited in a bank near the end of a calendar month may well not appear on the bank statement until early in the following month.

There are two types of cheques we will deal with:

- **Unpresented cheques** are those that have been paid out by the business and entered in the cash book but for which the bank has not yet paid out the money.
- **Lodgements not yet credited** are those cheques which we have received and entered in the cash book but for which the bank has not yet added the amount concerned to the balance as per the bank statement.

The bank reconciliation statement will appear as follows:

J Lyne
Bank reconciliation statement as at 31 October 2015

	£	£
Balance as per updated cash book		154
Add Unpresented cheques:		
R Wakeling	99	
D Doyle	204	303
		457
Less Lodgements not yet credited:		
L Webster		430
Balance as per bank statement		27

As you can see, the balance on the updated cash book can be reconciled with the balance on the bank statement. This would indicate that errors have not taken place and that the differences in the two balances can be accounted for.

You should now attempt review questions 13.5 to 13.10.

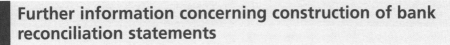

Further information concerning construction of bank reconciliation statements

There are alternative methods of attempting to reconcile the cash book and bank statement balances.

● Firstly, it is possible to include all the items in the bank reconciliation statement. This would eliminate the need to complete an updated cash book. However, this makes the procedure more complicated and increases the chances of errors occurring – even if it does take slightly longer. With the same example used earlier, the following bank reconciliation statement was completed *without* first updating the cash book.

J Lyne
Bank Reconciliation Statement as at 31 October 2015

	£	£
Balance as per cash book		514
Add:		
Credit transfer	240	
Interest received	4	
Unpresented cheque – Wakeling	99	
Unpresented cheque – Doyle	204	547
		1,061
Less:		
Direct debit (SE Electricity)	86	
Standing order	350	
Direct debit (Eastern Insurance)	92	
Dishonoured cheque	76	
Lodgements not yet credited – Webster	430	1,034
Balance as per bank statement		27

Items that have been added to the bank balance on the bank statement will need adding to the cash book balance in order to bring them in line.

Similarly, items that have been paid out of the bank account on the bank statement but have not yet appeared in the cash book will need subtracting from the cash book balance.

As in the earlier example, although the two closing balances differ they can be reconciled, which indicates that no errors have taken place.

● Secondly, the bank reconciliation statement can begin with the balance as per the bank statement. In this case, we would need to subtract unpresented cheques and add the lodgements not yet credited.

You should now attempt review questions 13.11 to 13.15.

Chapter review

By now you should understand the following:

- How to update a cash book from a given bank statement
- How to produce a bank reconciliation statement from an updated cash book
- How to construct a bank reconciliation statement without the need of an updated cash book.

Handy hints

The following hints will help you avoid errors.

- If you are given both the cash book closing balance and the closing balance on the bank statement then, to some degree, you already have the answer for any reconciliation statement – you should be confident that you have completed it correctly if the numbers are already there.
- Be careful with overdrafts – subtracting an amount will add to the size of the overdraft.
- Don't just rely on rote learning. It is possible that you will have to start with the cash book or the bank statement balance.

Key terms

Bank reconciliation statement   A statement which attempts to show if any disagreement between the cash book and the bank statement is due to error or due to timing differences

Updated cash book   A cash book which has items entered into it from the bank statement which were previously not included

Direct debit   A payment of varying amount taken out of a bank account by a third party on a regular basis

Standing order   A payment made to a third party of a fixed amount paid out on a regular basis

Dishonoured cheque   A cheque received which the bank of the issuer of the cheque fails to honour – i.e. will not pay out the amount for which the cheque is written

Unpresented cheque   A cheque paid out by a business for which the bank of the business has not yet paid out the amount concerned

Lodgements not yet credited   Cheques received by a business concerning which the money has yet to be paid into the bank account of the business

Clearing   The time taken by banks between a cheque being deposited and the funds been transferred to the account

REVIEW QUESTIONS

13.1   The following cash book was completed for the month of October 2019:

Cash book

2019		£	2019		£
Oct 01	Balance b/d	42	Oct 09	L Carey	439
Oct 08	J Hynes	534	Oct 19	K Andrews	226
Oct 26	H Smithson	123	Oct 31	Balance c/d	34
		699			699

However, it came to light shortly after completion that the following items had been omitted from the cash book:

	£
Interest paid	11
Bank charges	18
Direct debit: Northern Gas	56
Dividends received	23

Bring the cash book up to date with the above items.

13.2   The following cash book was completed for the month of January 2010:

Cash book

2010		£	2010		£
Jan 01	Balance b/d	489	Jan 07	G Taylor	320
Jan 13	K Gee	546	Jan 10	J Crouch	761
Jan 15	D Fish	432	Jan 22	M Lace	434
Jan 23	S Poole	76	Jan 31	Balance c/d	28
		1,543			1,543

However, it came to light shortly after completion that the following items have been omitted from the cash book:

	£
Interest paid	23
Credit transfer from M Armstrong	432
Bank charges	45
Standing order: J Rowe	323
Dividends received	56

Bring the cash book up to date with the above items.

13.3 The following cash book was completed for the month of March 2012:

Cash book

2012		£	2012		£
Mar 05	D Gahan	324	Mar 01	Balance b/d	190
Mar 09	V Clarke	127	Mar 18	M Lyne	34
Mar 14	F Sharkey	239	Mar 19	R Keenan	312
Mar 19	P Evans	132	Mar 22	L Webster	654
Mar 31	Balance c/d	821	Mar 26	C Webb	453
		1,643			1,643

However, it came to light shortly after completion that the following items have been omitted from the cash book:

	£
Interest received	18
Direct debit: Electricity	177
Bank charges	98
Dishonoured cheque	414
Credit transfer: H Morris	287
Dividends received	11

Bring the cash book up to date with the above items.

13.4 The following cash book was completed for the month of August 2013:

Cash book

2013		£	2013		£
Aug 02	M Kite	42	Aug 01	Balance b/d	55
Aug 06	L Scott	199	Aug 07	R Gutteridge	243
Aug 11	E Bowden	98	Aug 09	H Latham	34
Aug 16	C Becker	87	Aug 17	B Moody	57
Aug 20	A King	46	Aug 24	J Simpson	423
Aug 31	Balance c/d	340			
		812			812

However, it came to light shortly after completion that the following items have been omitted from the cash book:

	£
Standing order: H Reyes	300
Direct debit: B Williams	121
Interest received	17
Credit transfer: A Fender	290
Dishonoured cheque	55
Bank charges	35
Dividends received	42

Bring the cash book up to date with the above items.

13.5 The following are extracts from the cash book and the bank statement of P Jones:

Cash book

2011	Dr	£	2011	Cr	£
Oct 01	Balance b/d	129	Oct 08	B Eden	71
Oct 08	D Watts	45	Oct 21	L Green	335
Oct 14	C Milligan	221	Oct 28	R Keenan	150
Oct 27	T Wright	431	Oct 31	Balance c/d	270
		826			826

Bank statement

		Dr	Cr	Balance
2011		£	£	£
Oct 1	Balance b/d			129
Oct 11	D Watts		45	174
Oct 12	B Eden	71		103
Oct 16	Bank charges	45		58
Oct 18	C Milligan		221	279
Oct 24	M Green	335		56 o/d
Oct 29	Credit transfer: ABC Ltd		106	50

(a) Write up the cash book up to date and state the new balance as on 31 October 2011.
(b) Draw up a bank reconciliation statement as on 31 October 2011.

13.6 The bank columns in the cash book for November 2004 and the bank statement for that month for S Shaw are:

Cash book

2004	Dr	£	2004	Cr	£
Nov 5	G Peggs	80	Nov 1	Balance b/d	210
Nov 14	B Ford	115	Nov 4	S Haslem	74
Nov 18	N Renton	86	Nov 21	S Nower	95
Nov 25	B Hughes	190	Nov 24	L Black	167
Nov 26	I Yates	134	Nov 30	Balance c/d	59
		605			605

Bank statement

		Dr	Cr	Balance
2004		£	£	£
Nov 1	Balance b/d			210 (Dr)
Nov 9	11334	74		284 (Dr)
Nov 11	Sundries		80	204 (Dr)
Nov 12	Bank charges	41		245 (Dr)
Nov 18	Standing order: O Browne	75		320 (Dr)
Nov 17	Sundries		115	205 (Dr)
Nov 26	11335	95		300 (Dr)
Nov 27	Sundries		86	214 (Dr)
Nov 29	Dividends		64	150 (Dr)

(a) Write up the cash book up to date and state the new balance as on 30 November 2004.

(b) Draw up a bank reconciliation statement as on 30 November 2004.

13.7 The balance in the cash book and on the bank statement did not agree in the accounts of R Green for the month of June 2014.

Cash book

2014		£	2014		£
Jun 1	Balance b/d	45	Jun 18	T Tippett	67
Jun 10	J Manson	321	Jun 24	J Tunnerly	432
Jun 14	A Nair	532	Jun 26	J Merkel	133
Jun 27	W Thompson	213	Jun 30	Balance b/d	479
		1,111			1,111

Bank statement

June		Payments £	Receipts £	Balance £
1	Balance b/d			45
12	Cheque deposited		321	366
17	Cheque deposited		532	898
19	Bank charges	22		876
22	Sundries 3144	67		809
26	Sundries 3145	432		377
30	Credit transfer		150	527

From the above data:

(a) Update the cash book

(b) Produce a bank reconciliation statement as at 30 June 2014.

13.8 The balance in the cash book and on the bank statement did not agree in the accounts of R Alvefors for the month of July 2016.

Cash book

2016		£	2016		£
Jul 1	Balance b/d	38	Jul 18	F Benjamin	277
Jun 10	D Bellamy	452	Jul 28	F Harris	299
Jun 25	D Griffiths	119	Jul 31	Balance b/d	33
		609			609

Bank statement

June		Payments £	Receipts £	Balance £
1	Balance b/d			38
12	Cheque deposited		452	490
17	Interest		3	493
19	Direct debit	45		448
22	Cheque 1011	277		171
26	Standing order	67		104

From the above data:

(a) Update the cash book
(b) Produce a bank reconciliation statement as at 31 July 2016.

13.9 On 30 November 2017, L Venison's cash book had been brought up to date and showed a debit balance of £76. However, the balance on the bank statement still disagreed with the balance on the cash book. Unpresented cheques amounted to £108 and lodgements not yet credited by the bank totalled to £245.

Produce a bank reconciliation statement and ascertain the balance on the bank statement.

13.10 N Luck has just updated his cash book which now has a balance of £208.96 (Dr). However, this still disagrees with the balance on the bank statement at the end of May 2014. Based on the information that follows relating to outstanding cheques, produce a bank reconciliation statement as at 31 May 2014 and verify that the balance on the bank statement is £395.35.

- Unpresented cheque 100056: £190.56
- Unpresented cheque 100057: £214.33
- Unpresented cheque 100058: £646.75
- Lodgement: K Davies: £865.25

13.11 On 31 January 2013 T Tripp's bank statement showed an overdrawn balance of £111. However, the cash book contained two items that were not on the bank statement. There were unpresented cheques totalling £230 and lodgements not yet credited by the bank amounting to £404.

Produce a bank reconciliation statement and ascertain the balance on the cash book.

13.12 Complete the bank reconciliation again for question 13.5 but miss out the stage of updating the cash book and include all relevant items in the statement.

13.13 Complete the bank reconciliation again for question 13.6 but miss out the stage of updating the cash book and include all relevant items in the statement.

13.14 Complete the bank reconciliation again for question 13.7 but miss out the stage of updating the cash book and include all relevant items in the statement.

13.15 Starting with the balance as on the bank statement complete the bank reconciliation again for question 13.8 but miss out the stage of updating the cash book and include all relevant items in the statement.

CHAPTER 14

Manufacturing accounts

Learning objectives

By the end of this chapter you should be able to:

- Classify costs according to their relationship with the level of production
- Construct a manufacturing account for a business which manufactures its own output
- Show factory profit in the financial statements
- Adjust for unrealised profits on unsold inventory and make appropriate adjustments in the financial statements.

Introduction

In all the examples used in this textbook so far none of the businesses have produced goods for themselves. In each case, the gross profit for each business has been calculated as the difference between the sales revenue and the cost of these goods purchased (adjusted for inventory at the start and end of the business period).

If a business manufactures goods then the trading account will need to be adjusted as it can no longer contain an entry for the purchases of goods. Instead we will have to include a cost for the goods manufactured by the business. This cost of manufacture will be calculated in a separate statement, known as the **manufacturing account**.

The manufacturing account calculates the cost of manufacturing goods for a particular period of time by including all costs relevant to the production of goods. The manufacturing account is divided into two sections.

The two sections of the manufacturing account:	
Prime cost	The **direct costs** associated with manufacturing goods
Indirect manufacturing costs	The **indirect costs** associated with manufacturing goods

How costs are classified

In order to include costs in the correct section of the manufacturing account, we will need to understand how the cost is related to the manufacturing process.

Direct costs are those costs directly related to the production of output. These will increase in relation to the level of output in a linear (i.e. proportionate) manner. Common examples would include the cost of **raw materials**, **direct labour** and **royalties**.

Indirect costs are those costs indirectly related to the production of output. Although linked to the production of goods they will not increase in a linear manner in relation to the level of output. This is because they are only partly connected with the production of goods and are known collectively as **indirect manufacturing costs** (though these are sometimes labelled 'factory' costs). Examples include rent of the factory, indirect labour and equipment depreciation.

There will also be other costs incurred by the business which are not related to production. These will not appear in the manufacturing account and will instead appear in the statement of comprehensive income. Sometimes these are labelled as 'office' expenses. Examples include office salaries and depreciation of office fixtures.

You should now attempt review questions 14.1 and 14.2.

Prime cost

As mentioned earlier, the prime cost section of the manufacturing account contains the direct costs of manufacturing. These direct costs will consist of the cost of raw materials consumed and any other direct costs involved in the production of the goods.

Cost of raw materials consumed

The most obvious example of a cost directly related to the production of output would be the cost of the materials that are purchased in order to be transformed into finished goods. Any materials that are purchased will need adjusting based on the accruals concept. This means that we will need to adjust for any inventory of materials in hand at the start of trade and also at the close of trade (as well as for any returns of materials and the carriage on materials purchased).

The calculation for raw materials is known as the **cost of raw materials consumed**.

Example 14.1

The following data is available relating to raw materials purchased for Chillingworth Ltd for the year to 31 December 2005:

	£
Inventory of raw materials as at 1 January 2005	6,456
Inventory of raw materials as at 31 December 2005	5,353
Purchases of raw materials	42,322
Carriage inwards on raw materials	540
Returns outwards	725

The cost of raw materials consumed is calculated as follows:

Chillingworth Ltd
Cost of raw materials calculation for year ended 31 Dec 2005

	£	£
Inventory of raw materials as at 1 Dec 2005		6,456
Add Purchases	42,322	
Add Carriage inwards	540	
	42,862	
Less Returns outwards	725	42,137
		48,593
Inventory of raw materials as at 31 Dec 2005		5,353
Cost of raw materials consumed		43,240

You should now attempt review questions 14.3 and 14.4.

Direct costs

Other direct costs would be added to the cost of raw materials consumed to reach the prime cost of production. These are likely to be the direct labour costs and royalties, but will also include any other direct costs.

It is possible that some costs will need to be divided between the prime cost and the indirect manufacturing costs. This information would be provided in the additional information to the account. Any division of cost would be conducted after any adjustment is made for prepayments and accruals.

Example 14.2

The following data relates to the production activities of J Kite & Sons for the year ended 31 December 2009:

	£
Inventory of raw materials as at 1 Jan 2009	21,342
Inventory of raw materials as at 31 Dec 2009	18,787
Purchases of raw materials	231,440
Production wages	178,500
Royalties	12,430

Additional information:

(a) As at 31 December 2009, production wages prepaid amounted to £2,150.
(b) Production wages are allocated between direct costs and indirect costs in the ratio of 3:1.

We calculate the prime cost as follows:

J Kite & Sons
Prime cost calculation for the year ended 31 December 2009

	£
Inventory of raw materials as at 1 Jan 2009	21,342
Purchases of raw materials	231,440
	252,782
Inventory of raw materials as at 31 Dec 2009	18,787
	233,995
Production wages (£178,500 − £2,150) × 3/4	132,263
Royalties	12,430
Prime cost	378,688

Notice how we adjust for the prepaid production wages before we apportion the wages between the prime cost and the indirect manufacturing costs.

You should now attempt review questions 14.5 to 14.7.

Indirect manufacturing costs

Once prime cost has been calculated we would then proceed to add on the **indirect manufacturing costs**. These are the costs that are related to production but in a relationship less close than the direct costs of production.

As a general rule, to decide whether a cost is an indirect manufacturing cost, ask yourself, does the cost vary with the level of output? If it does, then it belongs in the manufacturing account. However, if the cost varies directly with the level of output then it will belong in the prime cost section. It is costs that vary with the level of output in a less than linear manner that would be considered indirect manufacturing costs and would belong in this section.

Once the indirect manufacturing costs are added on to the prime cost we would need to adjust for work-in-progress.

Work-in-progress

Any goods which are not yet completed are known as **work-in-progress**. As these goods are incomplete they cannot be added to the costs of production but they will be adjusted for as follows:

Total of prime cost and indirect factory costs
+ Opening balance of work-in-progress
− Closing balance of work-in-progress
= Production cost of goods completed

Once work-in-progress is adjusted for we can complete the manufacturing account by arriving at the total cost of production.

Example 14.3

The following data relates to the production of Testa Ltd for the year ended 31 March 2011:

	£
Inventory as at 1 April 2010:	
Raw materials	8,960
Work-in-progress	4,245
Purchases of raw materials	64,520
Carriage inwards on raw materials	453
Manufacturing wages	55,600
Royalties	3,255
Supervisory wages	11,210
Factory rent	6,546
Machinery depreciation	5,450
Factory maintenance	7,656

Additional information:

Inventory held at 31 March 2011 was valued as follows:

Raw materials   £8,678
Work-in-progress   £5,435

The manufacturing account can now be completed as follows:

Testa Ltd
Manufacturing account for year ended 31 March 2011

	£	£
Opening inventory of raw materials		8,960
Add Purchases	64,530	
Add Carriage inwards	453	64,983
		73,943
Less Closing inventory of raw materials		8,678
Cost of raw materials consumed		**65,265**
Manufacturing wages		55,600
Royalties		3,255
Prime cost		**124,120**
Add Indirect manufacturing costs:		
Supervisory wages	11,210	
Factory rent	6,546	
Machinery depreciation	5,450	
Factory maintenance	7,656	30,862
		154,982
Add Opening work-in-progress		4,245
		159,227
Less Closing work-in-progress		5,435
Production cost of goods completed		**153,792**

After the manufacturing account is completed

Once we have calculated the production cost of goods completed we can proceed to constructing the statement of comprehensive income as per normal. If we look at the statement of comprehensive income as per individual section then the trading account section will contain all the items that you would normally expect. However, the purchases figure will be replaced with the production cost of goods completed.

Replace the purchases figure in the trading account with the production cost of goods completed figure.

In addition, there will be no carriage inwards or returns outwards here as these (if present) would have both appeared in the prime cost section of the manufacturing account.

You should now attempt review questions 14.8 to 14.13.

Factory profit

Firms are likely to manufacture goods instead of purchasing them from an outside supplier for one or more of the following reasons:

- The firm can produce the goods at a lower cost than would be paid to purchase the same goods from another firm
- There are no firms that can supply the goods elsewhere
- The firm can produce goods to a higher quality than the goods available from other firms.

As a result, the firm manufacturing the goods will often generate higher profits as a result of manufacturing the goods. The savings made by a firm from manufacturing rather than purchasing goods is known as **factory profit**. This will usually be an estimated figure.

The amount of savings – factory profit – generated can be built into the manufacturing account presentation. The factory profit is added on to the production cost of goods completed at the end of the manufacturing account. This can be an estimated amount simply added on to the production cost or can be based on a percentage mark-up – by adding on a percentage of the cost on top of the production cost.

Example 14.4

The production cost of goods completed for the year ended 30 June 2006 was £280,000. Factory profit for the business is based on a mark-up of 25%.

	£
Production cost of goods completed	280,000
Add: Factory profit (25%)	70,000
Transfer price of goods completed	350,000

The £350,000, not the £280,000, would be transferred to the trading account.

One issue that you may have realised is that by boosting the production cost by the addition of factory profit, then when this is transferred to the trading account the cost of finished goods sold will be higher and gross and net profits will be lower as a result. This appears self-defeating – why bother including factory profit if it only leads to lower overall profit?

The solution to this issue is that we always add back the factory profit in the statement of comprehensive income to cancel out the effect of lowering profit by the addition of factory profit. This may raise the question of why we bother to adjust for factory profit.

The answer to this is that by including factory profit within the manufacturing account and income statement, we can analyse the composition of the business's over-all net profit. The net profit can be considered to consist of the profit on manufactur-ing (in the form of savings made) and the profit on other operations. For example, it is possible that the firm's net profit arises mainly from savings made in manufacturing.

You should now attempt review questions 14.14 and 14.15.

Provision for unrealised profit on unsold inventory

Allowing factory profit creates a problem in the valuation of any inventory remaining unsold at the end of the period. Notice that the factory profit adds to the value of the production costs of the finished goods. This means that any finished goods that remain within the business will include some of this profit. The factory profit included in the value of closing finished goods inventory is known as **unrealised profit**.

Unrealised profit goes against the concept of **prudence**, and we should not allow these 'profits' to be included in goods that have yet to be sold. We have to, in effect, remove this profit from the value of the closing inventory. The method of eliminating this unrealised profit is by the creation of a provision for unrealised profit.

Example 14.5

Inventory of finished goods at the end of the period was valued at £15,000. To allow for factory profit the production cost of goods completed had been marked up by 25%. How should the inventory be valued in the financial statements?

The £15,000 already includes the factory profit which we need to cancel out. Your first thought might be that we simply need to subtract 25% from £15,000 (i.e. £3,750) as unrealised profit. This would be wrong – if you think about it, if a number is marked up by 25% then subtracting 25% will not get you back to the original value. For example, £100 marked up by 25% results in £125. Subtracting 25% from £125 does not get you back to £100.

The correct approach is to use the following formula:

$$\frac{\text{Mark-up \%}}{100 + \text{Mark-up \%}} \times \text{Value of inventory} = \text{Unrealised profit}$$

In our example, the unrealised profit will be $(25/125 \times £15,000) = £3,000$.

This £3,000 would appear in the statement of comprehensive income as a deduction against the gross profit. We would show the value of closing inventory of finished goods on the statement of financial position as £15,000 − £3,000 = £12,000.

When a provision for unrealised profit already exists then we would need to make the following adjustments:

Treatment of unrealised profit in the financial statements		
Treatment in statement of comprehensive income		Treatment on statement of financial position
If provision increases:	If provision decreases:	
Deduct **INCREASE** only from profit	Add **DECREASE** only to profit	Deduct FULL provision from value of inventory of finished goods

Example 14.6

The following data was extracted from the books of a business as at 31 December 2012:

	£
Inventory of finished goods as at 1 January 2012	11,800
Inventory of finished goods as at 31 December 2012	12,500
Provision for unrealised profit as at 1 Jan 2012	2,360

The production cost of completed goods is marked up at the uniform rate of 25%. How would we account for the unrealised profit on the unsold inventory?

The new provision for unrealised profits would be $(25/125 \times £12,500) = £2,500$.

Given that there is already a provision on the books of £2,360, in the end-of-year statement of comprehensive income we would include a deduction from profit of $(£2,500 − £2,360) = £140$.

The ledger account for the provision for unrealised profit would appear as follows:

Provision for unrealised profit on unsold inventory

2012		£	2012		£
Dec 31	Balance c/d	2,500	Jan 1	Balance b/d	2,360
			Dec 31	Statement of Comp. Income	140
		2,500			2,500

Unless it is asked for, there is no need to construct the ledger account when calculating the adjustment for unrealised profit in a manufacturing account question.

The inventory of finished goods would appear on the statement of financial position as follows:

Statement of financial position (extract) as at 31 December 2012

Current assets	£	£
Inventory of finished goods	12,500	
Less: Provision for unrealised profit	2,500	10,000

Because of time constraints, examination questions are unlikely to require the completion of a full set of financial statements including the manufacturing accounts. However, questions could focus on any one part of the overall system so it is important that you familiarise yourself with the entire layout of the financial statements connected with manufacturing organisations.

You should now attempt review questions 14.16 to 14.20.

Chapter review

By now you should understand the following:

- How to construct a manufacturing account for a production-oriented business
- How to produce financial statements for a production-oriented business
- How to account for factory profit and the adjustments for unrealised profit that result from unsold inventory.

Handy hints

The following hints will help you avoid errors.

- Read any examination question carefully as the clues will be there for you to classify costs accurately. Look for the key words:
  - *Direct* – implies that the cost should appear within the prime cost
  - *Indirect* (or *Factory*) – implies that the cost should appear within indirect manufacturing costs
  - *Office* – implies a non-production expense that should appear in the statement of comprehensive income.
- Remember to adjust for prepayments and accruals before apportioning expenses between different sections of the financial statements.
- Factory profit needs adding back on in the statement of comprehensive income – this cancels the effect of marking up the cost of production.
- The provision for unrealised profit on unsold inventory should be treated like other provisions – it is the change in the size of the provision that appears in the statement of comprehensive income, but the full provision on the statement of financial position.

Key terms

Manufacturing account   Account used to calculate the cost of producing goods when a business manufactures goods rather than purchasing them from another firm

Prime cost   The total of all costs involved in physically manufacturing goods

Direct costs   Costs which are directly related to the level of output

Indirect costs   Costs which are indirectly related to the level of output

Direct labour   Labour costs directly related to the production of output – i.e. the cost incurred by those workers producing the output

Royalties   A cost incurred which is paid per unit of production which relates to the use of copyright or a patent owned by another business or person

Raw materials   The cost relating to the purchase of materials which are to be the base for the production of output – this will depend on the type of product

Cost of raw materials consumed   The cost incurred for a period relating to the purchase and use of raw materials and any associated costs involved in the acquisition of these materials

Work-in-progress   Goods which are partly finished and are at an intermediate stage in the production process

Indirect manufacturing costs   Costs related to the output of the business which vary in amount indirectly with the level of production

Factory profit   The difference between the costs of producing output and the anticipated costs of purchasing the same inventory from another business (the factory profit is often substituted by adding a mark-up to the costs of production)

Unrealised profit   The amount of factory profit included in each unit of unsold inventory of finished goods at the end of a period which must be eliminated from the value in the financial statements through the creation of a provision for unrealised profit on unsold inventory

REVIEW QUESTIONS

14.1   Classify the following costs by stating whether they will belong in the prime cost or indirect manufacturing costs section of the manufacturing account, or in the statement of comprehensive income.

- Purchases of raw materials
- Depreciation of machinery
- Carriage outwards
- Office insurance
- Factory foreman's wages
- Direct power
- Salaries of sales staff
- Machinery repairs
- Carriage inwards.

14.2   Classify the following costs by stating whether they will belong in the prime cost or indirect manufacturing costs section of the manufacturing account, or in the statement of comprehensive income.

- Wages of factory supervisors
- Returns inwards
- Returns outwards
- Depreciation of factory premises
- Wages of production staff
- Depreciation of delivery vehicles
- Wages of distribution staff
- Factory rent
- Royalties.

14.3 From the following data calculate the cost of raw materials consumed for the year ended 31 March 2006.

	£
Inventory of raw materials as at 1 April 2005	14,323
Inventory of raw materials as at 31 March 2006	11,543
Purchases of raw materials	64,544
Carriage inwards on raw materials	423
Returns outwards	565

14.4 From the following data calculate the cost of raw materials consumed.

	£
Opening inventory of raw materials	23,440
Closing inventory of raw materials	31,200
Purchases of raw materials	178,500
Carriage inwards	2,910
Carriage outwards	3,231
Returns inwards	1,765
Returns outwards	832

14.5 From the following data calculate the prime cost for the year to 31 May 2008.

	£
Inventory of raw materials as at 1 June 2007	5,645
Inventory of raw materials as at 31 May 2008	4,534
Purchases of raw materials	53,535
Direct wages	76,756
Royalties	3,143

14.6 From the following data calculate the prime cost for the year to 31 December 2009.

	£
Inventory of raw materials as at 1 Jan 2009	18,902
Inventory of raw materials as at 31 Dec 2009	23,134
Purchases of raw materials	154,535
Manufacturing wages	133,215
Royalties	9,898
Direct power	31,233

14.7 From the following data, calculate the value of the prime cost for the year ended 31 December 2007.

	£
Inventory of raw materials as at 1 Jan 2007	5,645
Inventory of raw materials as at 31 Dec 2007	6,577
Purchases of raw materials	54,322
Production wages	89,770
Direct expenses	13,443

Additional information:

(a) Production wages consisted of both direct and indirect wages. Direct wages account for 40% of the total production wages.
(b) Direct expenses accrued as at 31 December were £342.

14.8 For Jacoby Ltd, produce a manufacturing account for the year ended 30 June 2009 based on the following data.

	£
Inventory of raw materials as at 1 July 2008	23,212
Inventory of work-in-progress as at 1 July 2008	15,463
Purchases of raw materials	142,344
Direct power	7,868
Royalties	4,323
Supervisory wages	45,365
Factory rent	11,311
Machinery depreciation	8,600
Factory maintenance	7,863

Additional information:
Inventory as at 30 June 2009 was valued as follows:

Raw materials	£23,141
Work-in-progress	£15,767.

14.9 For Haynes Ltd, produce a manufacturing account for the year ended 31 March 2011 based on the following data.

	£
Inventory of raw materials as at 1 April 2010	8,960
Inventory of work-in-progress as at 1 April 2010	4,245
Purchases of raw materials	64,520
Carriage inwards on raw materials	453
Manufacturing wages	55,600
Royalties	3,255
Supervisory wages	11,210
Factory rent	6,546
Machinery depreciation	5,450
Factory maintenance	7,656

Additional information:
Inventory as at 31 March 2011 was valued as follows:

Raw materials	£8,678
Work-in-progress	£5,435.

14.10 For Barron Ltd, produce a manufacturing account for the year ended 31 October 2014 based on the following data.

	£
Inventory of raw materials as at 1 November 2013	16,560
Inventory of work-in-progress as at 1 November 2013	11,580
Purchases of raw materials	87,900
Direct wages	55,600
Royalties	3,255
Indirect wages	11,210
Factory rent	6,546
Heating and lighting	5,490
Machinery repairs	3,423

Additional information:

(a) Inventory as at 31 October 2014 was valued as follows:

Raw materials	£6,457
Work in progress	£9,780

(b) Machinery repairs owing as at 31 October 2014 were £211.

(c) Heating and lighting is split equally between the statement of comprehensive income and the manufacturing account.

14.11 For Martin Shine, produce a manufacturing account for the year ended 31 December 2016 based on the following data.

	£
Inventory of raw materials as at 1 January 2016	9,890
Inventory of work-in-progress as at 1 January 2016	12,340
Purchases of raw materials	78,500
Carriage inwards on raw materials	123
Returns outwards	1,123
Direct wages	67,675
Royalties	1,750
Indirect wages	39,500
Rent	7,650
Factory running costs	5,490
Equipment at cost	18,900
Provision for depreciation on equipment	5,200

Additional information:

1 Inventory as at 31 December 2016 was valued as follows:

Raw materials	£7,843
Work-in-progress	£14,233

2 Rent is to be apportioned between the factory and the office in the ratio of 3:1

3 Rent accrued as at 31 December 2016 was valued at £390

4 Factory running costs prepaid as at 31 December 2016 were valued at £190

5 Equipment is to be depreciated using reducing balance at a rate of 20%.

14.12 The following balances were taken from the trial balance of L Goburn as at 31 December 2007. From this data, construct the manufacturing account and statement of comprehensive income for the year ended 31 December 2007.

	£	£
Inventory as at 1 January 2007:		
Raw materials	8,989	
Work-in-progress	6,456	
Finished goods	13,134	
Manufacturing wages	87,990	
Purchases of raw materials	95,600	
Factory indirect wages	56,464	
Factory power	12,313	
Rent	8,680	
Machinery at cost	42,500	
Office equipment at cost	34,000	
Provision for depreciation: Machinery		5,433
Provision for depreciation: Office equipment		12,500
Carriage inwards	312	
Carriage outwards	453	
Sales		324,000
Royalties	3,123	
Administrative wages	53,455	
Insurance	3,214	

Additional information:

1 Inventory as at 31 December 2007:

    (a) Raw materials: £9,312
    (b) Work-in-progress: £5,420
    (c) Finished goods: £11,570

2 Manufacturing wages accrued at 31 December 2007: £1,250
3 Prepaid insurance at 31 December 2007: £444
4 Rent is to be apportioned between indirect overheads and the office in the proportion $^3/_4$:$^1/_4$
5 Insurance is to be apportioned between indirect overheads and the office in the proportion $^4/_5$:$^1/_5$
6 Machinery is to be depreciated at 10% on cost
7 Office equipment is to be depreciated at 20% using reducing balance.

14.13 The following balances were taken from the trial balance of S Stockley as at 31 December 2004. From this data, construct the manufacturing account and statement of comprehensive income for the year ended 31 December 2004.

	£	£
Inventory as at 1 January 2004:		
Raw materials	14,240	
Work-in-progress	17,331	
Finished goods	28,978	
Direct wages	145,300	
Indirect wages	89,000	
Factory maintenance	11,890	
Heating and lighting	6,786	
Returns outwards		1,213
Office salaries	43,500	
Sales		567,000
Purchases of raw materials	135,000	
Royalties	4,234	
Distribution costs	7,650	
Rent and rates	14,524	
Factory equipment	87,600	
Factory premises	250,000	
Provision for depreciation: Factory equipment		5,435

Additional information:

1 Inventory was valued at 31 December 2004 as follows:

Raw materials	£15,654
Work-in-progress	£16,544
Finished goods	£34,410

2 Rent and rates were to be allocated between the factory and the office equally
3 Heating and lighting was allocated between the factory and the office in the ratio of $^2/_3$:$^1/_3$
4 Rent and rates prepaid as at 31 December 2004 was £790
5 Heating and lighting prepaid as at 31 December 2004 was £432
6 Office salaries owing as at 31 December 2004 were £5,450
7 Factory equipment was to be depreciated at 25% using the reducing balance method
8 Factory premises were to be depreciated at 2% on cost.

14.14 The following data was extracted from the books of S Horsfield. Construct the manufacturing account for the year to 31 October 2014.

	£
Inventory of raw materials as at 1 November 2013	12,400
Inventory of work-in-progress as at 1 November 2013	8,950
Purchases of raw materials	89,500
Manufacturing wages	101,400
Royalties	5,200
Indirect factory expenses	11,240
Factory rent	17,800
Factory repair costs	2,375

Additional information:

1 Inventory as at 31 October 2014 was valued as follows:

Raw materials	£11,890
Work-in-progress	£9,850

2 Production costs are marked up at a uniform rate of 40%.

14.15 The following data was extracted from the books of H Thompson. Construct the manufacturing account for the year to 31 December 2010.

	£
Inventory of raw materials as at 1 January 2010	5,670
Inventory of work-in-progress as at 1 January 2010	4,230
Purchases of raw materials	54,356
Direct wages	67,670
Royalties	3,280
Indirect factory expenses	7,890
Factory rent and rates	4,234
Insurance	5,660
Indirect production wages	13,200
Factory rent and rates accrued	425

Additional information:

1 Inventory as at 31 December 2010 were valued as follows:

Raw materials	£6,547
Work-in-progress	£3,120

2 Insurance was assumed to split between production and non-production expenses equally
3 Factory rent and rates accrued as at 31 December 2010 was £425
4 Factory profit is calculated as 20% of total production costs.

14.16 The following data was available for Hyde Ltd:

	£
Inventory of finished goods as at 1 January 2010	12,500
Inventory of finished goods as at 31 December 2010	14,800

It is company policy to transfer goods from the manufacturing account to the statement of comprehensive income at cost plus 25%.

The provision for unrealised profit on unsold inventory as at 1 January 2010 amounted to £2,500.
Produce the ledger account for provision for unrealised profit on unsold inventory.

14.17 The following data was available for Sax Ltd:

	£
Inventory of finished goods as at 1 April 2012	24,640
Inventory of finished goods as at 31 March 2013	22,890

It is company policy to transfer goods from the manufacturing account to the statement of comprehensive income at cost plus 40%.

The provision for unrealised profit on unsold inventory as at 1 April 2012 amounted to £7,040.
Produce the ledger account for provision for unrealised profit on unsold inventory.

14.18   The following data is available for Bellwood Ltd:

	£
Inventory of finished goods as at 1 January 2006	5,250
Inventory of finished goods as at 31 December 2006	7,500

It is company policy to transfer goods from the manufacturing account to the statement of comprehensive income at cost plus 20%.

Produce the ledger account for provision for unrealised profit on unsold inventory.

14.19   The following balances were taken from the trial balance of G Northfield as at 31 December 2004. From this data, construct the manufacturing account and statement of comprehensive income for the year ended 31 December 2014.

	£	£
Inventory as at 1 April 2013:		
Raw materials	11,540	
Work-in-progress	7,890	
Finished goods	15,680	
Manufacturing wages	99,600	
Purchases of raw materials	86,500	
Indirect wages	45,680	
Factory power	15,340	
Heating and lighting	21,340	
Machinery at cost	89,000	
Equipment at cost	34,000	
Provision for depreciation: Machinery		12,240
Provision for depreciation: Equipment		18,500
Sales		325,000
Royalties	5,600	
Administrative wages	18,100	
Rent and rates	10,400	
Provision for unrealised profits on unsold inventory		3,136

Additional information:

1 Inventory as at 31 March 2014 was valued as follows:

Raw materials	£9,312
Work-in-progress	£5,420
Finished goods	£16,500

2 Factory profit is calculated as 25% of production costs.
3 As at 31 March 2014:

Indirect wages accrued were £1,250
Rent and rates prepaid were £420

4 Heating and lighting was apportioned to the factory and the office in the ratio of 2:1
5 Rent and rates was apportioned to the factory and the office in the ratio of 3:2
6 Non-current assets were to be depreciated as follows:

Machinery: 15% on cost
Equipment: 20% using reducing balance.

14.20 The following balances were taken from the trial balance of F Dawood as at 31 December 2005. From this data, construct the manufacturing account and statement of comprehensive income for the year ended 31 December 2005.

	£	£
Inventory as at 1 January 2005:		
Work-in-progress	16,782	
Finished goods	24,560	
Prime cost	195,000	
Factory power	13,450	
Factory wages	99,000	
Factory repairs	8,940	
Factory plant at cost	156,000	
Office fixtures at cost	54,000	
Administration expenses	9,100	
Sales		500,000
Distribution costs	13,500	
Insurance	8,700	
Provision for unrealised profits on unsold inventory		4,912
Provision for depreciation: Factory plant		18,900
Provision for depreciation: Office fixtures		5,600

Additional information:

1 Inventory as at 31 December 2005 was valued as follows:

Work-in-progress	£17,890
Finished goods	£22,450

2 Factory profit is calculated as 25% of production costs
3 As at 31 December 2005:

Factory wages accrued were £3,242
Insurance accrued was £580

4 Insurance was apportioned to the factory and the office in the ratio of 4:1
5 Non-current assets were to be depreciated using the reducing balance method as follows:

a Factory plant: 20%
b Office fixtures: 10%

CHAPTER 15

Limited companies

Learning objectives

By the end of this chapter you should be able to:

● Distinguish between types of limited company
● Explain the different types of share that can be issued by a company
● Calculate the dividends paid out on shares issued
● Construct the financial statements for a limited company.

Introduction

Sole traders and partnerships are, as business organisations, in effect, indistinguishable from the people who own and work for these businesses. They are known as **unincorporated** businesses. Limited companies are businesses that exist separately from the owners of the businesses. They are incorporated into businesses which are separate legal entities – which mean that they continue independently of the owners of the company.

The term 'limited' in the title **'limited company'** refers to the liability of each shareholder (shareholders being the owners of the company) being limited. The term **limited liability** means that, in the event of the company failing, each shareholder can only lose their original investment into the company – they can be forced to pay no more than this amount. This is different from sole traders and partnerships where the owners of these organisations can be forced to use personal possessions to settle any business debt.

Types of limited company

In the UK, there are two types of limited company – the **public limited company** (abbreviated as '**plc**') and the **private limited company** (abbreviated as '**Ltd**'). These companies are regulated by the Companies Acts of 1985, 1989 and 2006.

Types of limited company in the UK	
Public limited company	Known as a 'Plc'
Private limited company	Known as a 'Ltd'

As part of setting up each company will produce two documents: a Memorandum of Association, and Articles of Association.

Memorandum of Association

This document will set out the following details:

(a) The name of the company
(b) The size (in £s) of the **authorised share capital** of the company
(c) The activities of the company (this can be left in fairly general terms such as a 'general commercial company')
(d) In which country (England, Scotland or Wales) the company is registered
(e) A statement saying the liability of the members of the company is limited.

(The process of registering a company in Northern Ireland differs from the process for companies registering in England, Scotland or Wales.)

Articles of Association

This sets out the internal workings of the company. For example, it may outline the powers of the directors of the company.

Differences between public and private limited companies

Public limited companies

A public limited company will have the following features:

● Share capital of at least £50,000
● Two or more shareholders
● Two or more directors.

Public limited companies can raise share capital by selling shares to the general public. Shares can be sold on the stock market but it is not necessary for companies to do so. A common misconception is that all public limited companies are quoted companies. This is not the case as public limited companies do not have to have their shares quoted on the stock market.

Private limited companies

A private limited company has no minimum level of share capital and can also operate with only one shareholder and one director (who can be the same person as the shareholder). A key difference is that the shares in a private limited company cannot be bought by the general public. Shares in a private limited company are only made available to others by agreement of all existing shareholders.

It is possible for a private limited company to convert into a public limited company. However, it is harder to convert from public to private. This is because public limited companies are likely to have large numbers of individual shareholders who may not be willing to sell their shares 'back'.

In the UK there are many more private limited companies than public limited companies. However, it is more likely that we will have heard of the public limited companies as these are generally larger and more likely to be higher profile companies.

Shares and shareholders

As stated earlier the owners of limited companies are known as **shareholders**. Each shareholder owns a portion of the company. The more shares a shareholder owns, the greater portion of the company that shareholder owns. Ownership of shares gives the shareholder voting rights at the **AGM (Annual General Meeting)** of the company. Those with higher shareholdings gain more voting rights, meaning they will have greater influence over business decisions.

Shareholders do not usually run the business. The running of the company is undertaken by the directors of the business. **Directors** are elected by shareholders to run the company on behalf of the shareholders. The board of directors decides, with the shareholders' agreement, how the company is to be run. The board of directors is led by the chairperson.

- **Authorised share capital** is the maximum amount of share capital that can be issued by the company. This share capital will be bought in varying quantities by those who wish to invest in the company.
- **Issued share capital** is the amount of capital that the company has actually sold to shareholders. This amount represents the capital invested into the company and will be part of the calculations on the statement of financial position.

The main motivation for buying shares in a company is to gain returns in the form of either **capital gains** (whereby shares are sold at a later date for a higher value) or **dividends** (a portion of the profits). Once shares have been issued by a company it is unlikely that the shares will ever be redeemed (paid back) and as a result the shares issued represent the permanent capital of the company (even if the identity of the shareholders will change on a regular basis).

There are two types of shares that can be issued by a company. These are **ordinary shares** and **preference shares**. The differences between the two types of shares is summarised in the following table.

Ordinary shares	Preference shares
Dividends are not guaranteed	Dividends are (normally) guaranteed*
Shareholder gains voting rights	Shareholder doesn't gain voting rights

* Whether the preference shares are cumulative or non-cumulative will determine whether a dividend is given in full in the year it is due or whether it is carried forward and added to the next year's dividend if it cannot be paid in any one year.

The value of the share

The value of each share issued is known as the **nominal value** or **face value**. Issuing shares at their face value is also known as issuing them at **par**. This is the price at which the share was sold when it was originally issued by the company. (In reality shares are rarely issued at the face value. They are likely to be issued for a value in excess of their face value. This is explained later in this chapter in the section covering share premium.) The nominal value of a share is used for the calculation of dividends. Occasionally, shares may be issued by a company for a price in excess of the face value – where they are issued at a premium. This is dealt with later in this chapter in the section on reserves.

The current value of each share is known as the **market value**. This represents what it would cost to buy each individual share currently on the second-hand market (known as the stock market). The sale of shares on the stock market does not directly affect the company, but can affect the company in other ways. For example, a fall in the market value of a company's shares could indicate that investors do not view the future of the company positively. Factors which influence the market value of share prices would include:

● Expectations of future profits of the company
● Economic factors (e.g. GDP forecasts, likely changes in interest rates)
● The price of other investments (e.g. bonds and other securities).

To see which direction share prices are moving in general, there are a number of financial indicators. For example, the FTSE 100 index tracks the daily share prices of the leading 100 limited companies listed on the UK stock market.

Dividends

As already stated, a reward for owning shares in a company is the possibility that the shareholder will receive dividends. These are a portion of the company's profits that are paid out to shareholders and are paid per share owned, meaning that the dividend paid to each shareholder will rise as the size of the shareholding rises.

The dividends will be paid out of the year's profits. However, it is possible for a company to pay more in dividends than the current year's profits if it so wishes. This will draw on previous retained earnings.

Often dividends are paid in multiple instalments. Dividends paid out earlier in the financial year are known as **interim dividends**.

Example 15.1

Stebbings Ltd has the following share capital:

Authorised share capital:

● 200,000 ordinary shares of £1 each
● 100,000 5% preference shares of 50p each

Issued share capital:

● 100,000 ordinary shares of £1 each
● 50,000 5% preference shares of 50p each.

The company decides to pay a dividend of 8p per ordinary share. It also decides to pay the preference dividend in full. It is important to remember that the calculations for dividends are based on the *issued* share capital and not the authorised share capital.

The ordinary dividend paid by the company will be $100,000 \times 8p = £8,000$. The preference dividend paid will be $5\% \times 50p \times 50,000 = £1,250$.

You should now attempt review questions 15.1 to 15.4.

Debentures

In addition to the share capital, a company can raise further funds through the issue of debentures. These are a form of long-term borrowing issued by the company.

The company will decide how much money it wishes to raise from the debenture issue which will then be divided up into smaller 'packets' of debt which are sold individually as debenture certificates to those investors who wish to lend the company money. Each debenture certificate will pay the holder a guaranteed rate of interest each year which would be indicated on the certificate.

A *redemption date* will also be shown on the debenture certificate. At this date, the holder of the debenture will be repaid by the company. For example, if we see an item to be included in the company accounts reading '7% 2014 Debentures' then we would read this as meaning that the interest of 7% was paid to debenture holders each year and that the face value of the debentures would be repaid in full in the year 2014.

A debenture can be secured against the value of the company's assets. This means that, in the case of business failure, the holders of the debentures may be entitled to some of the revenue raised by selling the business assets. However, debentures can also be unsecured, making them a riskier investment.

Financial statements of limited companies

In this textbook we will only consider the internal accounts of the limited company. The external accounts are for publication and must comply with prescribed layouts set out by accounting standards and regulatory bodies. Although many accounting standards are relevant to the financial statements of limited companies, it is IAS 1 that sets out most of the prescribed formats.

Published accounts are expected to conform to guidelines set by accounting standards and regulations set out in the Companies Acts. Internal accounts – those used by user groups within the company – do not have to comply with required guidelines in the same way. This chapter will focus on the presentation of the internal accounts of the limited company.

One of the main differences between the financial statements of the sole trader and those of the company is that companies have a separate section called 'statement of changes in equity' which deals with the allocation of the company profits. This section is dealt with in more detail later.

The following example shows how the financial statements prepared for a limited company would appear.

Example 15.2

The following data relates to the accounts of Egan Ltd for the year ended 31 December 2012:

	£
Authorised ordinary share capital (£1 shares)	400,000
Authorised 5% preference share capital (5% 50p shares)	200,000
Issued ordinary share capital (£1 shares)	250,000
Issued 5% preference share capital (50p shares)	50,000
Retained earnings	7,700
Gross profit	70,000
Administration costs	20,500
Distribution costs	14,000
Debenture interest	4,800
Ordinary dividends paid	7,900
Preference dividends paid	2,500
Directors' remuneration	19,800
Non-current assets at cost	400,000
Provision for depreciation	38,000
Trade receivables	14,500
Trade payables	8,900
Closing inventories	22,600
Cash and cash equivalents	18,000
8% 2018 debentures	60,000

Additional information:

1 Depreciation is to be provided on non-current assets on the basis of 10% on cost (i.e. the straight line method is used).
2 A provision for tax on profits is made of £4,500.

Statement of comprehensive income

The statement of comprehensive income would appear as follows:

Egan Ltd
Statement of comprehensive income for the year ended 31 December 2012

	£	£
Gross profit		70,000
Less Expenses		
Administration costs	20,500	
Distribution costs	14,000	
Debenture interest	4,800	
Directors' remuneration	19,800	59,100
Profit before tax		10,900
Taxation		4,500
Profit for the year		6,400

Directors' remuneration is the amount paid to the directors of the company – this is often listed as separate from the other expenses.

Debenture interest is based on the fixed interest charge for the non-current liabilities of debentures. Some companies will calculate '**profit on operations**' which is, in effect, profit before interest charges are made.

The **profit for the year** refers to the profit after all expenses are deducted. This is equivalent to net profit.

Statement of changes in equity

For limited companies, there is a further statement once the profit for the year is calculated. This is known as the **statement of changes in equity**. This deals with the allocation of profit and any transfers to and from revenue reserves. This is explored in more detail later in this chapter in the section on reserves.

Statement of changes in equity for the year ended 31 December 2012

Retained earnings		£
Balance at start of year		7,700
Profit for the year		6,400
		14,100
Dividends paid:		
Ordinary dividends paid	7,900	
Preference dividends paid	2,500	10,400
Balance at end of year		3,700

Statement of financial position

The statement of financial position of a limited company is very similar to that of a sole trader.

The equity section outlines the share capital of the company as well as any capital and revenue reserves that the company has generated. Other than as a comparison with the capital balance, there is no equivalent to this in the sole trader's statement.

Egan Ltd
Statement of financial position as at 31 December 2012

	Cost £	Depreciation £	Net book value £
Non-current assets	400,000	78,000	322,000
Current assets			
Inventory		22,600	
Trade receivables		14,500	
Cash and cash equivalents		18,000	
		55,100	
Current liabilities			
Trade payables		8,900	
Tax owing		4,500	
		13,400	
Working capital			41,700
			363,700
Non-current liabilities			
8% debentures			60,000
NET ASSETS			303,700
Equity			
Authorised share capital			
Ordinary share capital (£1 shares)			400,000
5% preference share capital (50p shares)			200,000
			600,000
Issued share capital			
Ordinary share capital (£1 shares)			250,000
5% preference share capital (50p shares)			50,000
Revenue reserve			
Retained earnings			3,700
TOTAL EQUITY			303,700

Note the following on the above statement:

1 The tax owing represents the liability for tax which was based on the profit for the year. This will remain a liability until it is paid.
2 Authorised share capital can appear on the internal statement of financial position (though it equally may not appear) even though it is the issued share capital which 'counts' as far as being included in the calculations for equity. As a guide, it would not normally be expected that you include the authorised share capital on any internal statements of financial position.

Relationship between the statements

The statement of changes in equity shows how the profit for the business is allocated. This section provides a link between the statement of comprehensive income and the statement of financial position.

Any profits that have not been distributed as dividends will be kept within the business as 'retained earnings'. The retained earnings add to the resources used within the business and further profits earned over time (e.g. from the current year) will be added to this figure. The nature of retained earnings is explored in the following section.

It is often the case that the board of directors will propose to pay a dividend. It may seem that if we apply the accruals concept then these proposed dividends should appear as a deduction against the profit in the statement of changes of equity and as a current liability. However, given that proposed dividends have to be confirmed at the AGM it is not certain that the proposed dividends will become a future liability of the company. As a result, the proposed dividends could appear as a footnote to the statement of changes in equity.

You should now attempt review questions 15.5 to 15.7.

Reserves

When a sole trader earns profits, these will be added on to the capital figure which will (as long as the business remains profitable) increase, over time, the size of the capital. With a limited company, this does not happen in the same way.

Any profits retained within the firm are kept in **reserves**, which are listed alongside the share capital but are separate to the share capital. Reserves are part of the **equity** (issued share capital plus the total of the reserves). Unfortunately, the term reserve tends to conjure up images of amounts of money being set aside within the firm that can be used in the same way the money in the bank can be used. It is important to drop this idea as soon as is possible – reserves on the statement of financial position do not mean that there is any more cash set aside within the firm as a reserve. The money available to the firm will always be the cash at hand and the cash at bank figure.

In actual fact, there are two types of reserves that exist in the accounts of limited companies – these are **revenue reserves** and **capital reserves**.

Revenue reserves

These reserves are created out of the profits earned by the firm over a period of time. Once tax has been deducted, the firm can choose to allocate the remainder as dividends, or to retain this within the firm. Remaining profit is known as the retained earnings (this is a revenue reserve). However, the firm may also decide to transfer money to another designated reserve. This would then appear as a subtraction in the statement of changes in equity.

The name of a revenue reserve is not necessarily an indicator of why the profits have been transferred into this reserve. For example, if the firm transfers profits into a reserve called the '*fixed asset replacement reserve*', then this may mean that the firm would like to use some of its profits to replace the fixed assets. However, this is not necessarily the case. Profits are earned over a period of time and therefore they may be tied up in other assets, in stocks or in other investments. The name of the revenue reserve does not commit the firm to any type of actions. As a result, most revenue reserves are simply known as a '*general reserve*'.

Example 15.3

Look at the extracts from the statements of changes in equity for two companies. Both have profits for the year of £30,000 and both pay dividends of £10,000. Company A transfers some of the profits to the general reserve, but Company B does not.

	Company A		Company B	
	£	£	£	£
Profit for the year (after tax)		30,000		30,000
Less dividends	10,000		10,000	
Transfer to general reserve	5,000	15,000	0	10,000
Retained earnings		15,000		20,000

On the statements of financial position of these two companies would appear the following balances for the reserves:

	Company A	Company B
	£	£
General reserve	5,000	0
Retained earnings	15,000	20,000
	20,000	20,000

Notice that the total of the reserves is exactly the same – we are merely taking from one reserve and adding it to another reserve. Therefore transferring to other revenue reserves makes no difference to the overall size of the revenue reserves.

Capital reserves

Capital reserves do not arise out of profits, which means that they cannot be used for distribution as dividends. They arise largely out of changes involving the statement of financial position of the firm. There are two main capital reserves that you are likely to come across: the **revaluation reserve** and the **share premium account** (also a reserve).

Revaluation reserve

Non-current assets (with the exception of freehold land) should normally be depreciated annually. Although property does lose value it is possible that its value will increase significantly over a period of time. If the value of any non-current asset becomes significantly greater than the statement of financial position value then it is allowable for a firm to revalue – increase the value of – this asset. This requires a simple upwards adjustment to the asset's value on the statement of financial position.

However, if we simply increase the value of any non-current asset then the statement of financial position would no longer balance. To remedy this, we simply create a 'revaluation reserve' (or add to one if one already exists) by adding the amount equal to the increase in the value of the asset (i.e. both sections of the statement of financial position increase by the same amount – thus permitting the statement of financial position to balance).

Example 15.4

Freehold property is currently valued at £75,000 but the directors have decided to increase the value of the property on the statement of financial position to £250,000.

How would this affect the statement of financial position?

The new statement of financial position would have the new value for the property at £250,000. The increase in the value is £250,000 – £75,000 = £175,000.

The revaluation reserve would either be created or be added to with the amount of £175,000 – enabling the statement of financial position to balance.

Effect on statement of financial position	
Change in net assets	**Change in equity**
Non-current assets increase by £175,000	Revaluation reserve increases by £175,000

Share premium account

When limited companies issue shares, they may not always issue them all in one go. They may issue their shares in a number of stages. If this is the case, shares issued at a later date will still be issued at the same face (nominal) value as the shares that were originally issued. However, if the firm has been historically successful then the market value of the firm's shares is likely to be higher than the face value of the shares.

The shares issued later can be issued at a *premium*. This means that the price paid for these shares will be closer to their current market value. However, the face value of these shares will still be as originally set out in the memorandum of association. This means that the firm will receive more in cash than is indicated by the increase in the share capital (the value of the share capital is always based on the face value of the shares). This surplus money that is being received will be entered into the share premium account, which is a capital reserve.

Example 15.5

A firm issues 100,000 50p ordinary shares at a premium of 25p. How would this affect the statement of financial position?

Assuming the share issue is fully subscribed and paid for, the firm will be selling each share for 75p (50p face value plus 25p premium). Therefore, the firm will receive 75p × 100,000 and the cash at bank figure will increase by £75,000. The ordinary share capital will increase by the 50p (face value) × 100,000 = £50,000.

The extra £25,000 that is the money received because of the premium will be placed in the share premium account – a capital reserve which appears alongside the capital and reserves section of the statement of financial position. Thus, the statement of financial position will still balance.

You should now attempt review questions 15.8 to 15.13.

Example 15.6

The following example deals with the financial statements of a limited company and involves the transfer to revenue reserves.

Legood Ltd
Trial balance as at 31 December 2015

	£	£
Issued ordinary share capital (£1 shares)		200,000
Land and buildings	270,000	
Machinery	84,000	
Sales revenue		220,110
Purchases	121,333	
Inventory as at 1 January 2015	25,659	
Wages and salaries	32,322	
Administration and distribution	9,997	
Directors' remuneration	12,000	
Trade receivables and payables	19,824	16,465
Cash and cash equivalents	4,974	
Provision for depreciation on land and buildings		15,200
Provision for depreciation on machinery		8,000
Dividends paid	24,500	
General reserve		20,000
Share premium account		30,000
Revaluation reserve		60,000
Retained earnings		34,834
	604,609	604,609

Additional information:

1 Inventory as at 31 December 2015 was valued at £25,435
2 Depreciation is to be provided as follows:

   (a) Land and buildings: 1% on cost
   (b) Machinery: 10% using reducing balance

3 A provision for corporation tax was to be made for £7,647
4 A transfer of £5,000 was to be made to the general reserve.

Legood plc
Statement of comprehensive income for year ended 31 December 2015

	£	£
Sales		220,110
Less cost of goods sold:		
Opening inventory	25,659	
Add Purchases	121,333	
	146,992	
Less Closing inventory	25,435	121,557
Gross profit		98,553
Less Expenses		
Wages and salaries	32,322	
Administration and distribution	9,997	
Depreciation on property	2,700	
Depreciation on plant and equipment	7,600	
Directors' remuneration	12,000	64,619
Profit before tax		33,934
Tax		7,647
Profit for year		26,287

Legood plc
Statement of changes in equity for year ended 31 December 2015

Retained earnings		
Balance at start of year		34,834
Add Profit for year		26,287
		61,121
Less Dividends paid	24,500	
Less Transfer to general reserve	5,000	29,500
Balance at end of year		31,621

Legood plc
Statement of financial position as at 31 December 2015

	£	£	£
Non-current assets			
Land and buildings	270,000	17,900	252,100
Machinery	84,000	15,600	68,400
	354,000	33,500	320,500
Current assets			
Inventory		25,435	
Trade receivables		19,824	
Cash and cash equivalents		4,974	
		50,233	
Current liabilities			
Trade payables		16,465	
Tax owing		7,647	
		24,112	
Working capital			26,121
NET ASSETS			346,621
Equity			
Ordinary share capital			200,000
Capital reserves			
Share premium account			30,000
Revaluation reserve			60,000
Revenue reserves			
Retained earnings			31,621
General reserve			25,000
EQUITY			346,621

You should now attempt review questions 15.14 to 15.17.

Chapter review

By now you should understand the following:

- The difference between a sole trader and a company
- The difference between a public and private limited company
- The types of shares that a company can issue
- How to calculate the dividends for a company
- The nature of debentures
- How to construct the financial statements for a limited company
- What reserves are and how these feature in the accounts of a company
- The differences between revenue and capital reserves.

Relevant accounting standards

Most standards are relevant – check your course content.

Handy hints

The following hints will help you avoid errors.

- Dividends are paid on the face value, not the market value.
- Be careful when dealing with shares with a face value that is not £1 – this can make calculating the dividends more complicated.
- When transferring amounts to revenue reserves, ensure that the statement of financial position includes both the transferred amount and any existing reserve from the trial balance.
- If shares are issued at a premium, remember to separate out the share premium from the value of share capital on the statement of financial position.
- For the revaluation reserve, only include the amount the asset has increased by.

Key terms

Public limited company (plc)   A limited company whose shares are available to the general public

Private limited company (Ltd)   A limited company whose shares are not available to the general public

Shareholders   Those who own a limited company – each shareholder has invested a certain amount in the business to acquire a share of the business

Shares   The value of a company's capital divided up into smaller shares of this capital which can be acquired by investors

AGM   Annual general meeting, held by law to decide company policy and to elect the directors of the company

Directors   Those elected to run a company on behalf of the shareholders; normally directors are elected at the AGM

Authorised share capital   The maximum amount of share capital that can be raised by a company – normally set out in the memorandum of association

Issued share capital   The actual amount of share capital that has been raised by a company

Ordinary shares   The most common type of share: vote-carrying shares that have a variable non-guaranteed dividend

Preference shares   Shares which are not normally vote-carrying but have a fixed dividend which is usually expressed as a percentage of the face value of the share

Nominal value (face value)   The face value of a share used for calculation of dividends: normally, but not always, the price at which the share is originally sold by the company

Market value   What shares are worth at the point at which they are sold to a new investor

Dividends   A share of the profits given to shareholders in proportion to the size of their shareholdings

Interim dividends   Dividends which are paid out during the year (often half-yearly)

Debentures   Long-term borrowing by a company, held as certificates which can be traded by investors; the debentures pay a fixed rate of interest until the redemption date at which the original value of the debenture is repaid by the company

Equity   The value of issued capital and any reserves

Directors' remuneration   Fees paid to the directors for their services – treated as a business expense

Profit on operations   Profit after expenses but before interest charges have been deducted

Profit for the year   Profit after all other expenses have been deducted (otherwise known as net profit)

Capital gains   Selling an asset (e.g. shares) for a higher amount than the asset was purchased for – i.e. for a profit

Reserves   Increases in a company's capital that are either due to retained earnings or to changes in the capital structure of the company

Revenue reserves   Reserves created out of profits retained within the company which can be used for the distribution of dividends

Capital reserves   Reserves which cannot be used for distribution of dividends; capital reserves are created out of changes in the capital structure of the company

Retained earnings   Profits for the year which are not distributed as dividends and are kept for reinvestment in the business

Share premium account   The capital reserve used when shares are issued at a price which is in excess of their nominal value

Revaluation reserve   The capital reserve which is created when non-current assets are revalued in an upwards direction

Statement of changes in equity   The section of the financial statements of a company which deals with how profits are to be allocated within the company

REVIEW QUESTIONS

15.1   The following relates to the capital of Nisanci plc:

- Authorised share capital: 500,000 £1 ordinary shares
- Issued share capital: 350,000 £1 ordinary shares

If a dividend of 4.5p per share is paid, calculate the value of this dividend.

15.2   The following relates to the capital of Norfolk Ltd:

- Authorised share capital: 400,000 50p ordinary shares
- Issued share capital: 250,000 50p ordinary shares

If a dividend of 2.5p per share is paid, calculate the value of this dividend.

15.3   The following relates to the capital of Adams Ltd:

Issued share capital:

- 200,000 £1 ordinary shares
- 120,000 4% £1 preference shares

If a dividend of 3.5 pence per share is paid in full as well as the preference dividend, then calculate the total dividend paid by Adams Ltd.

15.4 The issued share capital of Dickenson plc is as follows:

- 25p Ordinary shares: £300,000
- 8% 50p Preference shares: £100,000

The preference dividend was paid in full and an ordinary dividend of 4p per share was paid. Calculate the amount paid out in dividends.

15.5 The following trial balance relates to the trading activities of Billingham Ltd. From this data and the additional information provided you are to construct a set of financial statements.

Billingham Ltd
Trial balance as at 31 March 2017

	£	£
Issued ordinary share capital (£1 shares)		150,000
Issued preference shares (£1 shares)		40,000
Retained earnings		11,450
Land	190,000	
Equipment	45,000	
Sales revenue		107,000
Purchases	45,000	
Opening inventory	8,950	
Wages and salaries	17,340	
Overheads	9,925	
Directors' remuneration	7,400	
Debentures		20,000
Debenture interest	2,000	
Trade receivables and payables	8,110	6,780
Cash and cash equivalents	3,305	
Provision for depreciation of equipment		4,800
Dividends (ordinary and preference) paid	3,000	
	340,030	340,030

Additional information:

1 Inventory at 31 March 2017 was £11,980
2 Tax due for the year was £7,650
3 Depreciation is provided on equipment at 10% using the straight line method.

15.6 The following trial balance was extracted for Smithson plc as at 31 December 2017:

Smithson plc
Trial balance as at 31 Dec 2017

	£	£
Issued ordinary share capital (50p shares)		200,000
Retained earnings		36,534
Property	190,000	
Plant and equipment	65,000	
Sales revenue		99,043
Purchases	56,456	
Inventory as at 1 January 2017	11,221	
Distribution costs	8,750	
Administration costs	5,784	
Directors' remuneration	6,456	
Trade receivables and payables	9,997	5,344
Cash and cash equivalents	4,242	
Provision for depreciation on property		18,000
Provision for depreciation on plant and equipment		8,855
Dividends paid	9,870	
	367,776	367,776

Additional information:

1 Inventory at 31 Dec 2017: £12,123
2 Tax charge for the year: £2,123
3 Depreciation is to be provided for as follows:

Property: 2% on cost
Plant and equipment: 10% on cost.

From the above data, construct the financial statements for Smithson plc.

15.7 The following trial balance was extracted at the year-end for Hynes plc.

Hynes plc
Trial balance as at 30 June 2014

	£	£
Issued ordinary share capital (£1 shares)		200,000
Retained earnings		36,534
Land and buildings	260,000	
Equipment and machinery	76,000	
Sales revenue		143,434
Purchases	99,788	
Opening inventory	8,548	
Salaries	8,750	
Overhead costs		
Administration costs	5,784	
Directors' remuneration	6,456	
Debentures		80,000
Debenture interest	3,200	
Trade receivables and payables	13,212	7,657
Cash and cash equivalents	4,242	
Provision for depreciation on land and buildings		18,000
Provision for depreciation on equipment and machinery		8,855
Dividends paid	8,500	
	494,480	494,480

Additional information:

1 Inventory as at 30 June 2014: £11,901
2 Depreciation is to be provided as follows:

Land and buildings: 1% on cost
Equipment and machinery: 10% using reducing balance

3 Tax due for the year amounted to £1,200
4 Debenture interest is paid in two instalments but the second payment was overdue at the end of the year.

15.8 The following data relates to the financial statements of Emery Ltd:

● Issued share capital: 200,000 £1 ordinary shares
● Profit for the year: £6,570
● Retained earnings at the start of the current year: £18,560.

If a dividend of 7p per share is paid, then show the statement of changes in equity.

15.9 The issued share capital of Rahman Ltd was as follows:

● 1,000,000 £1 ordinary shares
● 300,000 £1 7% preference shares.

Profits for the year were £64,140 and the retained earnings from the last statement of financial position were £87,554. The preference dividends were paid in full and the directors proposed and paid an ordinary dividend of 4p per share.
Construct the statement of changes in equity.

15.10 The following information relates to McCauley plc:

- Issued ordinary share capital: 500,000 50p shares
- Issued preference share capital: 50,000 6% £1 shares.

Profits for the year were £18,543 and retained earnings from the previous year's statement of financial position were £42,343. Dividends of 2p per share were paid and the preference dividend was paid in full.

  Construct the statement of changes in equity.

15.11 Hopgood plc issues 500,000 ordinary shares of 50p each at a 10p premium. The issue is fully subscribed and paid for.

  Show the journal entries required to record this share issue.

15.12 Woodbridge plc issues the following shares:

- 100,000 £1.50 ordinary shares at a 25p premium
- 50,000 £2 preference shares at face value.

  Show the journal entries required to record this share issue.

15.13 Ramshaw plc issues 2,000,000 25p ordinary shares at a premium of 5p per share. It also decides to revalue property originally valued at £700,000 to £1m.

  Show the journal entries required to record this share issue and revaluation.

15.14 From the following trial balance, construct the financial statements for Boothroyd Ltd for the year ended 31 December 2011.

Boothroyd Ltd
Trial balance as at 31 December 2011

	£	£
£2 ordinary shares		200,000
5% £1 preference shares		60,000
Retained earnings		40,003
Non-current assets	390,000	
Sales revenue		400,000
Purchases	260,000	
Opening inventory	35,600	
Distribution costs	23,000	
Administration costs	17,600	
Directors' remuneration	13,500	
Trade receivables and payables	25,400	21,900
Cash and cash equivalents	51,400	
Provision for depreciation on non-current assets		8,997
8% debentures		80,000
Share premium account		20,000
Debenture interest	6,400	
Ordinary dividends paid	5,000	
Preference dividends paid	3,000	
	830,900	830,900

Additional information:

1 Depreciation is to be provided on non-current assets at 10% on cost
2 Inventory as at 31 December 2017 was £27,880
3 Tax due for the year was £13,400.

15.15 The following statement of financial position has been drawn up for the directors of Cousins Ltd.

Cousins Ltd
Statement of financial position as at 31 March 2014

	£	£	£
Non-current assets			
Freehold land	175,000	–	175,000
Property	85,000	11,000	74,000
Equipment	18,000	12,400	5,600
	278,000	23,400	254,600
Current assets			
Inventory		17,455	
Trade receivables		11,899	
Cash and cash equivalents		5,345	
		34,699	
Current liabilities			
Trade payables		7,799	
Tax owing		12,500	
		20,299	
Working capital			14,400
			269,000
Non-current liabilities			
Debentures			50,000
NET ASSETS			219,000
Equity			
Ordinary share capital (50p shares)			150,000
Preference share capital (£1 shares)			50,000
Revenue reserves			
Retained earnings			19,000
EQUITY			219,000

However, it was drawn up before the following changes were implemented:

1 Property was to be revalued at £200,000
2 A further 50,000 £1 ordinary shares were issued at face value.

Based on this new information, redraft the statement of financial position.

15.16 The following statement of financial position has been drawn up for the directors of Gaurav plc as at 31 March 2018.

Gaurav plc
Statement of financial position as at 31 March 2018

	£	£	£
Non-current assets			
Freehold land	625,000	–	625,000
Plant and equipment	298,500	56,800	241,700
	923,500	56,800	866,700
Current assets			
Inventory		61,978	
Trade receivables		32,323	
		94,301	
Current liabilities			
Trade payables		28,423	
Tax owing		11,800	
Bank balance		13,233	
		53,456	
Working capital			40,845
			907,545
Non-current liabilities			
Debentures			90,000
NET ASSETS			817,545
Equity			
Ordinary share capital (£1 shares)			600,000
Preference share capital (50p shares)			100,000
Capital reserves			
Share premium account			50,000
Revenue reserves			
Retained earnings			67,545
EQUITY			817,545

However, the following changes were made after the first draft of the balance sheet was drawn up:

1 An issue of 100,000 ordinary shares was made at a premium of £1
2 Money from the successful share issue was used as follows:

   (a) The debenture was redeemed in full
   (b) The tax owing was paid
   (c) The bank overdraft was cleared

3 Freehold land was revalued to £900,000.

Redraft the statement of financial position after taking into account the above changes.

15.17 The following trial balance relates to the trading activities of Falhstrom Ltd. From this data and the additional information provided you are to construct a set of financial statements.

Falhstrom Ltd
Trial balance as at 31 December 2019

	£	£
Issued ordinary share capital (£1 shares)		250,000
Issued preference shares (£1 shares)		50,000
Retained earnings		36,313
Freehold land	320,000	
Other non-current assets	195,000	
Sales revenue		312,000
Purchases	165,090	
Opening inventory	29,808	
Business overheads	43,080	
Staffing costs	32,877	
General expenses	8,780	
Directors' remuneration	15,000	
Mortgage on property		100,000
Mortgage interest	6,700	
Trade receivables and payables	23,976	21,211
Cash and cash equivalents	9,013	
General reserve		45,000
Provision for depreciation of other non-current assets		45,800
Dividends paid	11,000	
	860,324	860,324

Additional information:

1 Inventory held at 31 December 2019 was £23,444
2 Depreciation is to be provided on other non-current assets at 5% using reducing balance
3 A provision for tax was to be made for £9,100
4 A transfer of £10,000 was to be made to the general reserve
5 Staff costs owing at the year-end were £2,233
6 Business overheads paid in advance for the following year were £820.

APPENDIX 1

Answers to review questions

Chapter 1

1.1
(a) No need to share profits.
(b) No need to consult on decision making.
(c) No conflict on direction of business.

1.2 Any three from:
(a) Generate more capital to expand the business
(b) Ability to specialise in different roles within the business
(c) Cover can be arranged for illness
(d) Holidays can be arranged without the business having to close
(e) More creative ideas may be generated.

1.3 Any three from:
(a) Limited liability – no risk of losing own money
(b) Higher profile – more publicity for business
(c) Easier to raise finance (esp. if plc)
(d) More chance of acquiring loans (due to less risk attached to business).

1.4 Limited companies are owned by shareholders who are not necessarily involved in running the business while control of the business lies in the hands of the directors or managers of the business.

1.5 Companies are owned by shareholders. It is likely that shareholders would have originally purchased shares in order to maximise their returns which is only likely to occur if the company is aiming to maximise profits. Companies that don't pursue this objective will not find it easy to attract shareholders.

1.6 Assets: (a), (c), (d), (f); liabilities: (b), (e), (g).

1.7 Assets: (b), (c), (d); liabilities: (a), (e), (f).

1.8 Assets: (b), (c), (d), (f); liabilities: (a), (e).

1.9

	Assets £	Liabilities £	Capital £
(a)	5,400	4,100	1,300
(b)	3,870	1,190	2,680
(c)	9,875	1,195	8,680
(d)	1,180	543	637
(e)	6,767	1,107	5,660

1.10

	Assets £	Liabilities £	Capital £
(a)	12,231	4,344	7,887
(b)	23,434	18,312	5,122
(c)	74,423	23,111	51,312
(d)	54,524	9,090	45,434
(e)	31,231	11,209	20,022

1.11

	Assets £	Liabilities £	Capital £
(a)	64,564	31,221	33,343
(b)	100,113	23,123	76,990
(c)	64,564	9,871	54,693
(d)	76,575	11,200	65,375
(e)	86,788	31,231	55,557

1.12 Capital is £47,450.

Chapter 2

2.1

	Account to be debited	Account to be credited
(a)	Equipment	M Sparks
(b)	Motor car	Bank
(c)	Bank	Capital
(d)	J Harker	Fixtures
(e)	A Johnson	Bank
(f)	Cash	P Shortland

2.2

Capital

		£
	1 Mar Cash	900
	19 Mar Computer	380

Cash

	£		£
1 Mar Capital	900	4 Mar Bank	500
13 Mar Machinery	200		

Bank

	£		£
4 Mar Cash	500	8 Mar Machinery	400

Machinery

	£		£
8 Mar Bank	400	13 Mar Cash	200

Computer

	£
19 Mar Capital	380

Shop fittings

	£
12 Mar M Yeates	200

M Yeates

		£
	12 Shop fittings	200

2.3

Capital

2009	£	2009	£
		Jan 2 Bank	25,000

Bank

2009	£	2009	£
Jan 2 Capital	25,000	Jan 7 Premises	15,000
		Jan 14 Cash	900

Premises

2009	£	2009	£
Jan 7 Bank	15,000		

Cash

2009	£	2009	£
Jan 14 Bank	900	Jan 19 Office supplies	500

Fixtures

2009	£	2009	£
Jan 17 C Platt	4,500	Jan 23 D Hammond	750

C Platt

2009	£	2009	£
		Jan 17 Fixtures	4,500

Office supplies

2009	£	2009	£
Jan 19 Cash	500		

D Hammond

2009	£	2009	£
Jan 23 Fixtures	750		

2.4

Bank

2011	£	2011	£
Apr 8 Bank loan	18,000	Apr 11 Plant	4,000
		Apr 26 J Bellwood	2,500

Bank loan

2011	£	2011	£
		Apr 8 Bank	18,000

2.5

Plant

2011	£	2011	£
Apr 11 Bank	4,000	Apr 23 C Roberts	800

Car

2011	£	2011	£
Apr 15 Capital	8,000		

Capital

2011	£	2011	£
		Apr 15 Car	8,000

Machinery

2011	£	2011	£
Apr 18 J Bellwood	2,500		

J Bellwood

2011	£	2011	£
Apr 26 Bank	2,500	Apr 18 Machinery	2,500

C Roberts

2011	£	2011	£
Apr 23 Plant	800		

Capital

2012	£	2012	£
		Aug 2 Cash	950

Cash

2012	£	2012	£
Aug 2 Capital	950	Aug 12 Machinery	340
		Aug 27 Bank	400

Bank

2012	£	2012	£
Aug 3 J Tahoulan	1,200	Aug 19 J Tahoulan	600
Aug 27 Cash	400	Aug 27 S Wells	1,000

J Tahoulan

2012	£	2012	£
Aug 19 Bank	600	Aug 3 Bank	1,200

2.6

Machinery

2012	£	2012	£
Aug 12 Cash	340		

Delivery van

2012	£	2012	£
Aug 7 S Wells	1,000		

S Wells

2012	£	2012	£
Aug 27 Bank	1,000	Aug 7 Delivery van	1,000

Capital

2013	£	2013	£
		Jul 1 Cash	300
		Jul 3 Bank	1,000

Bank

2013	£	2013	£
Jul 3 Capital	1,000	Jul 5 Machinery	400
Jul 21 Cash	200	Jul 18 B Street	250

Cash

2013	£	2013	£
Jul 1 Capital	300	Jul 21 Bank	200

Machinery

2013	£	2013	£
Jul 5 Bank	400		

Equipment

2013	£	2013	£
Jul 12 B Street	250		

B Street

2013	£	2013	£
Jul 18 Bank	250	Jul 12 Equipment	250

Motor car

2013	£	2013	£
Jul 14 C Alexander	1,300		

C Alexander

2013	£	2013	£
		Jul 14 Motor car	1,300

2.7

Essex Bank

2009	£	2009	£
		Mar 1 Bank	10,000

Bank

2009	£	2009	£
Mar 1 Essex Bank	10,000	Mar 3 Machinery	950
		Mar 5 Cash	1,000
		Mar 14 Motor vehicle	2,000

Cash

2009	£	2009	£
Mar 5 Bank	1,000	Mar 24 T Wilson	250

Machinery

2009	£	2009	£
Mar 3 Bank	950		

Motor vehicle

2009	£	2009	£
Mar 14 Bank	2,000		

Equipment

2009	£	2009	£
Mar 12 T Wilson	450	Mar 19 T Wilson	200

T Wilson

2009	£	2009	£
Mar 19 Equipment	200	Mar 12 Equipment	450
Mar 24 Cash	250		

2.8

	Account to be debited	Account to be credited
(a)	Purchases	Bank
(b)	A Rahman	Returns outwards
(c)	Purchases	Autocars Ltd
(d)	Purchases	Cash
(e)	Rescuecars Ltd	Recovery vehicle

2.9

	Account to be debited	Account to be credited
(a)	Returns inwards	K Jones
(b)	Bacon slicer (or Equipment)	Bank
(c)	A Francis	Returns outwards
(d)	Cash	Sales
(e)	E Polley	Counter (or Equipment)

2.10

Purchases

	£		£
1 Mar T Burke	32		
3 Mar W Randlesome	81		

Returns outwards

	£		£
		9 Mar T Burke	12

W Randlesome

	£		£
12 Mar Bank	81	3 Mar Purchases	81

Cash

	£		£
		15 Mar T Burke	20

Bank

	£		£
		12 Mar W Randlesome	81

T Burke

	£		£
9 Mar Returns outwards	12	1 Mar Purchases	32
15 Mar Cash	20		

2.11

Capital

	£	2014	£
		Dec 1 Bank	8,000

Bank

2014	£	2014	£
Dec 1 Capital	8,000	Dec 13 Purchases	41

2.12

Fixtures & fittings

	£	2014	£
Dec 4 P Lambert	2,200		

P Lambert

2014	£	2014	£
		Dec 4 Fixtures & fittings	2,200

Purchases

2014	£	2014	£
Dec 11 K Symons	85		
Dec 13 Bank	41		

K Symons

2014	£	2014	£
		Dec 11 Purchases	85

Sales

2014	£	2014	£
		Dec 15 G Williams	95
		Dec 17 P Parkinson	124

G Williams

2014	£	2014	£
Dec 15 Sales	95	Dec 22 Returns inwards	23

P Parkinson

2014	£	2014	£
Dec 22 Sales	124		

Returns inwards

2014	£	2014	£
Dec 22 G Williams	23		

Capital

2009	£	2009	£
		Feb 2 Cash	400

Cash

2009	£	2009	£
Feb 2 Capital	400	Feb 21 P Jackson	36
Feb 14 Sales	102		

2.13

Purchases

2009	£	2009	£
Feb 3 P Jackson	47		
Feb 5 K Sage	43		

P Jackson

2009	£	2009	£
Feb 8 Returns outwards	11	Feb 3 Purchases	47
Feb 21 Cash	36		

K Sage

2009	£	2009	£
		Feb 5 Purchases	43

Sales

2009	£	2009	£
		Feb 14 Cash	102
		Feb 17 L Burrell	95

L Burrell

2009	£	2009	£
Feb 17 Sales	95	Feb 24 Returns inwards	28

Returns outwards

2009	£	2009	£
		Feb 8 P Jackson	11

Returns inwards

2009	£	2009	£
Feb 24 L Burrell	28		

Capital

2015	£	2015	£
		Jun 1 Bank	6,000

Bank

2015	£	2015	£
Jun 1 Capital	6,000	Jun 26 Equipment	950
Jun 4 M Lockwood	4,000		

M Lockwood

2015	£	2015	£
		Jun 4 Bank	4,000

2.13 (cont'd)

Purchases

Dr	£	Cr	£
2015 Jun 8 P Reid	76	2015	
Jun 8 C Coyne	65		

P Reid

Dr	£	Cr	£
2015		2015 Jun 8 Purchases	76

C Coyne

Dr	£	Cr	£
2015		2015 Jun 8 Purchases	65

Premises

Dr	£	Cr	£
2015 Jun 16 Woodseats Building Society	50,000	2015	

Woodseats Building Society

Dr	£	Cr	£
2015		2015 Jun 16 Premises	50,000

Sales

Dr	£	Cr	£
2015		2015 Jun 21 P Baldwin	240
		Jun 21 J Dunne	340
		Jun 25 Cash	250

P Baldwin

Dr	£	Cr	£
2015 Jun 21 Sales	340	2015 Jun 29 Returns inwards	50

J Dunne

Dr	£	Cr	£
2015 Jun 21 Sales	340	2015	

Cash

Dr	£	Cr	£
2015 Jun 25 Sales	250	2015	

Equipment

Dr	£	Cr	£
2015 Jun 26 Bank	950	2015	

Returns inwards

Dr	£	Cr	£
2015 Jun 29 P Baldwin	50	2015	

2.14

Capital

Dr	£	Cr	£
		2008 Sep 1 Bank	4,500

Bank

Dr	£	Cr	£
2008 Sep 1 Capital	4,500	2008 Sep 12 Motor vehicle	2,900
		Sep 27 C Throup	89

Purchases

Dr	£	Cr	£
2008 Sep 3 S Painter	123	2008	
Sep 3 C Throup	89		

S Painter

Dr	£	Cr	£
2008 Sep 13 Returns outwards	87	2008 Sep 3 Purchases	123

C Throup

Dr	£	Cr	£
2008 Sep 27 Bank	89	2008 Sep 3 Purchases	89

Returns outwards

Dr	£	Cr	£
2008		2008 Sep 13 S Painter	87

Motor vehicle

Dr	£	Cr	£
2008 Sep 12 Bank	2,900	2008	

Sales

Dr	£	Cr	£
2008		2008 Sep 5 Cash	121
		Sep 18 J Brown	187

J Brown

Dr	£	Cr	£
2008 Sep 18 Sales	187	2008 Sep 21 Returns inwards	31
		Sep 29 Cash	156

Returns inwards

2008		£	2008		£
Sep 21	J Brown	31			

Cash

2008		£	2008		£
Sep 5	Sales	121			
Sep 29	J Brown	156			

2.15

	Account to be debited	Account to be credited
(a)	Rent	Bank
(b)	Purchases	Cash
(c)	A Stacey	Sales
(d)	Bank	Commission received
(e)	Drawings	Computer
(f)	Bank	Cash

2.16

	Account to be debited	Account to be credited
(a)	Insurance	Cash
(b)	J Nesbit	Returns outwards
(c)	Bank	Cash
(d)	Purchases	G Thompson
(e)	Marketing	Bank
(f)	Cash	Car

2.17

	Account to be debited	Account to be credited
(a)	Car	Capital
(b)	Wages	Cash
(c)	Drawings	Purchases
(d)	Bank	Rent received
(e)	Returns inwards	J Spillane
(f)	Cash	R Hinds

2.18

K Johnson

2014		£	2014		£
			Aug 1	Bank	5,000

Bank

2014		£	2014		£
Aug 1	K Johnson	5,000	Aug 1	Cash	1,000
			Aug 3	Wages	320

Cash

2014		£	2014		£
Aug 1	Bank	1,000	Aug 15	Insurance	85
Aug 11	Sales	340	Aug 20	Drawings	28

Wages

2014		£	2014		£
Aug 3	Cash	320			

Purchases

2014		£	2014		£
Aug 4	D Rooney	52			

Sales

2014		£	2014		£
			Aug 11	Cash	340

Drawings

2014		£	2014		£
Aug 20	Cash	28			

Insurance

2014		£	2014		£
Aug 15	Cash	85			

D Rooney

2014		£	2014		£
			Aug 4	Purchases	52

2.19

Purchases

	£	2009	£
2009 May 1 C Donner	32		
May 3 J Holmes	74		

C Donner

	£	2009	£
2009 May 8 Returns outwards	12	May 1 Purchases	32

J Holmes

	£	2009	£
2009 May 23 Cash	74	May 3 Purchases	74

Sales

	£	2009	£
2009		May 5 Bank	318
		May 19 N Bell	93

Bank

	£	2009	£
2009 May 5 Sales	318	May 11 Advertising	19
		May 24 Drawings	100

Rent received

	£	2009	£
2009		May 6 Cash	54

Cash

	£	2009	£
2009 May 6 Rent received	54	May 23 J Holmes	74

Returns outwards

	£	2009	£
2009		May 8 C Donner	12

Advertising

	£	2009	£
2009 May 11 Bank	19		

Fixtures and fittings

	£	2009	£
2009 May 14 J Read	820		

J Read

2009	£	2009	£
		May 14 Fixtures and fittings	820

N Bell

2009	£	2009	£
		May 19 Sales	93

Drawings

2009	£	2009	£
May 24 Bank	100		

2.20

Capital

2010	£	2010	£
Nov 30 Balance c/d	8,500	Nov 1 Bank	8,500
	8,500	Dec 1 Balance b/d	8,500

Machinery

2010	£	2010	£
Nov 3 Bank	1,500	Nov 30 Balance c/d	1,500
Dec 1 Balance b/d	1,500		

Bank

2010	£	2010	£
Nov 1 Capital	8,500	Nov 3 Machinery	1,500
Nov 18 M Smith	272	Nov 4 Machinery insurance	95
		Nov 21 B Bolder	21
		Nov 30 Balance c/d	7,156
	8,772		8,772
Dec 1 Balance b/d	7,156		

Machinery insurance

2010	£	2010	£
Nov 4 Bank	95	Nov 30 Balance c/d	95
	95		95
Dec 1 Balance b/d	95		

Purchases

2010	£	2010	£
Nov 7 M Hodge	65	Nov 30 Balance c/d	86
Nov 7 B Bolder	21		
	86		86
Dec 1 Balance b/d	86		

M Hodge

2010		£	2010		£
Nov 16	Returns outwards	34	Nov 7	Purchases	65
Nov 30	Balance c/d	31			
		65			65
			Dec 1	Balance b/d	31

Returns outwards

2010		£	2010		£
Nov 30	Balance c/d	34	Nov 16	M Hodge	34
		34			34
			Dec 1	Balance b/d	34

B Bolder

2010		£	2010		£
Nov 21	Bank	21	Nov 7	Purchases	21

Vehicle

2010		£	2010		£
Nov 10	M Sterland	4,300	Nov 30	Balance c/d	4,300
Dec 1	Balance b/d	4,300			

M Sterland

2010		£	2010		£
Nov 30	Balance c/d	4,300	Nov 10	Vehicle	4,300
		4,300			4,300
			Dec 1	Balance b/d	4,300

Sales

2010		£	2010		£
Nov 30	Balance c/d	452	Nov 14	M Smith	272
			Nov 24	T Curran	180
		452			452
			Dec 1	Balance b/d	452

M Smith

2010		£	2010		£
Nov 14	Sales	272	Nov 18	Bank	272
		272			

T Curran

2010		£
Nov 24	Sales	180
Dec 1	Balance b/d	180

2.21

Capital

2017		£	2017		£
Apr 30	Balance c/d	500	Apr 1	Bank	500
		500			500
			May 1	Balance b/d	500

Bank

2017		£	2017		£
Apr 1	Capital	500	Apr 24	Drawings	100
			Apr 28	Wages	134
			Apr 30	Balance c/d	266
		500			500
May 1	Balance b/d	266			

Purchases

2017		£	2017		£
Apr 4	J Sheridan	67	Apr 30	Balance c/d	165
Apr 5	P King	98			
		165			165
May 1	Balance b/d	165			

J Sheridan

2017		£	2017		£
Apr 30	Balance c/d	67	Apr 4	Purchases	67
		67			67
			May 1	Balance b/d	67

P King

2017		£	2017		£
Apr 12	Returns outwards	22	Apr 5	Purchases	98
Apr 30	Balance c/d	76			
		98			98
			May 1	Balance b/d	76

Sales

2017		£	2017		£
Apr 30		277	Apr 8	C Turner	99
			Apr 18	R Nilsson	178
		277			277
			May 1	Balance b/d	277

Returns outwards

2017		£	2017		£
Apr 30	Balance c/d	22	Apr 12	P King	22
		22			22
			May 1	Balance b/d	22

2.21 *(cont'd)*

Commission received

Dr	£	Cr	£
2017 Apr 30 Balance c/d	45	2017 Apr 16 Cash	45
	45		45
		May 1 Balance b/d	45

Cash

Dr	£	Cr	£
2017 Apr 16 Commission received	45	2017 Apr 30 Balance c/d	95
Apr 25 C Turner	50		
	95		95
May 1 Balance b/d	95		

C Turner

Dr	£	Cr	£
2017 Apr 8 Sales	99	2017 Apr 25 Cash	50
		Apr 30 Balance c/d	49
	99		99
May 1 Balance b/d	49		

R Nilsson

Dr	£	Cr	£
2017 Apr 18 Sales	178	2017 Apr 20 Returns inwards	58
		Apr 30 Balance c/d	120
	178		178
May 1 Balance b/d	120		

Returns inwards

Dr	£	Cr	£
2017 Apr 20 R Nilsson	58	2017 Apr 30 Balance c/d	58
	58		58
May 1 Balance b/d	58		

Wages

Dr	£	Cr	£
2017 Apr 28 Bank	134	2017 Apr 30 Balance c/d	134
	134		134
May 1 Balance b/d	134		

Drawings

Dr	£	Cr	£
2017 Apr 24 Bank	100	2017 Apr 30 Balance c/d	100
	100		100
May 1 Balance b/d	100		

2.22

Capital

Dr	£	Cr	£
2016 Jan 31 Balance c/d	3,000	2016 Jan 1 Bank	3,000
	3,000		3,000
		Feb 1 Balance b/d	3,000

Bank

Dr	£	Cr	£
2016 Jan 1 Capital	3,000	2016 Jan 13 Cash	600
Jan 28 S Welsh	100	Jan 16 Insurance	33
		Jan 31 Balance c/d	2,467
	3,100		3,100
Feb 1 Balance b/d	2,467		

Fixtures

Dr	£	Cr	£
2016 Jan 3 K Wesson	870	2016 Jan 31 Balance c/d	870
	870		870
Feb 1 Balance b/d	870		

K Wesson

Dr	£	Cr	£
2016 Jan 31 Balance c/d	870	2016 Jan 3 Fixtures	870
	870		870
		Feb 1 Balance b/d	870

Cash

Dr	£	Cr	£
2016 Jan 13 Bank	600	2016 Jan 14 P Jones	45
Jan 22 Rent received	70	Jan 19 Advertising	45
		Jan 31 Balance c/d	580
	670		670
Feb 1 Balance b/d	580		

Rent received

Dr	£	Cr	£
2016 Jan 31 Balance c/d	70	2016 Jan 22 Cash	70
	70		70
		Feb 1 Balance b/d	70

Purchases

Dr	£	Cr	£
2016 Jan 5 S Johnson	95	2016 Jan 31 Balance c/d	140
Jan 9 P Jones	45		
	140		140
Feb 1 Balance b/d	140		

Chapter 3

3.1

H Clews
Trial balance as at 30 November 2010

	Dr £	Cr £
Capital		8,500
Machinery	1,500	
Bank	7,156	
Machinery insurance	95	
Purchases	86	
M Hodge		31
Returns outwards		34
Vehicle	4,300	
M Sterland		4,300
Sales		452
T Curran	180	
	13,317	13,317

3.2

D Weir
Trial balance as at 30 April 2017

	Dr £	Cr £
Capital		500
Bank	266	
Purchases	165	
J Sheridan		67
P King		76
Sales		277
Returns outwards		22
Commission received		45
Cash	95	
C Turner	49	
R Nilsson	120	
Returns inwards	58	
Wages	134	
Drawings	100	
	987	987

S Johnson

	£		£
2016		2016	
Jan 31 Balance c/d	95	Jan 5 Purchases	95
	95		95
		Feb 1 Balance b/d	95

P Jones

	£		£
2016		2016	
Jan 14 Cash	45	Jan 9 Purchases	45

Insurance

	£		£
2016		2016	
Jan 16 Bank	33	Jan 31 Balance c/d	33
Feb 1 Balance b/d	33		

Advertising

	£		£
2016		2016	
Jan 19 Cash	45	Jan 31 Balance c/d	45
Feb 1 Balance b/d	45		

Sales

	£		£
2016		2016	
Jan 31 Balance c/d	205	Jan 20 S Welsh	205
	205		205
		Feb 1 Balance b/d	205

S Welsh

	£		£
2016		2016	
Jan 20 Sales	205	Jan 26 Returns inwards	60
		Jan 28 Bank	100
		Jan 31 Balance c/d	45
	205		205
Feb 1 Balance b/d	45		

Returns inwards

	£		£
2016		2016	
Jan 26 S Welsh	60	Jan 31 Balance c/d	60
Feb 1 Balance b/d	60		

3.3

N James
Trial balance as at 31 January 2016

	Dr £	Cr £
Capital		3,000
Bank	2,467	
Fixtures	870	
K Wesson		870
Cash	580	
Rent received		70
Purchases	140	
S Johnson		95
Insurance	33	
Advertising	45	
Sales		205
S Welsh	45	
Returns inwards	60	
	4,240	4,240

3.4

	Dr £	Cr £
Sales		118,944
Purchases	76,574	
Returns inwards	432	
Returns outwards		342
Equipment	21,000	
Rent received		1,220
Office expenses	314	
Motor vehicles	12,300	
Inventory at 1 January 2011	9,950	
Trade payables		6,900
Trade receivables	8,786	
Bank overdraft		2,246
Wages and salaries	12,330	
Insurance	841	
Capital		26,000
Drawings	13,125	
	155,652	155,652

Inventory at 31 December 2011 was valued at £8,722.

3.5

C Palmer
Statement of comprehensive income for year ended
31 March 2009

	£	£	£
Sales			81,400
Less Cost of goods sold			
Purchases		74,750	
Less Closing inventory		5,890	68,860
Gross profit			12,540
Less Expenses:			
Business rates		1,800	
Electricity		975	
Salaries		3,800	
Rent		4,200	10,775
Net profit			1,765

3.6

C Woods
Statement of comprehensive income for year ended
30 June 2001

	£	£	£
Sales			87,450
Less Cost of goods sold			
Purchases		65,264	
Less Closing inventory		9,810	55,454
Gross profit			31,996
Add: Commission received			1,045
			33,041
Less Expenses:			
Heating and lighting		4,310	
Marketing		7,866	
Wages and salaries		11,721	
Rent		3,290	27,187
Net profit			5,854

3.7

J Harkes
Statement of financial position as at 30 June 2005

	£	£
Non-current assets		
Property		56,000
Equipment		9,870
		65,870
Current assets		
Inventory	9,020	
Trade receivables	3,422	
Bank	1,878	
	14,320	
Less Current Liabilities		
Trade payables	4,321	9,999
		75,869
Capital		67,000
Add Net profit		17,656
		84,656
Less Drawings		8,787
		75,869

3.8

D Wilson
Statement of financial position as at 30 April 2019

	£	£
Non-current assets		
Fixtures and fittings		18,500
Equipment		3,400
		21,900
Current assets		
Inventory	5,322	
Trade receivables	2,324	
Bank	1,122	
Cash	98	
	8,866	
Less Current liabilities		
Trade payables	3,413	5,453
		27,353
Less Non-current liabilities		
Long-term loan		10,000
		17,353
Capital		16,000
Add Net profit		4,786
		20,786
Less Drawings		3,433
		17,353

3.9

L Madden
Statement of financial position as at 31 December 2008

	£	£
Non-current assets		
Premises		75,000
Fixtures and fittings		12,500
		87,500
Current assets		
Inventory	4,995	
Trade receivables	7,212	
Bank	3,323	
	15,530	
Less Current liabilities		
Trade payables	5,788	9,742
		97,242
Less Non-current liabilities		
Long-term loan		25,000
		72,242
Capital		62,132
Add Net profit		14,343
		76,475
Less Drawings		4,233
		72,242

3.10

T Quinn
Statement of financial position as at 30 June 2012

	£	£
Non-current assets		
Buildings		133,000
Machinery		19,342
		152,342
Current assets		
Inventory	7,565	
Trade receivables	6,285	
Bank	4,324	
Cash	314	
	18,488	
Less Current liabilities		
Trade payables	9,797	8,691
		161,033
Less Non-current liabilities		
Loan repayable in 2017		54,000
		107,033
Capital		95,000
Add Net profit		23,423
		118,423
Less Drawings		11,390
		107,033

3.11

N Pearson
Statement of financial position as at 28 February 2011

	£	£
Non-current assets		
Premises		105,000
Motor vehicles		9,100
Machinery		13,700
		127,800
Current assets		
Inventory	9,800	
Trade receivables	4,543	
Cash	323	
	14,666	
Less Current liabilities		
Bank overdraft	3,423	
Trade payables	7,565	
	10,988	
		3,678
		131,478
Less Non-current liabilities		
Loan repayable in 2014		27,000
		104,478
Capital		88,434
Add Net profit		23,434
		111,868
Less Drawings		7,390
		104,478

3.12

R Grime
Statement of comprehensive income for year to 30 September 2015

	£	£
Sales		323,423
Less Cost of goods sold		
Purchases	234,354	
Less Closing inventory	23,223	
		211,131
Gross profit		112,292
Less Expenses		
Heating expenses	4,233	
Salaries	16,565	
Office expenses	2,131	
Rent and rates	19,213	
		42,142
Net profit		70,150

R Grime
Statement of financial position as at 30 September 2015

	£	£	£
Non-current assets			
Property			194,000
Delivery van			18,700
			212,700
Current assets			
Inventory		23,223	
Trade receivables		18,793	
Bank		12,346	
		54,362	
Less Current liabilities			
Trade payables		20,912	
			33,450
			246,150
Less Non-current liabilities			
Long-term loan			50,000
			196,150
Capital			144,798
Add Net profit			70,150
			214,948
Less Drawings			18,798
			196,150

3.13

D Ferdinand
Statement of comprehensive income for year ended 31 December 2016

	£	£
Sales		42,321
Less Cost of goods sold		
Purchases	35,188	
Less Closing inventory	1,890	
		33,298
Gross profit		9,023
Less Expenses		
Heating	2,425	
Staff wages	9,891	
Sundry expenses	881	
Insurance	345	
Maintenance	2,667	
Marketing	2,866	
		19,075
Net loss		10,052

D Ferdinand
Statement of financial position as at 31 December 2016

	£	£
Non-current assets		
Machinery		8,000
Fixtures and fittings		3,422
		11,422
Current assets		
Inventory	1,890	
Trade receivables	6,453	
Cash	246	
	8,589	
Less Current liabilities		
Trade payables	7,585	
Bank overdraft	1,415	
	9,000	(411)
		11,011
Capital		29,808
Less Net loss		10,052
		19,756
Less Drawings		8,745
		11,011

3.14

P Miller
Statement of comprehensive income for year ended 31 December 2007

	£	£
Sales		265,000
Less Cost of goods sold		
Purchases	210,450	
Less Closing inventory	9,450	201,000
Gross profit		64,000
Less Expenses		
Administration	4,300	
Wages and salaries	15,328	
Rates and insurance	3,432	
Carriage outwards	1,100	
Repair costs	2,450	26,610
Net profit		37,390

P Miller
Statement of financial position as at 31 December 2007

	£	£	£
Non-current assets			
Premises			100,000
Motor van			8,500
Equipment			15,900
			124,400
Current assets			
Inventory		9,450	
Trade receivables		7,520	
Bank		6,500	
		23,470	
Less Current liabilities			
Trade payables		6,980	16,490
			140,890
Capital			120,000
Add Net profit			37,390
			157,390
Less Drawings			16,500
			140,890

3.15

A Bantick
Statement of comprehensive income for period ending 30 November 2011

	£	£
Sales		342,312
Less Cost of goods sold		
Purchases	311,769	
Less Closing inventory	27,655	284,114
Gross profit		58,198
Less Expenses		
Heating and lighting	7,891	
Wages and salaries	23,141	
Rent and rates	6,543	
Vehicle expenses	3,212	
Repairs	4,234	
Advertising	2,313	47,334
Net profit		10,864

3.15 (*cont'd*)

A Bantick

Statement of financial position as at 30 November 2011

	£	£
Non-current assets		
Premises		87,000
Plant		23,000
Motor vehicle		13,000
		123,000
Current assets		
Inventory	27,655	
Trade receivables	27,878	
Bank	4,354	
	59,887	
Less Current liabilities		
Trade payables	29,090	
		30,797
		153,797
Capital		155,121
Add Net profit		10,864
		165,985
Less Drawings		12,188
		153,797

3.16 Trading account for year ended 31 December 2010

	£	£
Sales		15,432
Less Cost of goods sold		
Opening inventory	2,341	
Add Purchases	9,807	
	12,148	
Add Carriage inwards	332	
	12,480	
Less Closing inventory	3,298	
		9,182
Gross profit		6,250

3.17

	£	£
Sales		54,353
Less Returns inwards		122
Net turnover		54,231
Less Cost of goods sold		
Opening inventory	8,798	
Add Purchases	45,434	
	54,232	
Add Carriage inwards	767	
	54,999	
Less Returns outwards	453	
	54,546	
Less Closing inventory	12,773	
		41,773
Gross profit		12,458

3.18 Trading account for year ended 30 June 2007

	£	£
Sales		43,555
Less Returns inwards		544
Net turnover		43,011
Less Cost of goods sold		
Opening inventory	3,780	
Add Purchases	27,800	
	31,580	
Less Returns outwards	763	
	30,817	
Less Closing inventory	2,943	
		27,874
Gross Profit		15,137

3.19 Trading account for year ended 31 March 2006

	£	£
Sales		86,500
Less Returns inwards		390
Net turnover		86,110
Less Cost of goods sold		
Opening inventory	5,670	
Add Purchases	49,800	
	55,470	
Add Carriage inwards	540	
	56,010	
Less Returns outwards	1,010	
	55,000	
Less Closing inventory	6,500	
		48,500
Gross profit		37,610

3.20

Trading account for year ended 31 October 2012

	£	£
Sales		17,424
Less Returns inwards		123
Net turnover		17,301
Less Cost of goods sold		
Opening inventory	3,189	
Add Purchases	12,342	
	15,531	
Add Carriage inwards	787	
	16,318	
Less Returns outwards	432	
	15,886	
Less Closing inventory	4,123	11,763
Gross profit		5,538

3.21

D Hirst
Statement of comprehensive income for the year ended 31 Dec 2014

	£	£
Sales		143,244
Less Returns inwards		780
Net turnover		142,464
Less Cost of goods sold		
Opening inventory	14,300	
Add Purchases	105,400	
	119,700	
Add Carriage inwards	650	
	120,350	
Less Returns outwards	1,010	
	119,340	
Less Closing inventory	17,630	101,710
Gross profit		40,754
Add Rent received		1,899
		42,653
Less Expenses:		
Advertising	3,230	
Insurance	2,767	
Wages	22,321	
Carriage outwards	812	29,130
Net profit		13,523

3.22

P Warhurst
Statement of comprehensive income for year ended 31 December 2003

	£	£
Sales		243,233
Less Returns inwards		2,122
Net turnover		241,111
Less Cost of goods sold		
Opening inventory	43,545	
Add Purchases	165,764	
	209,309	
Add Carriage inwards	1,898	
	211,207	
Less Returns outwards	3,413	
	207,794	
Less Closing inventory	39,898	167,896
Gross profit		73,215
Less Expenses:		
Heating costs	2,865	
Office salaries	16,754	
Wages	26,323	
Rent and rates	8,778	
Carriage outwards	976	55,696
Net profit		17,519

3.23

C Hopkins
Statement of comprehensive income for year ended 31 March 2011

	£	£
Sales		43,244
Less Returns inwards		342
Net turnover		42,902
Less Cost of goods sold		
Opening inventory	4,346	
Add Purchases	28,879	
	33,225	
Add Carriage inwards	756	
	33,981	
Less Returns outwards	453	
	33,528	
Less Closing inventory	6,519	27,009
Gross profit		15,893
Less Expenses:		
Heating	3,423	
Insurance	2,767	
Wages	8,787	
Carriage outwards	812	15,789
Net profit		104

3.24

R Millward
Statement of comprehensive income for the period ended 31 December 2014

	£	£
Sales		78,678
Less Cost of goods sold		
Opening inventory	8,984	
Add Purchases	56,545	
	65,529	
Add Carriage inwards	321	
	65,850	
Less Closing inventory	5,467	60,383
Gross profit		18,295
Add Commission received		870
		19,165
Less Expenses		
Gas and electricity	4,212	
Wages	14,234	
General expenses	1,254	
Carriage outwards	345	
Maintenance	2,667	
Advertising	3,221	25,933
Net loss		6,768

R Millward
Statement of financial position as at 31 December 2014

	£	£
Non-current assets		
Machinery		15,000
Equipment		4,300
Fixtures and fittings		8,450
		27,750
Current assets		
Inventory	5,467	
Trade receivables	9,876	
	15,343	
Less Current liabilities		
Trade payables	5,676	
Bank overdraft	5,344	
	11,020	4,323
		32,073
Capital		48,740
Less Net loss		6,768
		41,972
Less Drawings		9,899
		32,073

3.25

D Wilcox
Statement of comprehensive income for year ended 31 July 2015

	£	£
Sales		141,000
Less Returns inwards		321
Net turnover		140,679
Less Cost of goods sold		
Opening inventory	6,788	
Add Purchases	96,500	
	103,288	
Less Returns outwards	423	
	102,865	
Add Carriage inwards	433	
	103,298	
Less Closing inventory	5,454	97,844
Gross profit		42,835
Less Expenses		
Lighting and heating	4,233	
Wages and salaries	14,312	
Insurance	2,131	
Carriage outwards	534	
Rent	7,705	28,915
Net profit		13,920

D Wilcox
Statement of financial position as at 31 July 2015

	£	£
Non-current assets		
Machinery		13,200
Vehicles		7,800
		21,000
Current assets		
Inventory	5,454	
Trade receivables	8,232	
Bank	3,453	
	17,139	
Less Current liabilities		
Trade payables	7,564	9,575
		30,575
Less Non-current liabilities		
Long-term loan		7,000
		23,575
Capital		15,000
Add Net profit		13,920
		28,920
Less Drawings		5,345
		23,575

3.26

E Soormally
Statement of comprehensive income for period ending
30 September 2017

	£	£
Sales		534,534
Less Returns inwards		5,435
Net turnover		529,099
Less Cost of goods sold		
Opening inventory	67,809	
Add Purchases	412,312	
	480,121	
Less Returns outwards	4,233	
	475,888	
Add Carriage inwards	989	
	476,877	423,204
Less Closing inventory	53,673	105,895
Gross profit		18,980
Add Sundry income		124,875
Less Expenses		
Power costs	23,432	
Wages	42,423	
Business rates	8,723	
Carriage outwards	2,123	
Maintenance	6,805	
Marketing expenses	5,132	88,638
Net profit		36,237

E Soormally
Statement of financial position as at 30 September 2017

	£	£	£
Non-current assets			
Plant			55,000
Equipment			45,400
Motor van			19,800
			120,200
Current assets			
Inventory		53,673	
Trade receivables		43,242	
Bank		19,809	
		116,724	
Less Current liabilities			
Trade payables		32,132	84,592
			204,792
Less Non-current liabilities			
Long-term loan			75,000
			129,792
Capital			121,211
Add Net profit			36,237
			157,448
Less Drawings			27,656
			129,792

3.27

S Rogers
Statement of comprehensive income for the year ended
31 July 2018

	£	£
Sales		765,755
Less Returns inwards		5,424
Net turnover		760,331
Less Cost of goods sold		
Opening inventory	63,443	
Add Purchases	545,343	
	608,786	
Less Returns outwards	6,562	
	602,224	
Add Carriage inwards	1,213	
	603,437	
Less Closing inventory	75,343	528,094
Gross profit		232,237
Add Commission received		8,676
		240,913
Less Expenses		
Heating and lighting	24,211	
Wages and salaries	43,243	
General expenses	8,787	
Carriage outwards	5,343	
Maintenance	2,667	
Distribution costs	5,989	90,240
Net profit		150,673

S Rogers
Statement of financial position as at 31 July 2018

	£	£	£
Non-current assets			
Machinery			88,500
Equipment			24,500
Fixtures and fittings			49,600
			162,600
Current assets			
Inventory		75,343	
Trade receivables		42,540	
Bank		23,123	
Cash		877	
		141,883	
Less Current liabilities			
Trade payables		53,453	
			88,430
			251,030
Less Non-current liabilities			
Loan			25,000
			226,030
Capital			99,700
Add Net profit			150,673
			250,373
Less Drawings			24,343
			226,030

Chapter 4

4.1
(a) Sales
(b) Returns outwards
(c) Journal
(d) Cash book
(e) Cash book
(f) Purchases

4.2
(a) Cash book
(b) Journal
(c) Returns inwards
(d) Cash book
(e) Journal
(f) Cash book

4.3
(a) Journal
(b) Journal
(c) Sales
(d) Returns outwards
(e) Purchases
(f) Cash book

4.4

Cash book

Debit

2010		Cash £	Bank £
Mar 01	Balance b/d	45	560
Mar 04	Sales	89	
Mar 09	Capital		430
Mar 13	Commission received	76	
		210	990
Apr 01	Balance b/d	187	449

Credit

2010		Cash £	Bank £
Mar 02	Rent		240
Mar 07	M Harold		110
Mar 12	Wages		135
Mar 18	Purchases	23	
Mar 22	Electricity		56
Mar 31	Balance c/d	187	449
		210	990

4.5

Cash book

Debit

2011		Cash £	Bank £
May 01	Balance b/d	21	430
May 05	Bank	120	
May 11	K Maher		255
May 21	Sales	99	
May 31	Cash		149
		240	855
Jun 01	Balance b/d	20	544

Credit

2011		Cash £	Bank £
May 03	Equipment		50
May 09	Purchases		42
May 12	Rent	71	
May 15	Office supplies		120
May 31	Bank	149	
May 31	Balance c/d	20	544
		240	855

4.6

Cash book

Debit

2011		Cash £	Bank £
Jun 01	Balances b/d	198	450
Jun 03	J Blakeley	125	
Jun 07	Loan		800
Jun 12	Sales		96
Jun 15	Rent received		89
Jun 20	Cash		100
Jun 25	N Standen	43	
Jun 28	Office equipment	65	
		431	1,535
Jul 01	Balances b/d	105	709

Credit

2011		Cash £	Bank £
Jun 02	S Cowling		276
Jun 05	Fixtures		355
Jun 10	Drawings	50	
Jun 18	Purchases	176	
Jun 20	Bank	100	
Jun 21	Insurance		145
Jun 29	Drawings		50
Jun 30	Balances c/d	105	709
		431	1,535

4.7

Cash book

Debit

2011		Cash £	Bank £
May 01	Balance b/d	23.92	
May 04	Sales		215.00
May 09	A Kanner		800.00
May 17	Bank	30.00	
May 23	Computer	150.00	
May 24	Commission received	24.00	
May 26	P Cargill	56.00	
May 30	Cash		100.00
		283.92	1,115.00
Jun 01	Balances b/d	72.08	365.24

Credit

2011		Cash £	Bank £
May 01	Balance b/d		45.62
May 02	Petrol	16.23	
May 06	Sundry expenses	6.11	
May 12	A Rogers		56.00
May 14	Rent		67.00
May 17	Cash		30.00
May 19	Vehicle		450.00
May 22	Drawings		90.00
May 28	Interest		11.14
May 29	Purchases	89.50	
May 30	Bank	100.00	
May 31	Balances c/d	72.08	365.24
		283.92	1,115.00

4.8

Cash book

Debit

2013		Discount £	Cash £	Bank £
Oct 01	Balances b/d		41	320
Oct 12	A Ardley	10		190
Oct 12	J Thorogood	28		532
Oct 12	N Goody	4		76
Oct 17	Bank		66	
Oct 19	S Wilson	10		96
Oct 23	Motor vehicle			280
Oct 29	Cash			32
		52	107	1,526
Nov 01	Balances b/d		25	294

Credit

2013		Discount £	Cash £	Bank £
Oct 02	D Von Geete	21		399
Oct 03	C Baron	9		171
Oct 04	Heating			
Oct 08	Insurance			
Oct 13	Office equipment			
Oct 17	Cash			66
Oct 22	Office expenses		25	
Oct 26	B Rivers	20		300
Oct 27	Drawings		25	89
Oct 29	Bank		32	
Oct 31	Balances c/d		25	294
		50	107	1,526

4.9

Cash book

Date	Detail	Discount £	Cash £	Bank £	Date	Detail	Discount £	Cash £	Bank £
2012					2012				
Nov 01	Balance b/d		11		Nov 01	Balance b/d			289
Nov 02	E Allston	7		430	Nov 08	Wages			177
Nov 04	T Joyner			273	Nov 10	P Yarrow	15		285
Nov 04	S Platt	4		156	Nov 12	Computer			320
Nov 04	M Brookes	10		390	Nov 15	Cash			50
Nov 15	Bank		50		Nov 17	M Skipsey	14		266
Nov 21	Commission received		48		Nov 17	P Muskett	11		209
Nov 24	E Dixon	12			Nov 19	Purchases		79	
Nov 24	J Shephardson	5			Nov 28	Bank		100	
Nov 26	Sales		189		Nov 30	Equipment			290
Nov 28	Cash			100	Nov 30	Balance c/d		119	
Nov 29	J Terry	8		120					
Nov 30	Balance c/d			94					
		46	298	1,886			40	298	1,886
Dec 01	Balance c/d		119		Dec 01	Balance c/d			94

4.10

Cash book

Date	Detail	Discount £	Cash £	Bank £	Date	Detail	Discount £	Cash £	Bank £
2015					2015				
Feb 01	Balances b/d		101	878	Feb 02	Equipment			325
Feb 10	Sales		60	60	Feb 03	Purchases			192
Feb 12	D Clough	12		132	Feb 05	Motor repairs		33	
Feb 17	Bank		50		Feb 08	S Jens	8		152
Feb 25	D Vanian	22		418	Feb 08	S Lee	3		57
Feb 25	I Astbury	7		133	Feb 14	Drawings		68	
Feb 26	Rent received		76		Feb 17	Cash			50
					Feb 20	D West	28		252
					Feb 24	K Hawley	5		195
					Feb 24	A Vincent	4		156
					Feb 27	Drawings		80	
					Feb 28	Balances c/d		106	242
		41	287	1,621			48	287	1,621
Mar 01	Balance c/d		119	242					

4.11

Cash book

Date	Detail	Discount £	Cash £	Bank £	Date	Detail	Discount £	Cash £	Bank £
Aug 01	Balance b/d		54.50		Aug 01	Balance b/d			190.67
Aug 31	C Roberts	14.25		460.75	Aug 31	Sundry expenses		32.80	
Aug 31	J Bellwood	3.75		121.25	Aug 31	S Arora	4.70		89.30
Aug 31	P Shortland	2.52		81.48	Aug 31	E Hawkins	4.20		100.80
Aug 31	Balance c/d			153.05	Aug 31	J Clover	10.24		245.76
					Aug 31	Rent			190.00
					Aug 31	Balance c/d		21.70	
		20.52	54.50	816.53			19.14	54.50	816.53
Sep 01	Balance c/d		21.70		Sep 01	Balance c/d			153.05

4.12

Cash book

Date	Detail	Discount £	Cash £	Bank £	Date	Detail	Discount £	Cash £	Bank £
2010					2010				
Dec 01	Balances b/d		45.00	231.97	Dec 02	R Wheatcroft	5.00		126.00
Dec 03	R Armitage	10.00		215.00	Dec 04	P Cocking	12.50		320.00
Dec 05	G Gregory	8.50		160.00	Dec 06	M Clegg	3.75		87.00
Dec 31	Credit transfer (A Stroish)			111.30	Dec 31	Bank charges			14.50
Dec 31	Receipts		327.31		Dec 31	Interest			3.55
Dec 31	Cash			280.01	Dec 31	Petrol		28.54	
					Dec 31	Office expenses		18.76	
					Dec 31	Bank		280.01	
					Dec 31	Balance c/d		45.00	447.23
		18.50	372.31	998.28			21.25	372.31	998.28
Jan 01	Balances c/d		45.00	447.23					

4.13

S Donnelly – petty cash book – August 2005

Receipts £	Date	Details	Total £	Travel costs £	Stationery £	Cleaning £
100	Aug 1	Cash				
	Aug 2	Rail fares	17	17		
	Aug 4	Petrol	8	8		
	Aug 8	Stationery	4		4	
	Aug 10	Cleaning	11			11
	Aug 18	Petrol	16	16		
	Aug 21	Cleaning	10			10
	Aug 22	Bus fares	4	4		
	Aug 25	Cleaning	2			2
	Aug 28	Stationery	5		5	
	Aug 30	Petrol	6	6		
83	Aug 31	Cash				
	Aug 31	Balance c/d	100			
183			183	51	9	23
100	Sep 1	Balance b/d				

4.14

Received £	Date 2005	Details	Voucher number	Total £	Travel costs £	Stationery £	Office expenses £
100.00	Nov 6	Balance b/d					
	Nov 7	Bus fares	31	15.20	15.20		
	Nov 7	Stamps	32	0.40		0.40	
	Nov 8	Printer paper	33	21.20			21.20
	Nov 8	Coffee	34	2.40			2.40
	Nov 10	Petrol	35	17.80	17.80		
	Nov 11	Envelopes	36	4.56		4.56	
	Nov 11	Cleaner	37	8.75			8.75
	Nov 13	Balance c/d		70.31	33.00	4.96	32.35
100.00				29.69			
				100.00			
29.69	Nov 14	Balance b/d					
70.31	Nov 14	Bank					

255

4.15

Sales day book

2010		£
Jan 3	A Genn	45
Jan 8	T Wright	89
Jan 11	S Gill	111
Jan 12	J Gillot	76
Jan 18	A Genn	21
Jan 27	T Wright	54
Total for month		396

Sales Ledger

A Genn

2010		£
Jan 3	Sales	45
Jan 18	Sales	21

T Wright

2010		£
Jan 8	Sales	89
Jan 27	Sales	54

S Gill

2010		£
Jan 11	Sales	111

J Gillot

2010		£
Jan 12	Sales	76

General Ledger

Sales

	2010		£
	Jan 31	Total for month	396

4.16

Sales day book

2012		£
Oct 3	I Sharp	197
Oct 6	T Wilson	224
Oct 9	J Dolman	96
Oct 14	T Wilson	302
Oct 19	N Jackson	561
Oct 24	T Wilson	177
Total for month		1,557

Sales Ledger

I Sharp

2012		£
Oct 3	Sales	197

T Wilson

2012		£
Oct 6	Sales	224
Oct 14	Sales	302
Oct 24	Sales	177

J Dolman

2012		£
Oct 9	Sales	96

N Jackson

2012		£
Oct 19	Sales	561

General Ledger

Sales

	2012		£
	Oct 31	Total for month	1,557

4.17

Purchases day book

2014		£
Aug 4	W Cann	43
Aug 11	G Michael	19
Aug 12	B Currie	27
Aug 17	J Taylor	86
Aug 21	M King	24
Aug 26	G Michael	91
Total for month		290

Purchases Ledger

W Cann

	2014		£
	Aug 4	Purchases	43

G Michael

	2014		£
	Aug 11	Purchases	19
	Aug 26	Purchases	91

4.18

B Currie

2014			£	2014			£
				Aug 12	Purchases		27

J Taylor

2014			£	2014			£
				Aug 17	Purchases		86

M King

2014			£	2014			£
				Aug 21	Purchases		24

General Ledger

Purchases

2014			£	2014		£
Aug 31	Total for month		290			

Purchases day book

2012		£
Mar 2	J Austen	78
Mar 6	P Chang	118
Mar 9	L Martins	21
Mar 18	L Martins	65
Mar 21	E Blindefelt	43
Mar 31	P Chang	76
	Total for month	401

Purchases Ledger

J Austen

2012			£	2012			£
				Mar 2	Purchases		78

P Chang

2012			£	2012			£
				Mar 6	Purchases		118
				Mar 31	Purchases		76

L Martins

2012			£	2012			£
				Mar 9	Purchases		21
				Mar 18	Purchases		65

E Blindefelt

2012			£	2012			£
				Mar 21	Purchases		43

General Ledger

Purchases

2012			£	2012		£
Mar 31	Total for month		401			

4.19

Sales day book

2010		£
Apr 1	E Ram	125
Apr 6	B Lomus	210
Apr 12	E Ram	82
Apr 30	Total for month	417

Purchases day book

2010		£
Apr 8	P Alport	96
Apr 19	J Widmare	140
Apr 30	Total for month	236

Sales Ledger

E Ram

2010		£	2010		£
Apr 1	Sales	125			
Apr 12	Sales	82			

B Lomus

2010		£	2010		£
Apr 6	Sales	210			

Purchases Ledger

P Alport

2010			£	2010			£
				Apr 8	Purchases		96

J Widmare

2010			£	2010			£
				Apr 19	Purchases		140

4.19 (cont'd)

General Ledger

Sales

2010	£	2010		£
		Apr 30	Total for month	417

Purchases

2010		£	2010	
Apr 30	Total for month	236		

4.20

Sales day book

2016		£
Jun 2	J Lahr	76
Jun 12	S Aitken	56
Jun 16	M Armitage	87
Jun 30	Total for month	219

Purchases day book

2016		£
Jun 5	K Oldman	39
Jun 8	K Oldman	17
Jun 22	D Nichols	41
Jun 30	Total for month	97

Sales Ledger

J Lahr

2016	£	2016
Jun 2 Sales	76	

S Aitken

2016	£	2016
Jun 12 Sales	56	

M Armitage

2016	£	2016
Jun 16 Sales	87	

Purchases Ledger

K Oldman

2016	£	2016	
		Jun 5 Purchases	39
		Jun 8 Purchases	17

D Nichols

	£	2016		£
		Jun 22	Purchases	41

General Ledger

Sales

	£	2016		£
		Jun 30	Total for month	219

Purchases

2016		£	2016
Jun 30	Total for month	97	

4.21

Sales day book

2017		£
Nov 2	D Pearce	49
Nov 4	A Haslem	214
Nov 9	R Compton	76
Nov 15	D Pearce	181
Nov 30	Total for month	520

Returns inwards day book

2017		£
Nov 12	A Haslem	54
Nov 18	R Compton	19
Nov 30	Total for month	73

Sales Ledger

D Pearce

2017	£	2017
Nov 2 Sales	49	
Nov 15 Sales	181	

A Haslem

2017	£	2017	£
Nov 4 Sales	214	Nov 12 Returns inwards	54

R Compton

2017	£	2017	£
Nov 9 Sales	76	Nov 18 Returns inwards	19

4.22

General Ledger

Sales

	£	2017	£
		Nov 30 Total for month	520

Returns inwards

2017	£	2017	£
Nov 30 Total for month	73		

Purchases day book

2019		£
Mar 1	M Swann	97
Mar 3	G Denton	65
Mar 11	L Webster	114
Mar 14	M Swann	52
Mar 31	Total for month	328

Returns outwards day book

2019		£
Mar 4	M Swann	12
Mar 18	M Swann	21
Mar 21	G Denton	8
Mar 31	Total for month	41

Purchases Ledger

M Swann

2019		£	2019		£
Mar 4	Returns outwards	12	Mar 1	Purchases	97
Mar 18	Returns outwards	21	Mar 14	Purchases	52

G Denton

2019		£	2019		£
Mar 21	Returns outwards	8	Mar 3	Purchases	65

L Webster

	£	2019		£
		Mar 11	Purchases	114

General Ledger

Purchases

2019	£	2019	£
Mar 31 Total for month	328		

4.23

Returns outwards

2019	£	2019	£
		Mar 31 Total for month	41

Sales day book

2013		£
Jul 1	S Wilkins	87
Jul 3	J Nesbit	118
Jul 11	P Jones	240
Jul 31	Total for month	445

Purchases day book

2013		£
Jul 4	S Johnson	62
Jul 15	N James	88
Jul 22	P Wesson	55
Jul 31	Total for month	205

Returns inwards day book

2013		£
Jul 8	S Wilkins	23
Jul 28	P Jones	24
Jul 31	Total for month	47

Returns outwards day book

2013		£
Jul 19	S Johnson	25
Jul 31	Total for month	25

Sales Ledger

S Wilkins

2013		£	2013		£
Jul 1	Sales	87	Jul 8	Returns inwards	23

J Nesbit

2013		£	2013		£
Jul 3	Sales	118			

P Jones

2013		£	2013		£
Jul 11	Sales	240	Jul 28	Returns inwards	24

4.23 *(cont'd)*

Purchases Ledger

S Johnson

	£			£
2013 Jul 19 Returns outwards	25		2013 Jul 4 Purchases	62

N James

	£			£
			2013 Jul 15 Purchases	88

P Wesson

	£			£
			2013 Jul 22 Purchases	55

General Ledger

Sales

	£			£
2013			2013 Jul 31 Total for month	445

Purchases

	£			£
2013 Jul 31 Total for month	205		2013	

Returns inwards

	£			£
2013 Jul 31 Total for month	47		2013	

Returns outwards

	£			£
2013			2013 Jul 31 Total for month	25

4.24

Sales day book

2015		£
May 5	S Luscombe	165
May 18	J Keeble	101
May 22	J Keeble	145
May 31	Total for month	411

Purchases day book

2015		£
May 1	L Schmidt	75
May 4	M Rogers	54
May 16	N Arthur	81
May 31	Total for month	210

Returns inwards day book

2015		£
May 11	S Luscombe	31
May 25	J Keeble	32
May 31	Total for month	63

Returns outwards day book

2015		£
May 8	L Schmidt	24
May 21	N Arthur	11
May 31	Total for month	35

General Ledger

Sales

	£			£
2015			2015 May 31 Total for month	411

Purchases

	£			£
2015 May 31 Total for month	210		2015	

Returns inwards

	£			£
2015 May 31 Total for month	63		2015	

Returns outwards

	£			£
2015			2015 May 31 Total for month	35

Sales Ledger

S Luscombe

	£			£
2015 May 5 Sales	165		2015 May 11 Returns inwards	31

J Keeble

	£			£
2015 May 18 Sales	101		2015 May 25 Returns inwards	32
May 22 Sales	145			

Purchases Ledger

L Schmidt

2015	£	2015	£
May 8 Returns outwards	24	May 1 Purchases	75

M Rogers

2015	£	2015	£
		May 4 Purchases	54

N Arthur

2015	£	2015	£
May 21 Returns outwards	11	May 16 Purchases	81

4.25

The Journal

2006		Dr £	Cr £
June 1	Equipment	900	
	B Eden		900
June 5	Bad debts	38	
	M Sparks		38
June 8	W Bohanna	180	
	C Hurford		180
June 13	Drawings	690	
	Computer		690
June 19	Van	1,900	
	Vans R Us Ltd		1,900
June 25	Furniture	425	
	R Denys		425

4.26

The Journal

2006		Dr £	Cr £
August 1	Bad debts	15	
	F Grew		15
August 5	Van	900	
	Equipment		900
August 8	Bank	25	
	Bad debts	175	
	J Harker		200
August 13	Sales	25	
	Commission received		25
August 19	Office equipment	670	
	Fantastic Drawers Ltd		670
August 25	Drawings	40	
	Typewriter		40

4.27

The Journal

2007		Dr £	Cr £
May 1	N Johnston	500	
	Equipment		500
May 3	P Kenny	30	
	H Jagielka		30
May 12	Motor vehicle	1,200	
	Capital		1,200
May 13	M Burns	189	
	Equipment		189
May 21	Machinery	2,700	
	Jacks Ltd		2,700

4.28

The Journal

2003		Dr £	Cr £
April 5	Machinery	1,300	
	Fixtures and fittings		1,300
April 8	Bank	25	
	Bad debts	100	
	J Large		125
April 12	Bad debts	33	
	N Yarrow		33
April 22	Fixtures and fittings	450	
	Magic Fittings Ltd		450
April 25	Drawings	2,300	
	Car		2,300

4.29

The Journal

	Dr £	Cr £
Van	800	
P Gray		800
Purchases	75	
Drawings		75
Computer	180	
Capital		180
Desk	50	
L Skipsey		50
J Rowell	250	
Car		250
Office fixtures	95	
L Palmer		95

4.30

The Journal

	Dr £	Cr £
K Hodgson	355	
Motor van		355
Bad debts	27	
T Fairhurst		27
Car	295	
Capital		295
Office equipment	820	
S Merrills		820
S Merrills	75	
Office equipment		75
Drawings	25	
Insurance		25

4.31

The Journal

	Dr £	Cr £
Bad debt	45	
Cash	15	
R Marshall		60
Drawings	47	
Purchases		47
Machinery	172	
M Wainwright		172
M Wainwright	31	
Machinery		31
Drawings	160	
Electricity		160
H17 Ltd	425	
Plant		425

Chapter 5

5.1

VAT

2007	£	2007	£
Jul 31 VAT on purchases	196.88	Jul 31 VAT on sales	306.25
Jul 31 VAT on returns inwards	40.25	Jul 31 VAT on returns outwards	31.15
Jul 31 Balance c/d	100.27		
	337.40		337.40
		Aug 1 Balance b/d	100.27

5.2

VAT

2008	£	2008	£
Oct 31 VAT on purchases	1,538.25	Oct 31 VAT on sales	2,198.00
Oct 31 VAT on returns inwards	79.80	Oct 31 VAT on returns outwards	117.25
Oct 31 Balance c/d	697.20		
	2,315.25		2,315.25
		Nov 1 Balance b/d	697.20

5.3

VAT

2003	£	2003	£
Mar 9 Bank	145.00	Mar 1 Balance b/d	26.00
Mar 31 VAT on purchases	137.38	Mar 31 VAT on sales	156.63
Mar 31 VAT on returns inwards	3.15	Mar 31 VAT on returns outwards	1.58
		Mar 31 Balance c/d	101.32
	285.53		285.53
Apr 1 Balance b/d	101.32		

5.4

(i) VAT owing as at 1 May 2003
(ii) £308 (credit)
(iii) Current liabilities

5.5

£528.61

5.6

VAT

2019	£	2019	£
May 31 VAT on purchases	134.01	May 31 VAT on sales	196.61
May 31 VAT on returns inwards	17.15	May 31 VAT on returns outwards	18.03
		May 31 VAT on cash sales	72.10
May 31 Balance c/d	135.58		
	286.74		286.74
		Jun 1 Balance b/d	135.58

5.7

VAT

2007	£	2007	£
Jun 30 VAT on purchases	1,011.50	Jun 30 VAT on sales	1,303.75
Jun 30 VAT on returns inwards	152.95	Jun 30 VAT on returns outwards	176.75
Jun 30 VAT on fixed assets	350.00	Jun 30 VAT on cash sales	146.70
Jun 30 Balance c/d	112.75		
	1,627.20		1,627.20
		Jun 1 Balance b/d	112.75

5.8

VAT

2005		£	2005		£
Mar 31	VAT on purchases	498.75	Mar 31	Balance b/d	320.00
Mar 31	VAT on returns inwards	37.45	Mar 31	VAT on sales	567.00
			Mar 31	VAT on returns outwards	31.50
Mar 31	VAT on petty cash exp.	18.32	Mar 31	VAT on cash sales	189.15
Mar 31	Balance c/d	553.13			
		1,107.65			1,107.65
			Apr 1	Balance b/d	553.13

5.9

VAT

2006		£	2006		£
Apr 18	Bank	299.00	Apr 1	Balance b/d	220.73
Apr 30	VAT on purchases	691.25	Apr 30	VAT on sales	917.00
Apr 30	VAT on returns inwards	72.10	Apr 30	VAT on returns outwards	66.50
Apr 30	VAT on petty cash exp.	50.94	Apr 30	VAT on cash sales	129.57
Apr 30	VAT on fixed assets	450.00	Apr 30	Balance c/d	229.49
		1,563.29			1,563.29
May 1	Balance b/d	229.49			

5.10

VAT

2004		£	2004		£
Apr 1	Balance b/d	117.00	Jun 30	VAT on sales	137.38
May 24	Bank	183.00	Jun 30	VAT on returns outwards	7.70
Jun 30	VAT on expenses	58.00	Jun 30	Balance c/d	323.17
Jun 30	VAT on purchases	98.35			
Jun 30	VAT on returns inwards	11.90			
		468.25			468.25
Jul 1	Balance b/d	323.17			

5.11

Sales day book

2001		Net £	VAT £	Gross £
May 8	M Cousins	800.00	140.00	940.00
May 15	F Connelly	550.00	96.25	646.25
May 22	M Cousins	280.00	49.00	329.00
	Transferred to General Ledger	1,630.00	285.25	1,915.25

Purchases day book

2001		Net £	VAT £	Gross £
May 1	A Davidson	300.00	52.50	352.50
May 1	C Platt	200.00	35.00	235.00
May 12	G Guy	250.00	43.75	293.75
	Transferred to General Ledger	750.00	131.25	881.25

Returns inwards day book

2008		Net £	VAT £	Gross £
May 25	F Connelly	120.00	21.00	141.00
May 28	M Cousins	82.00	14.35	96.35
	Transferred to General Ledger	202.00	35.35	237.35

Returns outwards day book

2008		Net £	VAT £	Gross £
May 18	C Platt	36.00	6.30	42.30
	Transferred to General Ledger	36.00	6.30	42.30

Sales Ledger:

M Cousins

2001		£	2001		£
May 8	Sales	940.00	May 28	Returns inwards	96.35
May 22	Sales	329.00			

F Connelly

2001		£	2001		£
May 15	Sales	646.25	May 25	Returns inwards	141.00

Purchases Ledger:

A Davidson

2001		£	2001		£
			May 1	Purchases	352.50

C Platt

2001		£	2001		£
May 18	Returns outwards	42.30	May 1	Purchases	235.00

G Guy

2001		£	2001		£
			May 12	Purchases	293.75

5.11 (cont'd)
General Ledger:

Sales

2001	£	2001	
		May 31 Total for month	1,630.00

Purchases

2001	£	2001	
May 31 Total for month	750.00		

Returns inwards

2001	£	2001	
May 31 Total for month	202.00		

Returns outwards

2001	£	2001	
		May 31 Total for month	36.00

VAT

2001	£	2001	£
May 31 VAT on purchases	131.25	May 31 VAT on sales	285.25
May 31 VAT on returns inwards	35.35	May 31 VAT on returns outwards	6.30
May 31 Balance c/d	124.95		
	291.55		291.55
		June 1 Balance b/d	124.95

5.12 (a) (i) £1,749.38; (ii) £1,674.38;
(b) (i) £936.50; (ii) £916.50;
(c) (i) £2,111.06; (ii) £2,088.56;
(d) (i) £561.48; (ii) £547.08.

5.13 (a) £40.95
(b) £235.38
(c) £5.77.

5.14 £149.28.

5.15 £175.59.

5.16 £2,410.25.

Chapter 6

6.1 Capital expenditure: (b), (c), (d), (f); revenue expenditure: (a), (e).

6.2 Capital expenditure: (a), (b), (e), (h); revenue expenditure: (c), (d), (f), (g).

6.3 Capital receipts: (b), (c); revenue receipts: (a), (d), (e), (f).

6.4 Capital expenditure: (c), (f); revenue expenditure: (a), (b), (d), (e), (g).

6.5 Capital expenditure: (a), (b), (c), (h); revenue expenditure: (d), (e), (f), (g).

6.6 Capital expenditure: (a), (f), (g); revenue expenditure: (b), (c), (d), (e), (h).

6.7 Capital expenditure: (d), (e), (f), (i); revenue expenditure: (a), (b), (c), (g).

6.8 Capital expenditure: (a), (d), (e), (g), (h); revenue expenditure: (b), (c), (f).

6.9

Capital cost	£
Purchase price of land	140,000
Construction charges of factory	85,000
Installation costs of plant & equipment	3,600
Legal fees (*assuming they are one-offs*)	12,000
Total capital costs	240,600

6.10 Capital expenditure: £5,347; revenue expenditure: £1,337.

6.11 Capital expenditure: £53,930 (£48,000 + £1,600 + £4,330); revenue expenditure: £4,900 (£1,800 + £3,100).

6.12 Capital expenditure: £6,310 (£5,600 + £460 + £250); revenue expenditure: £10,924 (£710 + £226 + £9,800 + £188).

6.13 Capital expenditure: £2,746 (£2,670 + £76); revenue expenditure: £1,404 (£312 + £661 + £431).

6.14 £2,500 + £600 + £120 = £3,220.

6.15 Capital expenditure: £6,358 (£5,488 + £870); revenue expenditure: £4,657 (£1,990 + £1,656 + £868 + £143).

6.16 Capital expenditure: (b), (e), (f); revenue expenditure: (c), (d), (g), (h); capital receipt: (i); revenue receipts: (a), (j).

6.17 Capital expenditure £859 (£750 + £109); revenue expenditure £622 (£312 + £89 + £221); capital income £1,760 (£560 + £1,200); revenue income £408.

6.18 Net profit would be higher as revenue expenditure would be lower than it would otherwise be.

6.19

	£	£
Gross profit		5,133
Less expenses		
Insurance	423	
Wages	3,123	
Carriage outwards on goods sold	123	
Marketing costs	765	
		4,434
Net profit		699

6.20 **Chappell Ltd: Corrected Trading Account**

	£	£
Sales		9,075
Less cost of goods sold:		
Opening inventory	590	
Add Purchases	3,403	
	3,993	
Add carriage inwards	279	
	4,272	
Less Closing inventory	667	
		3,605
Gross profit		5,470

Chapter 7

7.1 Investors and the advisors to investors will want to invest with confidence. If a business does not comply with accounting standards then investors may be suspicious and consider that the business has something to hide – why not comply with the standards if all is well? This is likely to have a negative effect on the business in terms of attracting investors.

7.2 If the company is small and unlikely to need to attract European or international investment then it may consider that it is not worth adopting international standards. Also, there is a period of time where a business may be considering the switch but is not yet ready to adopt the international standards.

7.3 Financial statements should be accessible enough to be understood by the users of the information.

7.4 Any four from: investors, employees, lenders, suppliers, customers, government and the public.

7.5 Profits would be distorted by the effect of capital expenditure and capital receipts. For example, the purchase of a non-current asset could significantly reduce and or nullify a year's profits. Similarly, any business that delays in paying its expenses would artificially boost its profits.

7.6
(a) Prudence, historical cost
(b) Business entity
(c) Prudence, historical cost
(d) Accruals, prudence, realisation.

7.7
(a) Accruals
(b) Consistency
(c) Historical cost, prudence
(d) Going concern, prudence, historical cost.

7.8
(a) Going concern/historical cost
● Assets should be valued at cost not expected selling price
● Internal goodwill should not really be included in asset valuations unless the firm is expected to be sold.
(b) Accruals/prudence
● It is not prudent to include sales before the order is actually received
● The accruals concept infers that sales should be included when they are made
(c) Consistency
● To enable meaningful comparisons with earlier years, the same methods should be applied for depreciation – even if not entirely 'accurate'
● Depreciation is not about showing realistic valuations for assets anyway.
(d) Accruals/realisation
● Sales should be matched to the period in which they were incurred
● The sale is made when the order is received, not when the account is settled.

7.9
(a) £11,650 (£10,000 + £600 + £350 + £700)
(b) Prudence (there is also a case for referring to historical cost or consistency)
(c) Net realisable value is equal to the selling price less any costs involved in getting stock into saleable condition (e.g. repair costs).

7.10
(a) IAS 16
(b) IAS 2
(c) IAS 8
(d) IAS 17

Chapter 8

8.1

(a) Advertising

		£			£
2010			2010		
Dec 31	Bank	712	Dec 31	Statement of comprehensive income	757
Dec 31	Balance c/d	45			
		757			757

(b) Insurance

		£			£
2010			2010		
Dec 31	Bank	556	Dec 31	Statement of comprehensive income	535
			Dec 31	Balance c/d	21
		556			556

(c) Heating and lighting

		£			£
2010			2010		
Dec 31	Bank	650	Dec 31	Statement of comprehensive income	400
			Dec 31	Balance c/d	250
		650			650

(d) Rent received

		£			£
2010			2010		
Dec 31	Statement of comprehensive income	1,280	Dec 31	Bank	1,100
			Dec 31	Balance c/d	180
		1,280			1,280

8.2

(a) Commission Received

		£			£
2012			2012		
Dec 31	Statement of comprehensive income	420	Dec 31	Bank	560
Dec 31	Balance c/d	140			
		560			560

(b) Wages

		£			£
2012			2012		
Dec 31	Bank	3,200	Dec 31	Statement of comprehensive income	3,670
Dec 31	Balance c/d	470			
		3,670			3,670

(c) Rent received

		£			£
2012			2012		
Dec 31	Statement of comprehensive income	1,200	Dec 31	Bank	1,600
Dec 31	Balance c/d	400			
		1,600			1,600

(d) Insurance

		£			£
2012			2012		
Jan 1	Bank	400	Dec 31	Statement of comprehensive income	960
May 14	Bank	400	Dec 31	Balance c/d	240
Nov 10	Bank	400			
		1,200			1,200

8.3

(a) Insurance

		£			£
2012/13			2012/13		
Mar 31	Bank	725	Mar 31	Statement of comprehensive income	930
Mar 31	Balance c/d	205			
		930			930

(b) Heating and lighting

		£			£
2012/13			2012/13		
Apr 1	Bank	400	Mar 31	Statement of comprehensive income	1,340
Jul 1	Bank	400	Mar 31	Balance c/d	260
Oct 1	Bank	400			
Jan 1	Bank	400			
		1,600			1,600

(c) Rent received

		£			£
2012/13			2012/13		
Mar 31	Statement of comprehensive income	5,800	Mar 31	Bank	4,750
			Mar 31	Balance c/d	1,050
		5,800			5,800

(d) Motor expenses

		£			£
2012/13			2012/13		
Mar 31	Bank	750	Mar 31	Statement of comprehensive income	450
			Mar 31	Balance c/d	300
		750			750

8.4

J Churchard
Statement of comprehensive income for the year ended
31 July 2005

	£	£
Sales		56,193
Less Cost of goods sold		
Opening inventory	6,105	
Add Purchases	30,010	
	36,115	
Less Closing inventory	7,230	28,885
Gross profit		27,308
Less: Expenses		
Office expenses (£3,980 + £510)	4,490	
Rent (£1,750 + £230)	1,980	
Wages (£11,325 – £995)	10,330	16,800
Net profit		10,508

J Churchard
Statement of financial position as at 31 July 2005

	£	£	£
Non-current assets			
Premises		26,500	
Equipment		4,990	
		31,490	
Current assets			
Inventory		7,230	
Trade receivables		2,655	
Prepayments		995	
Bank		1,074	
		11,954	
Less Current liabilities			
Trade payables	3,156		
Accruals	740	3,896	
		8,058	
		39,548	
Capital		34,500	
Add Net profit		10,508	
		45,008	
Less Drawings		5,460	
		39,548	

8.5

B Wright
Statement of comprehensive income for the year ending
31 December 2014

	£	£	£
Sales			45,312
Less Cost of goods sold			
Opening inventory		3,231	
Add Purchases		31,980	
		35,211	
Less Closing inventory		5,670	29,541
Gross profit			15,771
Less: Expenses			
Insurance		1,013	
Salaries (£6,409 + £703)		7,112	
Rent (£3,870 + £540)		4,410	12,535
Net profit			3,236

B Wright
Statement of financial position as at 31 December 2013

	£	£	£
Non-current assets			
Equipment		11,400	
Machinery		5,340	
		16,740	
Current assets			
Inventory		5,670	
Trade receivables		4,231	
Bank		891	
		10,792	
Less Current liabilities			
Trade payables	5,436		
Accruals (£540 + £703)	1,243	6,679	4,113
			20,853
Capital			24,500
Add Net profit			3,236
			27,736
Less Drawings			6,883
			20,853

8.6

C Wattison
Statement of comprehensive income for the year ending 31 December 2013

	£	£
Sales		119,000
Less Cost of goods sold		
Opening inventory	12,560	
Add Purchases	71,500	
	84,060	
Less Closing inventory	13,420	70,640
Gross profit		48,360
Less: Expenses		
Insurance (£8,930 − £190)	8,740	
Heating and lighting (£2,360 − £312)	2,048	
Wages and salaries (£23,400 + £799)	24,199	34,987
Net profit		13,373

C Wattison
Statement of financial position as at 31 December 2013

	£	£	£
Non-current assets			
Property			74,000
Plant			7,560
			81,560
Current assets			
Inventory		13,420	
Trade receivables		8,340	
Prepayments (£190 + £312)		502	
Bank		2,210	
		24,472	
Less Current liabilities			
Trade payables	7,431		
Accruals	799	8,230	16,242
			97,802
Capital			91,312
Add Net profit			13,373
			104,685
Less Drawings			6,883
			97,802

8.7

M Krause
Statement of comprehensive income for the year ending 31 December 2012

	£	£
Sales		379,000
Less Cost of goods sold		
Opening inventory	23,450	
Add Purchases	256,000	
	279,450	
Less Closing inventory	16,740	262,710
Gross profit		116,290
Less: Expenses		
Administration expenses	4,720	
Power costs (£3,780 + £235)	4,015	
Salaries (£28,900 − £1,150)	27,750	
Insurance (£2,890 − £312)	2,578	
Sundry expenses (£990 + £90)	1,080	
Selling expenses	6,725	46,868
Net profit		69,422

M Krause
Statement of financial position as at 31 December 2012

	£	£	£
Non-current assets			
Premises			220,000
Plant, machinery and equipment			31,500
Vehicles			18,900
			270,400
Current assets			
Inventory		16,740	
Trade receivables		12,772	
Prepayments		1,462	
		30,974	
Less Current liabilities			
Trade payables	9,995		
Bank overdraft	3,132		
Accruals	325	13,452	17,522
			287,922
Capital			242,000
Add Net profit			69,422
			311,422
Less Drawings			23,500
			287,922

8.8

(a) Heating and lighting

	£			£
2016			2016	
Dec 31 Bank	453		Jan 1 Balance b/d	32
Dec 31 Balance c/d	56		Dec 31 Statement of Comprehensive Income	477
	509			509

(b) Insurance

	£			£
2016			2016	
Dec 31 Bank	955		Jan 1 Balance b/d	187
			Dec 31 Statement of Comprehensive Income	726
			Dec 31 Balance c/d	42
	955			955

(c) Wages

	£			£
2016			2016	
Jan 1 Balance b/d	211		Dec 31 Statement of Comprehensive Income	7,735
Dec 31 Bank	6,980			
Dec 31 Balance c/d	544			
	7,735			7,735

(d) Telephone

	£			£
2016			2016	
Jan 1 Balance b/d	17		Dec 31 Statement of Comprehensive Income	334
Dec 31 Bank	378		Dec 31 Balance c/d	61
	395			395

8.9

(a) Commission received

	£			£
2017			2017	
Jan 1 Balance b/d	50		Dec 31 Bank	750
Dec 31 Statement of Comprehensive Income	788		Dec 31 Balance c/d	88
	838			838

(b) Rent received

	£			£
2017			2017	
Dec 31 Statement of Comprehensive Income	3,357		Jan 1 Balance b/d	195
			Dec 31 Bank	2,800
			Dec 31 Balance c/d	362
	3,357			3,357

Royalties received

	£			£
2017			2017	
Jan 1 Balance b/d	94		Dec 31 Bank	899
Dec 31 Statement of Comprehensive Income	784			
Dec 31 Balance c/d	21			
	899			899

8.10

Heating

	£			£
2015			2015	
Jan 1 Balance b/d	12		Jan 1 Balance b/d	45
Jan 1 Bank (Elec)	250		Dec 31 Statement of comprehensive income	1,211
Jun 15 Bank (Elec)	460			
Dec 31 Bank (Gas × 12)	420			
Dec 31 Balance c/d	114			
	1,256			1,256

8.11

Rent received

	£			£
2016			2016	
Jan 1 Balance b/d	240		Jan 1 Balance b/d	130
Dec 31 Statement of comprehensive income	11,311		Jan 23 Bank	780
Dec 31 Balance c/d	76		Mar 12 Bank	1,430
			Jun 15 Bank	2,810
			Sep 30 Bank	4,520
			Nov 28 Bank	1,575
			Dec 31 Balance c/d	382
	11,627			11,627

8.12 Rent: £482 (£500 – £74 + £56); insurance: £274 (£245 +£18 +£11); wages £1,056 (£1,280 – £94 – £130).

8.13 Salaries: £4,881 (£5,600 – £439 – £280); rent received: £2,898 (£2,750 – £117 +£265); motor expenses: £830 (£843 +£42 – £55).

8.14

G Norfolk

Statement of comprehensive income extract for year ended 31 December 2003

	Debit	Credit
	£	£
Advertising	165	
Heating	317	
Rent received		1,000
Insurance	545	

8.15

Liz King
Statement of comprehensive income extract for year ended 31 December 2011

	Debit £	Credit £
Rent	430	
Marketing	145	240
Royalties		
Insurance	897	
Wages	532	

8.16

A Westwood
Statement of comprehensive income for year ended 30 June 2003

	£	£
Sales		52,000
Less Returns inwards		340
Net turnover		51,660
Less Cost of goods sold		
Opening inventory	8,550	
Add purchases	23,000	
	31,550	
Less Returns outwards	450	
	31,100	
Less Closing inventory	10,660	
		20,440
Gross profit		31,220
Less Expenses		
Wages	6,950	
Insurance	270	
Advertising	260	
Rent	1,561	
Depreciation: premises	7,500	
Depreciation: equipment	3,600	
Provision for doubtful debts	325	
		20,466
Net profit		10,754

8.17

I Mellor
Statement of comprehensive income for year ending 31 March 2011

	£	£
Sales		143,750
Less Cost of goods sold		
Opening inventory	9,875	
Add Purchases	99,600	
	109,475	
Less Closing inventory	8,760	
		100,715
Gross profit		43,035
Less: Expenses		
Electricity (£1,231 + £67)	1,298	
Wages and salaries (£18,721 + £540)	19,261	
Rent (£3,233 − £119)	3,114	
Insurance (£787 − £53)	734	
Office expenses	5,345	
Bad debts	280	
		30,032
Net profit		13,003

I Mellor
Statement of financial position as at 31 March 2011

	£	£	£
Non-current assets			
Buildings			32,000
Equipment			9,060
			41,060
Current assets			
Inventory		8,760	
Trade receivables		7,861	
Prepayments		172	
Bank		3,132	
		19,925	
Less Current liabilities			
Trade payables	6,546		
Accruals	607		
		7,153	
			12,772
			53,832
Capital			52,440
Add Net profit			13,003
			65,443
Less Drawings			11,611
			53,832

8.18

N Dorritt
Statement of comprehensive income for the year ended 31 March 2018

	£	£
Sales		98,787
Less Cost of goods sold		
Opening inventory	11,423	
Add Purchases	79,121	
	90,544	
Less Closing inventory	13,490	77,054
Gross profit		21,733
Add Provision for doubtful debts		40
		21,773
Less: Expenses		
Heating and lighting (£893 – £134)	759	
Wages (£7,121 + £1,120)	8,241	
Distribution costs (£2,321 + £435)	2,756	
Machine repairs (£989 + £87)	1,076	
Discounts allowed	864	
Bad debts	187	13,883
Net profit		7,890

N Dorritt
Statement of financial position as at 31 March 2018

	£	£	£
Non-current assets			
Machinery			25,400
Vehicles			9,250
			34,650
Current assets			
Inventory		13,490	
Trade receivables	6,000		
Less Provision for doubtful debts	240	5,760	
Prepayments		134	
Bank		1,400	
		20,784	
Less Current liabilities			
Trade payables	5,402		
Accruals	1,642	7,044	13,740
			48,390
Non-current liabilities			
Loan			10,000
			38,390
Capital			39,000
Add Net profit			7,890
			46,890
Less Drawings			8,500
			38,390

8.19

R Booth
Statement of comprehensive income for year ending 31 December 2009

	£	£
Sales		449,000
Less Cost of goods sold		
Opening inventory	20,672	
Add Purchases	312,000	
	332,672	
Less Closing inventory	19,122	313,550
Gross profit		135,450
Less: Expenses		
General expenses	8,881	
Provision for doubtful debts	230	
Salaries	59,970	
Administration costs	13,435	
Insurance	3,770	
Rent	9,789	
Depreciation of plant	12,400	
Depreciation of equipment	2,560	
Bad debts	545	111,580
Net profit		23,870

R Booth
Statement of financial position as at 31 December 2009

	£	£	£
Non-current assets			
Plant	62,000		
Less Provision for depreciation	21,900	40,100	
Equipment	18,000		
Less Provision for depreciation	7,760	10,240	
			50,340
Current assets			
Inventory		19,122	
Trade receivables	10,200		
Less Provision for doubtful debts	510	9,690	
Prepayments		765	
Bank		8,500	
		38,077	
Less Current liabilities			
Trade payables	7,800		
Accruals	5,747	13,547	24,530
			74,870
Capital			72,000
Add Net profit			23,870
			95,870
Less Drawings			21,000
			74,870

Chapter 9

9.1

Bad debts

2009		£	2009		£
Apr 15	D Hirst	65	Dec 31	Statement of comp. income	199
May 31	M Bright	24			
Aug 19	P Williams	110			
		199			199

9.2

L Farthing

Bad debts

2008		£	2008		£
Oct 19	Sales	950	Dec 15	Bank	285
			Dec 15	Bad debts	665
		950			950

9.3

S Peck

Bad debts

2011		£	2011		£
Mar 31	Balance owing	860	Mar 31	Bank	172
			Mar 31	Bad debts	688
		860			860

9.4

Year	Size of the provision (£)	Entry in statement of comprehensive income
2009	300	£300 (debit)
2010	360	£60 (debit)
2011	390	£30 (debit)
2012	330	£60 (credit)

9.5

Year	Size of the provision (£)	Entry in statement of comprehensive income
2009	6,200	£6,200 (debit)
2010	7,208	£1,008 (debit)
2011	7,380	£172 (debit)
2012	7,324	£56 (credit)

9.6

Year	Size of the provision (£)	Entry in statement of comprehensive income
2005	390	£115 (credit)
2006	365	£25 (credit)
2007	433	£68 (debit)
2008	450	£17 (debit)

9.7

Provision for doubtful debts

2008–9		£	2008–9		£
Jun 30	Balance c/d	890	Jul 1	Balance b/d	650
			Jun 30	Statement of comprehensive income	240
		890			890

P Brothers

Statement of financial position extract as at 30 June 2009

Current assets	£	£
Debtors	13,450	
Less Provision for doubtful debts	890	
		12,560

9.8

Provision for doubtful debts

2006		£	2006		£
Dec 31	Balance c/d	912	Dec 31	Statement of comprehensive income	912
		912			912

L Cornelius

Statement of financial position extract as at 31 December 2006

Current assets	£	£
Debtors	18,240	
Less Provision for doubtful debts	912	
		17,328

9.9

Provision for doubtful debts

2005		£	2005		£
Dec 31	Balance c/d	1,000	Jan 1	Balance b/d	850
			Dec 31	Statement of comp. income	150
		1,000			1,000
2006			2006		
Dec 31	Statement of comp. income	625	Jan 1	Balance b/d	1,000
Dec 31	Balance c/d	375			
		1,000			1,000
			2007		
			Jan 1	Balance b/d	375

9.10

Provision for doubtful debts

		£			£
2009			2009		
Dec 31	Balance c/d	800	Dec 31	Statement of comprehensive income	800
2010			2010		
Dec 31	Balance c/d	900	Jan 1	Balance b/d	800
			Dec 31	Statement of comprehensive income	100
		900			900
2011			2011		
Dec 31	Balance c/d	950	Jan 1	Balance b/d	900
			Dec 31	Statement of comprehensive income	50
		950			950
2012			2012		
Dec 31	Statement of comprehensive income	200	Jan 1	Balance b/d	950
Dec 31	Balance c/d	750			
		950			950
			2013		
			Jan 1	Balance b/d	750

9.11

Provision for doubtful debts

		£			£
2004			2004		
Dec 31	Balance c/d	1,045	Dec 31	Statement of comprehensive income	1,045
2005			2005		
Dec 31	Statement of comprehensive income	133	Jan 1	Balance b/d	1,045
Dec 31	Balance c/d	912			
		1,045			1,045
2006			2006		
Dec 31	Balance c/d	1,008	Jan 1	Balance b/d	912
			Dec 31	Statement of comprehensive income	96
		1,008			1,008
2007			2007		
Dec 31	Balance c/d	1,560	Jan 1	Balance b/d	1,008
			Dec 31	Statement of comprehensive income	552
		1,560			1,560
			2008		
			Jan 1	Balance b/d	1,560

9.12

Provision for doubtful debts

		£			£
2010			2010		
Dec 31	Balance c/d	500	Dec 31	Statement of comprehensive income	500
2011			2011		
Dec 31	Statement of comprehensive income	108	Jan 1	Balance b/d	500
Dec 31	Balance c/d	392			
		500			500
2012			2012		
Dec 31	Balance c/d	466	Jan 1	Balance b/d	392
			Dec 31	Statement of comprehensive income	74
		466			466
2013			2013		
Dec 31	Balance c/d	540	Jan 1	Balance b/d	466
			Dec 31	Statement of comprehensive income	74
		540			540
			2014		
			Jan 1	Balance b/d	540

9.13

Provision for doubtful debts

		£			£
2010			2010		
Dec 31	Balance c/d	714	Dec 31	Statement of comprehensive income	714
2011			2011		
Dec 31	Balance c/d	768	Jan 1	Balance b/d	714
			Dec 31	Statement of comprehensive income	54
		768			768
2012			2012		
Dec 31	Balance c/d	768	Jan 1	Balance b/d	768
2013			2013		
Dec 31	Statement of comprehensive income	69	Jan 1	Balance b/d	768
Dec 31	Balance c/d	699			
		768			768
			2014		
			Jan 1	Balance b/d	540

9.14

Provision for doubtful debts

2007		£	2007		£
Dec 31	Statement of comprehensive income	80	Jan 1	Balance b/d	420
Dec 31	Balance c/d	340			
		420			420

9.15

Provision for doubtful debts

2009		£	2009		£
Dec 31	Balance c/d	552	Jan 1	Balance b/d	250
			Dec 31	Statement of comprehensive income	302
		552			552

9.16

	2004	2005	2006	2007
Effect on profit	(£600)	(£450)	(£475)	(£380)

9.17

	2007	2008	2009	2010
Effect on profit	(£1,325)	(£1,455)	(£910)	£35

9.18

	2002	2003	2004	2005
Effect on profit	(£844)	(£554)	(£820)	(£614)

9.19

Provision for doubtful debts

2003		£	2003		£
Dec 31	Balance c/d	200	Dec 31	Statement of comprehensive income	200
2004			2004		
Dec 31	Balance c/d	325	Jan 1	Balance b/d	200
			Dec 31	Statement of comprehensive income	125
		325			325
2005			2005		
Dec 31	Balance c/d	525	Jan 1	Balance b/d	325
			Dec 31	Statement of comprehensive income	200
		525			525
2006			2006		
Dec 31	Statement of comprehensive income	136	Jan 1	Balance b/d	525
Dec 31	Balance c/d	389			
		525			525
			2007		
			Jan 1	Balance b/d	389

9.20

Statement of financial position extract as at 31 December 2009

Current assets	£	£
Debtors		15,000
Less Provision for doubtful debts		600
Less Provision for discounts on debtors		288	14,112

Effect on net profit is to reduce the net profit by £20 + £176 = £196.

Chapter 10

10.1

	Straight line	Reducing balance
	£	£
Cost	50,000	50,000
Depreciation: Year 1	12,500	25,000
NBV: End of year 1	37,500	25,000
Depreciation: Year 2	12,500	12,500
NBV: End of year 2	25,000	12,500
Depreciation: Year 3	12,500	6,250
NBV: End of year 3	12,500	6,250
Depreciation: Year 4	12,500	3,125
NBV: End of year 4	0	3,125

10.2

	Straight line	Reducing balance
	£	£
Cost	16,000	16,000
Depreciation: Year 1	3,100	8,000
NBV: End of year 1	12,900	8,000
Depreciation: Year 2	3,100	4,000
NBV: End of year 2	9,800	4,000
Depreciation: Year 3	3,100	2,000
NBV: End of year 3	6,700	2,000
Depreciation: Year 4	3,100	1,000
NBV: End of year 4	3,600	1,000
Depreciation: Year 5	3,100	500
NBV: End of year 5	500	500

10.3

	Straight line	Reducing balance
	£	£
Cost	2,500	2,500
Depreciation: Year 1	575	750
NBV: End of year 1	1,925	1,750
Depreciation: Year 2	575	525
NBV: End of year 2	1,350	1,225
Depreciation: Year 3	575	368
NBV: End of year 3	775	857
Depreciation: Year 4	575	257
NBV: End of year 4	200	600

10.4

	Straight line	Reducing balance
	£	£
Cost	14,000	14,000
Depreciation: Year 1	3,667	5,600
NBV: End of year 1	10,333	8,400
Depreciation: Year 2	3,667	3,360
NBV: End of year 2	6,667	5,040
Depreciation: Year 3	3,667	2,016
NBV: End of year 3	3,000	3,024

10.5 Straight line: £12,000 each year; Reducing balance: Year 1 £25,200; Year 2 £7,560; Year 3 £2,268.

10.6 Provision for depreciation

		£			£
2017			2017		
Dec 31	Balance c/d	6,000	Dec 31	Statement of Comp Inc	6,000
		6,000			6,000
2018			2018		
Dec 31	Balance c/d	10,800	Jan 1	Balance b/d	6,000
			Dec 31	Statement of Comp Inc	4,800
		10,800			10,800
2019			2019		
Dec 31	Balance c/d	14,640	Jan 1	Balance b/d	10,800
			Dec 31	Statement of Comp Inc	3,840
		14,640			14,640

10.7 Provision for depreciation of machinery

		£			£
2015			2015		
Dec 31	Balance c/d	4,000	Dec 31	Statement of Comp Inc	4,000
2016			2016		
Dec 31	Balance c/d	7,200	Jan 1	Balance b/d	4,000
			Dec 31	Statement of Comp Inc	3,200
		7,200			7,200
2017			2017		
Dec 31	Balance c/d	9,760	Jan 1	Balance b/d	7,200
			Dec 31	Statement of Comp Inc	2,560
		9,760			9,760

10.8 Provision for depreciation of equipment

		£			£
2013			2013		
Dec 31	Balance c/d	1,875	Dec 31	Statement of Comp Inc	1,875
2014			2014		
Dec 31	Balance c/d	5,625	Jan 1	Balance b/d	1,875
			Dec 31	Statement of Comp Inc	3,750
		5,625			5,625
2015			2015		
Dec 31	Balance c/d	9,375	Jan 1	Balance b/d	5,625
			Dec 31	Statement of Comp Inc	3,750
		9,375			9,375

10.9 Provision for depreciation of equipment

		£			£
2012			2012		
Dec 31	Balance c/d	500	Dec 31	Statement of Comp Inc	500
2013			2013		
Dec 31	Balance c/d	1,750	Jan 1	Balance b/d	500
			Dec 31	Statement of Comp Inc	1,250
2014			2014		
Dec 31	Balance c/d	3,750	Jan 1	Balance b/d	1,750
			Dec 31	Statement of Comp Inc	2,000
		3,750			3,750

10.10 Provision for depreciation of equipment

		£			£
2013			2013		
Dec 31	Balance c/d	5,000	Dec 31	Statement of Comp Inc	5,000
2014			2014		
Dec 31	Balance c/d	13,250	Jan 1	Balance b/d	5,000
			Dec 31	Statement of Comp Inc	8,250
		13,250			13,250
2015			2015		
Dec 31	Balance c/d	21,750	Jan 1	Balance b/d	13,250
			Dec 31	Statement of Comp Inc	8,500
		21,750			21,750

10.11 (a) Annual depreciation = £1,600. Asset owned for 3.5 years. Accumulated depreciation = £5,600. Therefore NBV = £4,400. Therefore loss of £500.

(b) Depreciation for 2014 = £3,000, for 2015 = £2,100, for 2016 = £1,470. NBV = £3,430. Therefore profit of £470.

10.12 Depreciation in year 2016 = £5,800 × 20% = £1,160
Depreciation in year 2017 = £4,640 × 20% = £928

Computer system disposal

	£			£
2017		2017		
Apr 4 Van at cost	5,800	Apr 26	Depreciation	2,088
		Apr 26	Bank	3,250
		Dec 31	Statement of Comp Inc	462
	5,800			5,800

10.13

Van disposal

	£			£
2019		2019		
Apr 4 Van at cost	32,000	Apr 4	Depreciation	18,500
		Apr 4	Bank	13,000
		Dec 31	Statement of Comp Inc	500
	32,000			32,000

10.14

Equipment disposal

	£			£
2016		2016		
Sep 30 Equipment at cost	14,000	Apr 1	Depreciation	3,000
		Apr 1	Bank	8,800
		Dec 31	Statement of Comp Inc	2,200
	14,000			14,000

10.15

Delivery truck disposal

	£			£
2017		2017		
May 23 Truck at cost	50,000	May 23	Depreciation	24,400
		May 23	Bank	21,500
		Dec 31	Statement of Comp Inc	4,100
	50,000			50,000

10.16 Depreciation = £2,400 per year. Owned for $2^{1}/_{3}$ years. Therefore accumulated depreciation = £5,600.
NBV = £12,000 − £5,600 = £6,400.
Trade-in value = £19,000 − £12,000 = £7,000.
Therefore profit of £600 on trade-in.

10.17 (a) NBV = £70,000 − £59,000 = £11,000.
Loss on disposal = £7,500 − £11,000 = £3,500.
(b) Depreciation = £125,000 − £59,000 + (£200,000 × $^{1}/_{4}$ = £50,000).

Gerken Ltd

Statement of financial position extract as at 31 Dec 2007

	£
Non-current assets	
Equipment	170,000
Less: Depreciation	116,000
	54,000

10.18 (a)

Machinery at cost

	£			£
2012		2012		
Jan 1 Balance b/d	21,000	Dec 31	Balance c/d	43,000
Jan 1 Bank	10,000			
Jun 30 Bank	12,000			
	43,000			43,000
2013		2013		
Jan 1 Balance b/d	43,000	Dec 31	Balance c/d	59,000
Mar 31 Bank	16,000			
	59,000			59,000
2014		2016		
Jan 1 Balance b/d	59,000	Dec 31	Balance c/d	79,000
Sep 30 Bank	20,000			
	79,000			79,000
2015		2015		
Jan 1 Balance b/d	79,000	Mar 31	Machinery disposal	6,000
		Dec 31	Balance c/d	73,000
	79,000			79,000

(b)   **Provision for depreciation of machinery**

		£			£
2012			2012		
Dec 31	Balance c/d	17,850	Jan 1	Balance b/d	8,600
			Dec 31	Statement of Comp Inc	9,250
		17,850			17,850
2013			2013		
Dec 31	Balance c/d	31,600	Jan 1	Balance b/d	17,850
			Dec 31	Statement of Comp Inc	13,750
		31,600			31,600
2014			2014		
Dec 31	Balance c/d	47,600	Jan 1	Balance b/d	31,600
			Dec 31	Statement of Comp Inc	16,000
		47,600			47,600
2015			2015		
Jul 27	Machinery disposal	3,750	Jan 1	Balance b/d	47,600
Dec 31	Balance c/d	62,475	Dec 31	Statement of Comp Inc	18,625
		66,225			66,225

Workings for depreciation:

		£
2012:	25% × £31,000	7,750
	25% × £12,000 × 1/2	1,500
		9,250
2013:	25% × £43,000	10,750
	25% × £16,000 × 3/4	3,000
		13,750
2014:	25% × £59,000	14,750
	25% × £20,000 × 1/4	1,250
		16,000
2015:	25% × £73,000	18,250
	25% × £6,000 × 1/4	375
		18,625
Disposal	25% × £6,000 × 3.75	5,625

(c)   **Machinery disposal**

2015		£	2015		£
Mar 31	Machinery at cost	6,000	Mar 31	Depreciation	5,625
			Mar 31	Bank	300
			Mar 31	Statement of Comp Inc	75
		6,000			6,000

(d)   **Yeates Ltd**
Statement of financial position extract as at 31 Dec 2015

Fixed assets	Cost (£)	Depreciation (£)	Net book value (£)
Machinery	73,000	62,475	10,525

10.19

(a)   **Machinery at cost**

		£			£
2016			2016		
Jan 1	Balance b/d	14,800	Dec 31	Machinery disposal	5,200
Jan 1	Bank	5,200	Dec 31	Balance c/d	25,000
Apr 30	Bank	4,200			
Jun 30	Bank	6,000			
		30,200			30,200

(b)   **Provision for depreciation of machinery**

2016		£	2016		£
Dec 31	Machinery disposal	520	Jan 1	Balance b/d	520
Dec 31	Balance c/d	9,660	Dec 31	Statement of Comp Inc	9,660
		10,180			10,180

Workings for machinery depreciation

	£
14,800 × 1 × 10%	1,480
5,200 × 1 × 10%	520
4,200 × 2/3 × 10%	280
6,000 × 1/2 × 10%	300
	2,580

(c)   **Machinery disposal**

2016		£	2016		£
Dec 31	Machinery at cost	5,200	Dec 31	Depreciation	520
			Dec 31	Bank	2,500
			Dec 31	Statement of Comp Inc	2,180
				Balance b/d	
		5,200			5,200

(d)   **Fixtures at cost**

2016		£	2016		£
Mar 31	Bank	3,800	Dec 31	Balance c/d	7,700
Aug 31	Bank	2,400			
Sep 30	Bank	1,500			
		7,700			7,700

10.19 (cont'd)

(e) Provision for depreciation of fixtures

2016	£	2016	£
Dec 31 Balance c/d	1,540	Dec 31 Statement of Comp Inc	1,540

(f) Lisbie Ltd
Statement of financial position extract as at 31 Dec 2016

Fixed Assets	Cost (£)	Depreciation (£)	Net Book Value (£)
Machinery	25,000	9,960	15,040
Fixtures	7,700	1,540	6,160
	32,700	11,500	21,200

10.20 (a)

(i) Machinery at cost

2014	£	2014	£
Jan 1 Bank	25,000	Dec 31 Balance c/d	55,000
Mar 31 Bank	30,000		
	55,000		55,000
2015		2015	
Jan 1 Balance b/d	55,000	Dec 31 Balance c/d	55,000
2016		2016	
Jan 1 Balance b/d	55,000	Dec 31 Balance c/d	75,000
Jun 30 Bank	20,000		
	75,000		75,000
2017		2017	
Jan 1 Balance b/d	75,000	Jul 27 Machinery disposal	30,000
Oct 1 Bank	12,000	Dec 31 Balance c/d	57,000
	87,000		87,000

(ii) Provision for depreciation of machinery

2014	£	2014	£
Dec 31 Balance c/d	11,000	Dec 31 Statement of Comp Inc	11,000
2015		2015	
Dec 31 Balance c/d	22,000	Jan 1 Balance b/d	11,000
		Dec 31 Statement of Comp Inc	11,000
	22,000		22,000
2016		2016	
Dec 31 Balance c/d	37,000	Jan 1 Balance b/d	22,000
		Dec 31 Statement of Comp Inc	15,000
	37,000		37,000
2017		2017	
Jul 27 Machinery disposal	18,000	Jan 1 Balance b/d	37,000
Dec 31 Balance c/d	30,400	Dec 31 Statement of Comp Inc	11,400
	48,400		48,400

(iii) Machinery disposal

2017	£	2017	£
Jul 27 Machinery at cost	30,000	Jul 27 Depreciation	18,000
		Jul 27 Bank	7,000
		Dec 31 Statement of Comp Inc	5,000
	30,000		30,000

(b) Morris Ltd
Statement of financial position extract as at 31 Dec 2017

Non-current assets	Cost (£)	Depreciation (£)	Net book value (£)
Machinery	57,000	30,400	26,600

Chapter 11

11.1
(a) Original entry
(b) Reversal
(c) Principle
(d) Commission
(e) Principle

11.2
(a) Omission
(b) Original entry
(c) Principle
(d) Reversal
(e) Principle

11.3
(a) Principle
(b) Principle
(c) Commission
(d) Omission
(e) Reversal

11.4

The Journal

	£	£
Motor vehicles	200	
Sales		200
Purchases	100	
Cash		100
T White	82	
W White		82
Returns outwards	54	
M Chase		54
Cash	64	
Bank		64

11.5

The Journal

	£	£
Discounts received	18	
Wages		18
Drawings	47	
Sundry expenses		47
Motor vehicle	300	
Motor expenses		300
H Cowe	32	
C Howe		32
Purchases	29	
S Prince		29

11.6

The Journal

	£	£
Wages	280	
Machinery		280
Sales	9	
S Painter		9
Sales	500	
Capital		500
Returns inwards	64	
C Throup		64
Drawings	38	
Insurance		38

11.7

The Journal

	£	£
S Baines	38	
S Barnes		38
M Brassington	18	
Bank		18
Motor repairs	32	
Motor vehicles		32
A Stacey	97	
Bank		97
Sales	11	
J Spillane		11

11.8

The Journal

	£	£
Repairs	18	
Cash (book)		18
C Quinn	64	
Sales		64
Bank	156	
Commission received		156
Drawings	420	
Rent		420
Cash	9	
Advertising		9

11.9
(a) Yes
(b) Yes
(c) No
(d) Yes
(e) No
(f) No
(g) Yes
(h) No

11.10

The Journal

	£	£
Discounts allowed	750	
Suspense		750
Rent received	630	
Suspense		630
Sales	950	
Suspense		950
Drawings	810	
Sundry expenses		810

Suspense

	£		£
May 31 Rent received	630	May 1 Balance b/d	830
May 31 Sales	950	May 31 Discounts allowed	750
	1,580		1,580

11.11

The Journal

	£	£
Suspense	240	
Bank		240
Cash	63	
T Curran		63
Suspense	68	
G Oliver		68
Suspense	114	
Purchases		114

Suspense

	£		£
2009		2009	
Apr 30 Bank	240	Apr 1 Balance b/d	422
Apr 30 G Oliver	68		
Apr 30 Purchases	114		
	422		422

11.12

The Journal

	£	£
Sales	150	
Suspense		150
Wages	100	
Suspense		100
Machinery	480	
I Fraser		480
Returns inwards	40	
Suspense		40

Suspense

	£		£
2009		2009	
Jan 1 Balance b/d	90	Jan 31 Sales	150
Jan 31 Wages	100	Jan 31 Returns inwards	40
	190		190

11.13

The Journal

	£	£
Bank	88	
Suspense		88
Bank	9	
Insurance		9
Suspense	180	
Returns inwards		90
Returns outwards		90
J Saunders	158	
Suspense		158
Suspense	90	
Capital		90

Suspense

	£		£
2012		2012	
Jan 31 Returns (both)	180	Jan 1 Balance b/d	24
Jan 31 Capital	90	Jan 31 Bank	88
		Jan 31 J Saunders	158
	270		270

11.14

The Journal

	£	£
Suspense	100	
Discounts allowed		50
Discounts received		50
Carriage inwards	78	
Carriage outwards		78
Suspense	18	
Bank		18
F Glue	17	
F Grew		17
Silly Sausage Ltd	152	
Sales		152
Purchases	64	
Suspense		64

Suspense

	£		£
30 Apr Discounts (both)	100	30 Apr Balance b/d (by inference)	54
30 Apr Bank	18	30 Apr Purchases	64
	118		118

11.15

Statement of corrected net profit

	£	£
Net profit		1,340
Add:		
Sales undercast	96	
Purchases overcast	63	159
		1,499
Less:		
Insurance omitted	76	
Repairs (double)	84	160
Net profit		1,339

11.16

Statement of corrected net profit

	£	£
Net profit		2,510
Add:		
Equipment		3,200
		5,710
Less:		
Returns	480	
Discounts received overcast	9	
Returns/Sales	128	
Bad debt	112	729
Net profit		4,981

11.17

Statement of corrected net profit

	£	£
Net loss		(130)
Add:		
Wages overcast	235	
Drawings	76	311
		181
Less:		
Sales	750	
Motor expenses	39	789
Corrected net loss		(608)

11.18 (a)

The Journal

	£	£
Returns inwards	82	
Suspense		82
Drawings	12	
Insurance		12
Discounts allowed	50	
Suspense		50
A Wood	9	
Purchases		9
Suspense	10	
Carriage outwards		10

(b)

Suspense

	£			£
2007			2007	
Apr 1 Balance b/d	122		Apr 30 Returns inwards	82
Apr 30 Carriage outwards	10		Apr 30 Discounts allowed	50
	132			132

M Jeffs

Statement of corrected net profit as at 31 March 2007

	£	£
Net profit		390
Add:		
Insurance overcast	12	
Purchases overcast	9	21
		411
Less:		
Returns inwards undercast	82	
Discounts allowed	50	132
Corrected net profit		279

11.19 (a)

The Journal

	£	£
B Street	860	
Suspense		860
Returns inwards	65	
Returns outwards	95	
Suspense		160
Suspense	9	
Motor expenses		9
Sales	580	
Motor van		580
Wages	1,520	
Cash		1,520

11.19 (cont'd)

(b)

Suspense

2010	£	2010	£
June 1 Balance b/d	1,011	June 30 B Street	860
June 30 Motor expenses	9	June 30 Returns	160
	1,020		1,020

(c)

D Madgett

Statement of corrected net profit as at 31 May 2010

	£	£
Net profit		1,760
Add:		
Motor expenses		9
		1,769
Less:		
Returns	160	
Sales	580	
Wages	1,520	
		2,260
Corrected net loss		(491)

11.20 (a)

The Journal

	£	£
Suspense	320	
Returns inwards		320
Suspense	190	
Sales		190
Sales	295	
Capital		295
Sundry expenses	152	
Suspense		152
Bank	227	
M Smith		227

(b)

Suspense

2018	£	2018	£
Jan 31 Returns inwards	320	Jan 1 Balance b/d	358
Jan 31 Sales	190	Jan 31 Sundry expenses	152
	510		510

(c)

B Bolder

Statement of corrected net profit as at 31 December 2017

	£	£	£
Net profit			3,897
Add:			
Returns inwards		320	
Sales		190	
			510
			4,407
Less:			
Sales		295	
Sundry expenses		152	
			447
Corrected net loss			3,960

Chapter 12

12.1

Sales ledger control account

2018	£	2018	£
Nov 1 Balances b/d	1,142	Nov 30 Cash book	9,201
Nov 30 Credit sales	8,899	Nov 30 Discounts allowed	54
		Nov 30 Returns inwards	88
		Nov 30 Balances c/d	698
	10,041		10,041

12.2

Sales ledger control account

2017	£	2017	£
Jan 1 Balances b/d	21,787	Jan 31 Cash book	81,312
Jan 31 Credit sales	77,520	Jan 31 Discounts allowed	2,211
		Jan 31 Returns inwards	342
		Jan 31 Bad debts	99
		Jan 31 Balances c/d	15,343
	99,307		99,307

12.3

Sales ledger control account

2012	£	2012	£
Jun 1 Balances b/d	22,323	Jun 30 Cash book	199,131
Jun 30 Credit sales	213,753	Jun 30 Discounts allowed	15,435
		Jun 30 Returns inwards	7,887
		Jun 30 Bad debts	500
		Jun 30 Balances c/d	13,123
	236,076		236,076

12.4

Purchases ledger control account

2018		£	2018		£
Jul 31	Cash book	4,898	Jul 01	Balances b/d	997
Jul 31	Discounts received	89	Jul 31	Credit purchases	4,113
Jul 31	Balances c/d	123			
		5,110			5,110

12.5

Purchases ledger control account

2013		£	2013		£
Nov 30	Cash book	45,767	Nov 01	Balances b/d	5,111
Nov 30	Discounts received	555	Nov 30	Credit purchases	50,909
Nov 30	Returns outwards	811			
Nov 30	Balances c/d	8,887			
		56,020			56,020

12.6

Purchases ledger control account

2014		£	2014		£
May 31	Cash book	69,998	May 01	Balances b/d	4,324
May 31	Returns outwards	1,294	May 31	Credit purchases	72,313
May 31	Balances c/d	5,345			
		76,637			76,637

12.7

Sales ledger control account

2016		£	2016		£
01 Mar	Balances b/d	6,646	31 Mar	Cash book	35,559
31 Mar	Credit sales	34,530	31 Mar	Discounts allowed	755
			31 Mar	Bad debts	760
			31 Mar	Returns inwards	2,090
			31 Mar	Set-offs	190
			31 Mar	Balances c/d	1,822
		41,176			41,176

Purchases ledger control account

2016		£	2016		£
Mar 31	Cash book	24,043	Mar 01	Balances b/d	3,424
Mar 31	Discounts received	543	Mar 31	Credit purchases	27,671
Mar 31	Returns outwards	1,785			
Mar 31	Set-offs	190			
Mar 31	Balances c/d	4,534			
		31,095			31,095

12.8

Sales ledger control account

2019		£	2019		£
01 Jun	Balances b/d	19,048	30 Jun	Cash book	83,499
30 Jun	Credit sales	87,870	30 Jun	Discounts allowed	334
			30 Jun	Bad debts	659
			30 Jun	Returns inwards	342
			30 Jun	Set-offs	994
			30 Jun	Balances c/d	21,090
		106,918			106,918

Purchases ledger control account

2019		£	2019		£
Jun 30	Cash book	56,312	Jun 01	Balances b/d	21,343
Jun 30	Discounts received	213	Jun 30	Credit purchases	53,535
Jun 30	Returns outwards	876			
Jun 30	Set-offs	994			
Jun 30	Balances c/d	16,483			
		74,878			74,878

12.9

Sales ledger control account

2011		£	2011		£
Apr 01	Balances b/d	2,313	Apr 30	Balance b/d	190
Apr 30	Credit sales	53,299	Apr 30	Cash book	48,912
			Apr 30	Discounts allowed	455
			Apr 30	Bad debts	534
			Apr 30	Returns inwards	756
			Apr 30	Set-offs	423
			Apr 30	Balances c/d	4,342
		55,612			55,612

Purchases ledger control account

2011		£	2011		£
Apr 01	Balances b/d	223	Apr 01	Balances b/d	1,767
Apr 30	Cash book	25,660	Apr 30	Credit purchases	27,777
Apr 30	Discounts received	433			
Apr 30	Returns outwards	765			
Apr 30	Set-offs	423			
Apr 30	Balances c/d	2,040			
		29,544			29,544

12.10

Sales ledger control account

2010		£	2010		£
01 Sep	Balances b/d	10,321	30 Sep	Cash book	59,977
30 Sep	Credit sales	70,213	30 Sep	Discounts allowed	1,432
30 Sep	Dishonoured cheques	765	30 Sep	Bad debts	10,121
			30 Sep	Returns inwards	1,123
			30 Sep	Set-offs	756
			30 Sep	Balances c/d	7,890
		81,299			81,299

Purchases ledger control account

2010		£	2010		£
Sep 30	Cash book	59,808	Sep 01	Balances b/d	11,233
Sep 30	Discounts received	433	Sep 30	Credit purchases	64,565
Sep 30	Returns outwards	765			
Sep 30	Set-offs	756			
Sep 30	Balances c/d	14,036			
		75,798			75,798

12.11

Sales ledger control account

2010		£	2010		£
01 Jul	Balances b/d	785	31 Jul	Cash book	3,989
31 Jul	Credit sales	4,342	31 Jul	Discounts allowed	99
31 Jul	Dishonoured cheques	115	31 Jul	Bad debts	65
			31 Jul	Returns inwards	78
			31 Jul	Set-offs	52
			31 Jul	Balances c/d	959
		5,242			5,242

Purchases ledger control account

2010		£	2010		£
Jul 31	Cash book	2,761	Jul 01	Balances b/d	1,010
Jul 31	Discounts received	82	Jul 31	Credit purchases	2,390
Jul 31	Returns outwards	290			
Jul 31	Set-offs	52			
Jul 31	Balances c/d	215			
		3,400			3,400

12.12

Sales ledger control account

2012		£	2012		£
01 Jan	Balances b/d	54,255	31 Jan	Balances b/d	913
31 Jan	Credit sales	509,483	31 Jan	Cash book	490,790
31 Jan	Dishonoured cheques	867	31 Jan	Discounts allowed	5,353
31 Jan	Balances c/d	2,190	31 Jan	Bad debts	2,111
			31 Jan	Returns inwards	767
			31 Jan	Set-offs	3,210
			31 Jan	Balances c/d	63,651
		566,795			566,795

Purchases ledger control account

2012		£	2012		£
Jan 31	Cash book	398,080	Jan 01	Balances b/d	42,331
Jan 31	Discounts received	6,438	Jan 31	Credit purchases	408,850
Jan 31	Returns outwards	1,109			
Jan 31	Set-offs	3,210			
Jan 31	Balances c/d	42,344			
		451,181			451,181

Chapter 13

13.1

Updated cash book

2019		£	2019		£
Oct 01	Balance b/d	42	Oct 09	L Carey	439
Oct 08	J Hynes	534	Oct 19	K Andrews	226
Oct 26	H Smithson	123	Oct 31	Interest paid	11
Oct 31	Dividends received	23	Oct 31	Bank charges	18
Oct 31	Balance c/d	28	Oct 31	Direct debit: Northern Gas	56
		750			750

13.2

Updated cash book

2010		£	2010		£
Jan 01	Balance b/d	489	Jan 07	G Taylor	320
Jan 13	K Gee	546	Jan 10	J Crouch	761
Jan 15	D Fish	432	Jan 22	M Lace	434
Jan 23	S Poole	76	Jan 31	Interest	23
Jan 31	Credit transfer	432	Jan 31	Bank charges	45
Jan 31	Dividends	56	Jan 31	Standing order	323
			Jan 31	Balance c/d	125
		2,031			2,031

13.3

Cash book

2012		£	2012		£
Mar 05	D Gahan	324	Mar 01	Balance b/d	190
Mar 09	V Clarke	127	Mar 18	M Lyne	34
Mar 14	F Sharkey	239	Mar 19	R Keenan	312
Mar 19	P Evans	132	Mar 22	L Webster	654
Mar 31	Interest	18	Mar 26	C Webb	453
Mar 31	Credit transfer	287	Mar 31	Electricity	177
Mar 31	Dividends	11	Mar 31	Bank charges	98
Mar 31	Balance c/d	1,194	Mar 31	Dishonoured cheque	414
		2,332			2,332

13.4

Cash book

2013		£	2013		£
Aug 02	M Kite	42	Aug 01	Balance b/d	55
Aug 06	L Scott	199	Aug 07	R Gutteridge	243
Aug 11	E Bowden	98	Aug 09	H Latham	34
Aug 16	C Becker	87	Aug 17	B Moody	57
Aug 20	A King	46	Aug 24	J Simpson	423
Aug 31	Interest received	17	Aug 31	Standing order: H Reyes	300
Aug 31	Credit transfer: A Fender	290	Aug 31	Direct debit: B Williams	121
Aug 31	Dividends received	42	Aug 31	Dishonoured cheque	55
Aug 31	Balance c/d	502	Aug 31	Bank charges	35
		1,323			1,323

13.5 (a)

Updated cash book

2011		£	2011		£
Oct 31	Balance b/d	270	Oct 31	Bank charges	45
Oct 31	Credit transfer: ABC Ltd	106	Oct 31	Balance c/d	331
		376			376

(b)

P Jones
Bank reconciliation statement as on 31 October 2011

	£
Balance as per updated cash book	331
Add Unpresented cheques	150
	481
Less Lodgements not yet credited	431
Balance as per bank statement	50

13.6 (a)

Updated cash book

2004	Dr	£	2004	Cr	£
Nov 28	Balance c/d	59	Nov 28	Standing order	75
Nov 14	Dividends	64	Nov 28	Bank charges	41
			Nov 30	Balance c/d	7
		123			123

(b)

S Shaw
Bank reconciliation statement as on 30 November 2004

		£
Balance as per updated cash book		7
Add Unpresented cheques		
L Black		167
		174
Less Lodgements not yet credited		
B Hughes	190	
I Yates	134	324
Balance as per bank statement		150 (o/d)

13.7 (a)

Updated cash book as at 30 June 2014

2014		£	2014		£
Jun 30	Balance b/d	479	Jun 30	Bank charges	22
Jun 30	Credit transfer	150	Jun 30	Balance c/d	607
		629			629

(b)

R Green
Bank reconciliation statement as at 30 June 2014

	£
Balance per updated cash book	607
Add Unpresented cheques	
J Merkel	133
	740
Less Lodgements	
W Thompson	213
Balance as per bank statement	527

13.8 (a) Updated cash book as at 31 July 2016

2016		£	2016		£
Jul 31	Balance b/d	33	Jul 31	Direct debit	45
Jul 31	Interest	3	Jul 31	Standing order	67
Jul 31	Balance c/d	76			112
		112			

(b) R Alvefors
Bank reconciliation statement as at 31 July 2016

	£
Balance per updated cash book	76 (o/d)
Add Unpresented cheques	
F Harris	299
	223
Less Lodgements	
D Griffiths	119
Balance as per bank statement	104

13.9 L Venison
Bank reconciliation statement as at 17 Nov 2017

	£
Balance as per cash book	76
Add: Unpresented cheques	108
	184
Less: Lodgements	245
Overdraft as per bank statement	(61)

13.10 N Luck
Bank reconciliation statement as at 31 May 2014

	£
Balance as per cash book	208.96
Add: Unpresented cheques	1,051.64
	1,260.60
Less: Lodgements	865.25
Balance as per bank statement	395.35

13.11 T Tripp
Bank reconciliation statement as at 31 January 2013

	£
Balance as per bank statement	(111) O/D
Less: Unpresented cheques	230
	(341)
Add: Lodgements	404
Balance as per cash book	63

13.12 P Jones
Bank reconciliation statement as on 31 October 2011

	£	£
Balance as per cash book		270
Add		
Unpresented cheques	150	
Credit transfer: ABC Ltd	106	256
		526
Less		
Lodgements not yet credited	431	
Bank charges	45	476
Balance as per bank statement		50

13.13 S Shaw
Bank reconciliation statement as on 30 November 2004

	£	£
Balance as per cash book		59
Add		
Unpresented cheques: L Black	167	
Dividends	64	231
		290
Less		
Standing order	75	
Bank charges	41	
Lodgements not yet credited (190 + 134)	324	440
Balance as per bank statement		(o/d) 150

13.14 R Green
Bank reconciliation statement as at 30 June 2014

	£	£
Balance per cash book		479
Add		
Unpresented cheques: J Merkel	133	
Credit transfer	150	283
		762
Less		
Lodgements not yet credited	213	
Bank charges	22	235
Balance as per bank statement		527

13.15

R Alvefors

Bank reconciliation statement as at 31 July 2016

	£	£
Balance as per bank statement		104
Less		
Unpresented cheques: F Harris	299	
Interest received	3	
	302	
		(198)
Add		
Lodgements not yet credited: D Griffiths	119	
Direct debit	45	
Standing order	67	
		231
Balance as per cash book		33

Chapter 14

14.1 Prime cost: purchases of raw materials, direct power, carriage inwards;
Indirect manufacturing costs: depreciation of machinery, factory foreman's wages, machinery repairs;
Statement of comprehensive income: carriage outwards, office insurance, salaries of sales staff.

14.2 Prime cost: returns inwards, wages of production staff, royalties;
Indirect manufacturing costs: wages of factory supervisors, depreciation of factory premises, factory rent;
Statement of comprehensive income: returns outwards, depreciation of delivery vehicles, wages of distribution staff.

14.3

	£
Inventory of raw materials as at 1 April 2005	14,323
Add Purchases	64,544
	78,867
Add Carriage inwards	423
	79,290
Less Returns outwards	565
	78,725
Inventory of raw materials as at 31 March 2006	11,543
Cost of raw materials consumed	67,182

14.4

	£	£
Opening inventory of raw materials		23,440
Add Purchases	178,500	
Add Carriage inwards	2,910	
	181,410	
Less Returns outwards	832	
		180,578
		204,018
Less Closing inventory of raw materials		31,200
Cost of raw materials consumed		172,818

14.5

Prime cost for year to 31 May 2008

	£
Inventory of raw materials as at 1 June 2007	5,645
Purchases of raw materials	53,535
	59,180
Inventory of raw materials as at 31 May 2008	4,534
Cost of raw materials consumed	54,646
Direct wages	76,756
Royalties	3,143
Prime cost	134,545

14.6

Prime cost for year to 31 December 2009

	£
Inventory of raw materials as at 1 Jan 2009	18,902
Purchases of raw materials	154,535
	173,437
Inventory of raw materials as at 31 Dec 2009	23,134
Cost of raw materials consumed	150,303
Manufacturing wages	133,215
Royalties	9,898
Direct power	31,233
Prime cost	324,649

14.7

Prime cost for year to 31 December 2007

	£
Inventory of raw materials as at 1 Jan 2007	5,645
Add Purchases of raw materials	54,322
	59,967
Inventory of raw materials as at 31 Dec 2007	6,577
Cost of raw materials consumed	53,390
Production wages (40%)	35,908
Direct expenses (13,443 + 342)	13,785
Prime cost	103,083

14.8

Jacoby Ltd
Manufacturing account for year to 30 June 2009

	£	£
Opening inventory of raw materials	23,212	
Add Purchases	142,344	
	165,556	
Less Closing inventory of raw materials	23,141	
Cost of raw materials consumed		142,415
Direct power		7,868
Royalties		4,323
Prime cost		154,606
Add Indirect factory overheads		
Supervisory wages	45,365	
Factory rent	11,311	
Machinery depreciation	8,600	
Factory maintenance	7,863	73,139
		227,745
Add Opening work-in-progress		15,463
		243,208
Less Closing work-in-progress		15,767
Production cost of goods completed		227,441

14.9

Haynes Ltd
Manufacturing account for the year ended 31 March 2011

	£	£
Opening inventory of raw materials	8,960	
Add Purchases	64,520	
	73,480	
Add Carriage inwards	453	
	73,933	
Less Closing inventory of raw materials	8,678	
Cost of raw materials consumed		65,255
Manufacturing wages		55,600
Royalties		3,255
Prime cost		124,110
Add Indirect factory overheads		
Supervisory wages	11,210	
Factory rent	6,546	
Machinery depreciation	5,450	
Factory maintenance	7,656	30,862
		154,972
Add Opening work-in-progress		4,245
		159,217
Less Closing work-in-progress		5,435
Production cost of goods completed		153,782

14.10

Barron Ltd
Manufacturing account for the year ended 31 October 2014

	£	£
Opening inventory of raw materials	16,560	
Add Purchases	87,900	
	104,460	
Less Closing inventory of raw materials	6,457	
Cost of raw materials consumed		98,003
Direct wages		55,600
Royalties		3,255
Prime cost		156,858
Add Indirect factory overheads		
Indirect wages	11,210	
Factory rent	6,546	
Heating and lighting	1,830	
Machinery repairs	3,634	23,220
		180,078
Add Opening work-in-progress		11,580
		191,658
Less Closing work-in-progress		9,780
Production cost of goods completed		181,878

14.11

Martin Shine
Manufacturing account for the year ended 31 December 2016

	£	£
Opening inventory of raw materials		9,890
Add Purchases	78,500	
Add Carriage inwards	123	
	78,623	
Less Returns outwards	1,123	
		77,500
		87,390
Less Closing inventory of raw materials	7,843	
Cost of raw materials consumed		79,547
Direct wages		67,675
Royalties		1,750
Prime cost		148,972
Add Indirect factory overheads		
Indirect wages	39,500	
Rent $(17,650 + 390] \times 3/4)$	6,030	
Factory running costs $(5,490 - 190)$	5,300	
Depreciation of equipment	2,740	53,570
		202,542
Add Opening work-in-progress		12,340
		214,882
Less Closing work-in-progress		14,233
		200,649

14.12

L Goburn
Manufacturing account and Statement of comprehensive income
for year ended 31 December 2007

	£	£
Opening inventory of raw materials		8,989
Add Purchases	95,600	
Carriage inwards	312	95,912
		104,901
Less: Closing inventory of raw materials		9,312
Cost of raw materials consumed		95,589
Manufacturing wages		89,240
Royalties		3,123
Prime cost		187,952
Add Indirect manufacturing costs		
Factory indirect wages	56,464	
Rent	6,510	
Depreciation: Machinery	4,250	
Insurance	2,216	69,440
		257,392
Add: Opening work-in-progress		6,456
		263,848
Less: Closing work-in-progress		5,420
Production cost of goods completed		258,428
Sales		324,000
Less: Cost of goods sold		
Opening inventory of finished goods	13,134	
Add: Production cost of goods completed	258,428	
	271,562	
Less: Closing inventory of goods completed	11,570	259,992
Gross profit		64,008
Less: Expenses		
Administrative wages	53,455	
Insurance	554	
Depreciation: Office equipment	4,300	
Rent	2,170	
Carriage outwards	453	60,932
Net profit		3,076

14.13

S Stockley
Manufacturing account and Statement of comprehensive income
for the year ended 31 December 2004

	£	£	£
Opening inventory of raw materials			14,240
Add Purchases		135,000	
Less Returns outwards		1,213	133,787
			148,027
Less: Closing inventory of raw materials			15,654
Cost of raw materials consumed			132,373
Direct wages			145,300
Royalties			4,234
Prime cost			281,907
Add Indirect manufacturing costs			
Indirect wages		89,000	
Heating and lighting		4,236	
Depreciation: Factory equipment		20,541	
Depreciation: Factory premises		5,000	
Rent and rates		6,867	125,644
			407,551
Add: Opening work-in-progress			17,331
			424,882
Less: Closing work-in-progress			16,544
Production cost of goods completed			408,338
Sales			567,000
Less: Cost of goods sold			
Opening inventory of finished goods		28,978	
Add: Production cost of goods completed		408,338	
		437,316	
Less: Closing inventory of goods completed		34,410	402,906
Gross profit			164,094
Less: Expenses			
Office salaries		48,950	
Rent and rates		6,867	
Distribution costs		7,650	
Heating and lighting		2,118	65,585
Net profit			98,509

14.16 Provision for unrealised profit on unsold inventory

	£			£
		2010		
Dec 31 Balance c/d	2,960	Jan 1 Balance b/d		2,500
		Dec 31 Statement of comprehensive income		460
	2,960			2,960

14.17 Provision for unrealised profit on unsold inventory

	£		£
2012/13		2012/13	
Mar 31 Statement of comprehensive income	500	Apr 1 Balance b/d	7,040
Mar 31 Balance c/d	6,540		
	7,040		7,040

14.18 Provision for unrealised profit on unsold inventory

	£			£
2006		2006		
Dec 31 Balance c/d	1,250	Jan 1 Balance b/d		875
		Dec 31 Statement of comprehensive income		375
	1,250			1,250

14.14

S Horsfield

Manufacturing account for year ended 31 October 2014

	£	£
Opening inventory of raw materials		12,400
Add Purchases		89,500
		101,900
Less Closing inventory of raw materials		11,890
Cost of raw materials consumed		90,010
Manufacturing wages		101,400
Royalties		5,200
Prime cost		196,610
Add Indirect factory overheads		
Indirect factory expenses	11,240	
Factory rent	17,800	
Factory repair costs	2,375	31,415
		228,025
Add Opening work-in-progress		8,950
		236,975
Less Closing work-in-progress		9,850
		227,125
Add Factory profit		90,850
Transfer price of completed goods		317,975

14.15

H Thompson

Manufacturing account for year ended 31 December 2010

	£	£
Opening inventory of raw materials		5,670
Add Purchases		54,356
		60,026
Less Closing inventory of raw materials		6,547
Cost of raw materials consumed		53,479
Direct wages		67,670
Royalties		3,280
Prime cost		124,429
Add Indirect factory overheads		
Indirect factory expenses	7,890	
Factory rent and rates (4,234 + 425)	4,659	
Insurance	2,830	
Indirect production wages	13,200	28,579
		153,008
Add Opening work-in-progress		4,230
		157,238
Less Closing work-in-progress		3,120
		154,118
Add Factory profit		30,824
Transfer price of completed goods		184,942

14.19

G Northfield
Manufacturing account and Statement of comprehensive income for year ended 31 March 2014

	£	£
Opening inventory of raw materials		11,540
Add Purchases		86,500
		98,040
Less: Closing inventory of raw materials		9,312
Cost of raw materials consumed		88,728
Manufacturing wages		46,930
Royalties		5,600
Prime cost		141,258
Add: Indirect manufacturing costs		
Factory indirect wages (45,680 + 1,250)	46,930	
Heating and lighting (2/3)	14,227	
Depreciation: Machinery	13,350	
Depreciation: Equipment	3,100	
Rent and rates ([10,400 – 420] × 3/5)	5,988	83,595
		224,853
Add: Opening work-in-progress		7,890
		232,743
Less: Closing work-in-progress		5,420
Production cost of goods completed		227,323
Add: Factory profit		56,831
Transfer price of goods completed		284,154
Sales		325,000
Less: Cost of goods sold		
Opening inventory of finished goods	15,680	
Add: Transfer price of goods completed	284,154	
	299,834	
Less: Closing inventory of goods completed	16,500	283,334
Gross profit		41,666
Less: Expenses		
Administrative wages	18,100	
Rent and rates ([10,400 – 420] × 2/5)	3,992	
Provision for unrealised profits	164	
Heating and lighting (1/3)	7,113	29,369
Net profit on trading		12,297
Add: Factory Profit		56,831
Net profit		69,128

14.20

F Dawood
Manufacturing account and Statement of comprehensive income for year ended 31 December 2005

	£	£
Prime cost		195,000
Add: Indirect manufacturing costs		
Factory wages (99,000 + 3,242)	102,242	
Factory repairs	8,940	
Depreciation: Factory plant	27,420	
Factory power	13,450	
Insurance ([8,700 + 580] × 4/5)	7,424	159,476
		354,476
Add: Opening work-in-progress		16,782
		371,258
Less: Closing work-in-progress		17,890
Production cost of goods completed		353,368
Add: Factory profit		88,342
Transfer price of goods completed		441,710
Sales		500,000
Less: Cost of goods sold		
Opening inventory of finished goods	24,560	
Add: Production cost of goods completed	441,710	
	466,270	
Less: Closing inventory of goods completed	22,450	443,820
Gross profit		56,180
Add: Provision for unrealised profits		422
		56,602
Less: Expenses		
Distribution costs	13,500	
Depreciation: Office fixtures	4,840	
Insurance ([8,700 + 580] × 1/5)	1,856	
Administration expenses	9,100	29,296
Net profit on trading		27,306
Add: Factory profit		88,342
Net profit		115,648

Chapter 15

15.1 4.5p × 350,000 = £15,750.

15.2 2.5p × 250,000 = £6,250.

15.3
Ordinary dividend = 3.5p × 200,000 =	£ 7,000
Preference dividend = 4% × 120,000 =	£ 4,800
Total	= £11,800

15.4
Ordinary dividend = 4p × 1,200,000 =	£48,000
Preference dividend = 8% × 100,000 =	£ 8,000
Total dividend	= £56,000

15.5

Billingham Ltd
Statement of comprehensive income for year ended 31 March 2017

	£	£
Sales		107,000
Less cost of goods sold		
Opening inventory	8,950	
Add Purchases	45,000	
	53,950	
Less Closing inventory	11,980	41,970
Gross profit		65,030
Less Expenses		
Wages and salaries	17,340	
Depreciation	4,500	
Debenture interest	2,000	
Overheads	9,925	
Directors' remuneration	7,400	41,165
Profit before tax		23,865
Tax		7,650
Profit for year		16,215

Billingham Ltd
Statement of changes in equity for year ended 31 March 2017

	£
Retained earnings	
Balance at start of year	11,450
Add Profit for year	16,215
	27,665
Less Dividends paid	3,000
Balance at end of year	24,665

Billingham Ltd
Statement of financial position as at 31 March 2017

	£	£	£
Non-current assets			
Land	190,000	–	190,000
Equipment	45,000	9,300	35,700
	235,000	9,300	225,700
Current assets			
Inventory		11,980	
Trade receivables		8,110	
Cash and cash equivalents		3,305	
		23,395	
Current liabilities			
Trade payables		6,780	
Tax owing		7,650	
		14,430	
			8,965
			234,665
Non-current liabilities			
Debentures			20,000
NET ASSETS			214,665
Equity			
Ordinary share capital			150,000
Preference share capital			40,000
Revenue reserves			
Retained earnings			24,665
EQUITY			214,665

15.6

Smithson plc
Statement of comprehensive income for year to 31 December 2017

	£	£
Sales		99,043
Less cost of goods sold		
Opening inventory	11,221	
Add Purchases	56,456	
	67,677	
Less Closing inventory	12,123	55,554
Gross profit		43,489
Less Expenses		
Distribution costs	8,750	
Administration costs	5,784	
Depreciation on property	3,800	
Depreciation on plant and equipment	6,500	
Directors' remuneration	6,456	31,290
Profit before tax		12,199
Tax		2,123
Profit for year		10,076

Smithson plc
Statement of changes in equity for year to 31 December 2017

	£
Retained earnings	
Balance at start of year	36,534
Add Profit for year	10,076
	46,610
Less Dividends paid	9,870
Balance at end of year	36,740

Smithson plc
Statement of financial position as at 31 December 2017

	£	£	£
Non-current assets			
Property	190,000	21,800	168,200
Plant and equipment	65,000	15,355	49,645
	255,000	37,155	217,845
Current assets			
Inventory		12,123	
Trade receivables		9,997	
Cash and cash equivalents		4,242	
		26,362	
Current liabilities			
Trade payables		5,344	
Tax owing		2,123	
		7,467	18,895
			236,740
Equity			
Ordinary share capital			200,000
Revenue reserves			
Retained earnings			36,740
			236,740

15.7

Hynes plc
Statement of comprehensive income for year ended 30 June 2014

	£	£
Sales		143,434
Less cost of goods sold		
Opening inventory	8,548	
Add Purchases	99,788	
	108,336	
Less Closing inventory	11,901	96,435
Gross profit		46,999
Less Expenses		
Salaries	8,750	
Administration costs	5,784	
Depreciation on land and buildings	2,600	
Depreciation on equipment and machinery	6,715	
Debenture interest	6,400	
Directors' remuneration	6,456	36,705
Profit before tax		10,294
Tax		1,200
Profit for year		9,094

Hynes plc
Statement of changes in equity for year ended 30 June 2014

	£
Retained earnings	
Balance at start of year	36,534
Add Profit for year	9,094
	45,628
Less Dividends paid	8,500
Balance at end of year	37,128

15.7 *(cont'd)*

Hynes plc
Statement of financial position as at 30 June 2014

	£	£	£
Non-current assets			
Land and buildings	260,000	20,600	239,400
Equipment and machinery	76,000	15,570	60,430
	336,000	36,170	299,830
Current assets			
Inventory		11,901	
Trade receivables		13,212	
Cash and cash equivalents		4,242	
		29,355	
Current liabilities			
Trade payables		7,657	
Tax owing		1,200	
Interest owing		3,200	
		12,057	
			17,298
			317,128
Non-current liabilities			
Debentures			80,000
NET ASSETS			237,128
Equity			
Ordinary share capital			200,000
Revenue reserves			
Retained earnings			37,128
EQUITY			237,128

15.8

Emery Ltd
Statement of changes in equity

	£
Retained earnings at start of year	18,560
Profit for year	6,570
	25,130
Less Dividends paid	14,000
Retained earnings at end of year	11,130

15.9

Rahman Ltd
Statement of changes in equity

	£	£
Retained earnings at start of year		87,554
Profit for year		64,140
		151,694
Ord. dividends	40,000	
Pref. dividends	21,000	
		61,000
Retained earnings at end of year		90,694

15.10

McCauley Ltd
Statement of changes in equity

	£	£
Retained earnings at start of year		42,343
Profit for year		18,543
		60,886
Less: Ordinary dividends	10,000	
Less: Preference dividends	3,000	
		13,000
Retained earnings at end of year		47,886

15.11

The Journal

	Dr £	Cr £
Bank	300,000	
Ordinary share capital		250,000
Share premium account		50,000

15.12

The Journal

	Dr £	Cr £
Bank	175,000	
Ordinary share capital		150,000
Share premium account		25,000
Bank	100,000	
Preference share capital		100,000

15.13

The Journal

	Dr £	Cr £
Bank	600,000	
Ordinary share capital		500,000
Share premium account		100,000
Property	300,000	
Revaluation reserve		300,000

15.14

Boothroyd Ltd

Statement of comprehensive income for year ended 31 December 2011

	£	£
Sales		400,000
Less cost of goods sold:		
Opening inventory	35,600	
Add Purchases	260,000	
	295,600	
Less Closing inventory	27,880	
		267,720
Gross profit		132,280
Less Expenses		
Distribution costs	23,000	
Administration costs	17,600	
Depreciation on non-current assets	39,000	
Debenture interest	6,400	
Directors' remuneration	13,500	
		99,500
Profit before tax		32,780
Tax		13,400
Profit for year		19,380

Boothroyd Ltd

Statement of changes in equity for year ended 31 December 2011

Retained earnings:		
Balance at start of year		40,003
Add Profit for year		19,380
		59,383
Ordinary dividends	5,000	
Preference dividends	3,000	
		8,000
Balance at end of year		51,383

Boothroyd Ltd

Statement of financial position as at 31 December 2011

	Cost £	Dep. £	NBV £
Non-current assets	390,000	47,997	342,003
Current assets			
Inventory		27,880	
Trade receivables		25,400	
Cash and cash equivalents		51,400	
		104,680	
Current liabilities			
Trade payables		21,900	
Tax owing		13,400	
		35,300	
Working capital			69,380
			411,383
Non-current liabilities			
Debentures			80,000
NET ASSETS			331,383
Equity			
Ordinary share capital			200,000
Preference share capital			60,000
Capital reserves			
Share premium account			20,000
Revenue reserves			
Retained earnings			51,383
EQUITY			331,383

15.15

Cousins Ltd
Statement of financial position as at 31 March 2014

	£	£	£
Non-current assets			
Freehold land	175,000	–	175,000
Property	200,000	–	200,000
Equipment	18,000	12,400	5,600
	393,000	12,400	380,600
Current assets			
Inventory		17,455	
Trade receivables		11,899	
Cash and cash equivalents		55,345	
		84,699	
Current liabilities			
Trade payables		7,799	
Tax owing		12,500	
		20,299	
Working capital			64,400
			445,000
Non-current liabilities			
Debentures			50,000
NET ASSETS			395,000
Equity			
Ordinary share capital (50p shares)			200,000
Preference share capital (£1 shares)			50,000
Capital reserves			
Revaluation reserve			126,000
Revenue reserves			
Retained earnings			19,000
EQUITY			395,000

15.16

Gaurav plc
Statement of financial position as at 31 March 2018

	£	£	£
Non-current assets			
Freehold land	900,000		900,000
Plant and equipment	298,500	56,800	241,700
	1,198,500	56,800	1,141,700
Current assets			
Inventory		61,978	
Trade receivables		32,323	
Bank balance		84,967	
		179,268	
Current liabilities			
Trade payables		28,423	
NET ASSETS			150,845
			1,292,545
Equity			
Ordinary share capital (£1 shares)			700,000
Preference share capital (50p shares)			100,000
Capital reserves			
Revaluation reserve			275,000
Share premium account			150,000
Revenue reserves			
Retained earnings			67,545
EQUTY			1,292,545

15.17

Falhstrom Ltd
Statement of comprehensive income for year ended
31 December 2019

	£	£
Sales		312,000
Less cost of goods sold		
Opening inventory	29,808	
Add Purchases	165,090	
	194,898	
Less Closing inventory	23,444	
		171,454
Gross profit		140,546
Less Expenses		
Business overheads	42,260	
General expenses	8,780	
Depreciation	7,460	
Mortgage interest	6,700	
Staffing costs	35,110	
Directors' remuneration	15,000	
		115,310
Profit before tax		25,236
Tax		9,100
Profit for year		16,136

Falhstrom Ltd
Statement of changes in equity for year ended
31 December 2019

	£	£
Retained earnings		
Balance at start of year		36,313
Add Profit for year		16,136
		52,449
Less Dividends paid	11,000	
Less Transfer to general reserve	10,000	
		21,000
Balance at end of year		31,449

Falhstrom Ltd
Statement of financial position as at 31 December 2019

	£	£	£
Non-current assets			
Freehold land	320,000	–	320,000
Other non-current assets	195,000	53,260	141,740
	515,000	53,260	461,740
Current assets			
Inventory		23,444	
Trade receivables		23,976	
Prepayments		820	
Cash and cash equivalents		9,013	
		57,253	
Current liabilities			
Trade payables		21,211	
Tax owing		9,100	
Accruals		2,233	
		32,544	
Working capital			24,709
			486,449
Non-current liabilities			
Mortgage on property			100,000
NET ASSETS			386,449
Equity			
Ordinary share capital			250,000
Preference share capital			50,000
Revenue reserves			
General reserve		55,000	
Retained earnings		31,449	
			86,449
EQUITY			386,449

Glossary

Account	A place where a particular type of transaction is recorded
Accounting concept	A guide as to how to deal with a certain type of transaction when preparing the accounts of a business
Accounting standards	A series of statements which act as guides for a variety of particular issues when preparing the accounts of a limited company
Accruals	Any expenses still owing at the end of the accounting period
Accruals concept	The accounting concept whereby all incomes and expenses are matched to the period in which they are incurred
Accrued revenue	Any revenue owing to a business which has not been received by the end of the period in which it was due
Aged debtors schedule	A system used to calculate the size of the provision for doubtful debts whereby trade receivables are classified according to age in order to estimate the likelihood of their becoming bad debts
AGM	Annual general meeting, held by law to decide company policy and to elect the directors of the company
Amortisation	Depreciation provided for intangible assets
Assets	Resources used within a business (e.g. equipment)
Authorised share capital	The maximum amount of share capital that can be raised by a company – normally set out in the memorandum of association
Bad debts	Debts which for which payment is not expected to be received and which are therefore written off against profits
Bad debts recovered	Debts previously written off as bad for which payment is eventually received
Balance	The outstanding amount remaining when an account is balanced – measured by the difference between the totals of the debit column and the credit column in an individual account
Bank reconciliation statement	A statement which attempts to show if any disagreement between the cash book and the bank statement is due to error or due to timing differences
Bookkeeping	The system of recording and maintaining financial transactions in accounts
Business objectives	The aim or purpose of a business – i.e. what it is trying to achieve
Capital (or **equity**)	Resources provided to a business by the owner(s) of the business

Capital expenditure	Expenditure on the purchase of, and any additional costs involved in the improvement, installation and acquisition of non-current assets
Capital gains	Selling an asset (e.g. shares) for a higher amount than the asset was purchased for – i.e. for a profit
Capital income	Income generated from one-off sources (e.g. the sale of non-current assets, loans acquired)
Capital reserves	Reserves which cannot be used for distribution of dividends; capital reserves are created out of changes in the capital structure of the company
Carriage inwards	The cost of delivering goods (purchases) into a business
Carriage outwards	The cost of delivering goods (sales) to the customers of a business
Carrying amount	The cost of an asset less accumulated depreciation to date (also known as the **net book value**)
Cash discount	Discount given to a customer in order to encourage prompt payment
Cash book	A day book and combined account recording all bank and cash transactions
Clearing	The time taken by banks between a cheque being deposited and the funds been transferred to the account
Compensating errors	Two errors which combine to ensure that the trial balance still agrees even though errors exist
Contra	A transaction in which both halves of the double-entry are contained within the same account
Control account	An account which checks the accuracy of a designated ledger
Cost of raw materials consumed	The cost incurred for a period relating to the purchase and use of raw materials and any associated costs involved in the acquisition of these materials
Credit	Accounting entry on the right-hand side of an account
Credit control	Systems used by a business to control and manage its trade receivables
Credit note	Document issued by the business when accepting returns inwards
Creditor	A person or business that a business owes money to and that is expected to be repaid within the near future
Current assets	Liquid assets which are held as part of the operations of a business, and which are unlikely to be held continuously for more than the next year
Current liabilities	Short-term borrowings and other debts incurred by a business which are to be repaid in the next year
Day book	Place where transactions are first classified and recorded according to type before they are posted to the ledger accounts
Debentures	Long-term borrowing by a company, held as certificates which can be traded by investors; debentures pay a fixed rate of interest until the redemption date at which the original value of the debenture is repaid by the company
Debit	Accounting entry on the left-hand side of an account
Debit note	Document issued when goods are returned to their original supplier

Debt factoring	The process of selling a debt of the business to a factor that specialises in debt collection
Debtor	A person or business that owes a business money and will repay in the near future
Depreciable amount	The cost of a non-current asset less any expected residual (scrap) value
Depreciation	The allocation of the depreciable amount (cost less residual value) of a non-current asset over its useful life
Direct costs	Costs which are directly related to the level of output
Direct debit	A payment of varying amount taken out of a bank account by a third party on a regular basis
Direct labour	Labour costs directly related to the production of output – i.e. the cost incurred by those workers producing the output
Directors	Those elected to run a company on behalf of the shareholders; normally directors are elected at the AGM
Directors' remuneration	Fees paid to the directors for their services – treated as a business expense
Discounts allowed	A reduction in the invoice total given to those owing the business money – treated as a revenue expense in the financial statements
Discounts received	A reduction in the invoice total received by the business when paying trade payables – treated as revenue income in the financial statements
Dishonoured cheque	A cheque received which the bank of the issuer of the cheque fails to honour – i.e. will not pay out the amount for which the cheque is written
Dividends	A share of the profits given to shareholders in proportion to the size of their shareholdings
Double-entry	The system by which accounting entries are recorded in two accounts
Drawings	Resources (e.g. cash) taken out of a business by the owner for private use
Equity	The value of issued capital and any reserves
Error of commission	Recording an entry in the wrong personal account
Error of omission	The missing out of a transaction from the double-entry accounts
Error of original entry	Recording the wrong amounts on both the debit and credit entries of a transaction
Error of principle	Recording an entry in the wrong type or class of account
Error of transposition	Recording a number entered in an account with the numerals in the wrong order
Expenses	Costs incurred by a business in the day-to-day running of the business
Factory profit	The difference between the costs of producing output and the anticipated costs of purchasing the same inventory from another business (the factory profit is often substituted by adding a mark-up to the costs of production)

Finance lease	An arrangement to obtain the right to use an asset where the risks and rewards of ownership are transferred to the lessee (the business paying to lease the asset)
Financial statements	The statements produced by a business to provide a summary of the overall performance and the financial position of the business
Float	The amount to be maintained at the start of each period in the petty cash book
Folio reference	An abbreviated reference accompanying an entry in a ledger or day book, which helps to locate where the transaction has been entered
GAAP	Generally Accepted Accounting Principles: the framework of accounting regulations and standards in a particular country or common area of harmonised accounting systems (e.g. UK GAAP, US GAAP)
General ledger	A book containing all accounts of the business that are not found in the sales or purchases ledgers
Gross profit	The difference between sales revenue and the cost of the goods sold, before taking other expenses into account
Imprest	System for running a petty cash book where the amount spent is reimbursed each month so as to restore the float
Income	Revenue earned by a business as part of the business's operations
Indirect costs	Costs which are indirectly related to the level of output
Indirect manufacturing costs	Costs related to the output of the business which vary in amount indirectly with the level of production
Intangible asset	An asset without physical presence, such as goodwill
Interim dividends	Dividends which are paid out during the year (often half-yearly)
Inventory	Goods purchased with the intention of being sold by the business for a profit
Issued share capital	The actual amount of share capital that has been raised by a company
Joint expenditure	Expenditure which contains elements of both capital and revenue expenditure
Journal	Day book used to record transactions (likely to be more unusual transactions) not contained within the other main day books
Ledger	A book containing double-entry accounts
Liabilities	Debts and other borrowings of a business
Limited company	A business organisation which has undergone incorporation and therefore exists as a legal entity separate from its owners
Limited liability	Where one is limited to losing no more than their original investment in a company
Lodgements not yet credited	Cheques received by a business concerning which the money has yet to be paid into the bank account of the business
Manufacturing account	Account used to calculate the cost of producing goods when a business manufactures goods rather than purchasing them from another firm
Market value	What shares are worth at the point at which they are sold to a new investor

Memorandum accounts	Accounts which are not part of the double-entry system and are used as a guide
Net assets	The total value of all assets of a business less the total value of any liabilities
Net book value	*See* **Carrying amount**
Net profit	The profit earned by deducting *all* expenses from the revenue for the period
Nominal value (face value)	The face value of a share used for calculation of dividends: normally, but not always, the price at which the share is originally sold by the company
Non-current assets	Assets held within a business in order to generate future economic benefits
Non-current liabilities	Borrowings by a business which are not expected to be repaid in the next year
Operating lease	An arrangement to obtain the right to use an asset where the risks and rewards of ownership remain with the lessor (the business supplying the asset)
Ordinary shares	The most common type of share: vote-carrying shares that have a variable non-guaranteed dividend
Overcasting	Entering an amount in excess of the correct amount in an account
Partnership	A business organisation owned and controlled by a small group of people
Preference shares	Shares which are not normally vote-carrying but have a fixed dividend which is usually expressed as a percentage of the face value of the share
Prepaid revenue	Any revenue which is received by a business in advance of the period in which it is due
Prepayments	Any expenses which are paid in advance of the accounting period in which they are due to be paid
Prime cost	The total of all costs involved in physically manufacturing goods
Private limited company (Ltd)	A limited company whose shares are not available to the general public
Private sector	Sector in the economy owned and controlled by private groups and individuals
Profit for the year	Profit after all other expenses have been deducted (otherwise known as net profit)
Profit maximisation	Where a business aims to generate as much profit as is possible
Profit on operations	Profit after expenses but before interest charges have been deducted
Provision	A future liability or future expectation of expenditure of uncertain value or timing
Provision for discounts on debtors	A provision created which estimates the likely size of cash discounts to be given to debtors in order to show a more realistic size for the debtors figure on the statement of financial position

Provision for doubtful debts	An estimate of the likely size of future debts – this is only an estimate in order to show a more realistic (and prudent) value of debts likely to be collected on the statement of financial position
Public limited company (plc)	A limited company whose shares are available to the general public
Public sector	Sector in the economy owned and controlled by the government
Purchases	Inventory purchased by a business for the purpose of resale
Purchases day book	Day book where all credit purchase transactions are first recorded
Purchases invoice	Sales invoice viewed from the perspective of the business making the purchase
Purchases ledger	A book containing all the accounts of the credit suppliers of the business
Purchases ledger control account	An account used to verify that the purchases ledger has been correctly maintained
Raw materials	The cost relating to the purchase of materials which are to be the base for the production of output – this will depend on the type of product
Reducing balance	A method of depreciation which charges more in earlier years due to the depreciation charge being based on the declining net book value of the asset
Reserves	Increases in a company's capital that are either due to retained earnings or changes in the capital structure of the company
Residual value	The value a business expects to receive for a non-current asset at the end of its useful life – often assumed to be zero
Retained earnings	Profits for the year which are not distributed as dividends and are kept for reinvestment in the business
Returns inwards	Inventory previously sold by a business which is returned to the firm by the customer (usually because of unsuitability of the inventory)
Returns inwards day book	Day book used to record all goods sold that are returned to the business
Returns outwards	Inventory previously purchased by a business which is returned to the original supplier (usually because of unsuitability of the inventory)
Returns outwards day book	Day book used to record all goods that are returned by the business to the original supplier
Revaluation reserve	The capital reserve which is created when non-current assets are revalued in an upwards direction
Revenue expenditure	Expenditure involved in the day-to-day running of a business
Revenue income	Income generated from the sale of goods and services provided by a business
Revenue reserves	Reserves created out of profits retained within the company which can be used for the distribution of dividends
Reversal of entries	Recording a transaction on the opposite side of both accounts
Royalties	A cost incurred which is paid per unit of production which relates to the use of copyright or a patent owned by another business or person

Sales	Inventory sold by a business
Sales day book	Day book where all credit sale transactions are first recorded
Sales invoice	Document issued by the business making a sale containing detailed information about the sale
Sales ledger	A book containing all the accounts of the credit customers of the business
Sales ledger control account	An account used to verify that the sales ledger has been correctly maintained
Setting off	Reducing an outstanding balance owed by one party to another by an amount owed the other way round
Share premium account	The capital reserve used when shares are issued at a price which is in excess of their nominal value
Shareholders	Those who own a limited company – each shareholder has invested a certain amount in the business to acquire a share of the business
Shares	The value of a company's capital divided up into smaller shares of this capital which can be acquired by investors
Sole trader	A business organisation owned and controlled by one person
Standing order	A payment made to a third party of a fixed amount paid out on a regular basis
Statement of changes in equity	The section of the financial statements of a company which deals with how profits are to be allocated within the company
Statement of comprehensive income	A statement which shows the profits (or losses) of a business calculated by comparing revenues and expenses
Statement of financial position	A statement which shows the assets, liabilities and capital of a business, enabling an assessment to be made of the strength of the business
Straight line	A method of depreciation which allocates the same depreciation charge each year
Suspense account	A temporary account used when the trial balance disagrees so as to facilitate the construction of the financial statements
Trade discount	Reduction in invoice total given to a customer – usually between businesses – which does not show up in the bookkeeping
Trade payables	The collective term used to represent the total of the creditors of a business
Trade receivables	The collective term used to represent the total of the debtors of a business
Trial balance	A list of all the balances from the double-entry accounts providing an arithmetical check on the accuracy of the bookkeeping
Undercasting	Entering an amount less than the correct amount in an account
Unincorporated business	A business organisation in which the owners and the business are, in legal terms, the same as each other
Unpresented cheque	A cheque paid out by a business for which the bank of the business has not yet paid out the amount concerned
Unrealised profit	The amount of factory profit included in each unit of unsold inventory of finished goods at the end of a period which must be eliminated

	from the value in the financial statements through the creation of a provision for unrealised profit on unsold inventory
Updated cash book	A cash book which has items entered into it from the bank statement which were previously not included
User group	A distinct group of people and/or organisations with a shared characteristic and a common interest in the financial statements of a business (e.g. shareholders or suppliers)
VAT (Value Added Tax)	A tax placed on most goods and services in the UK, currently normally levied at 17.5%
Work-in-progress	Goods which are partly finished and are at an intermediate stage in the production process
Working capital	The circulating capital of a business which is used to finance its day-to-day operations, calculated as current assists less current liabilities
Zero rated goods/services	Goods and services which are not subject to VAT, such as children's clothing

Index

Note: terms in Glossary and in end-of-chapter Key Terms are indicated by **emboldened page numbers**.